IMAGES of America

THE JEWISH COMMUNITY OF SHREVEPORT

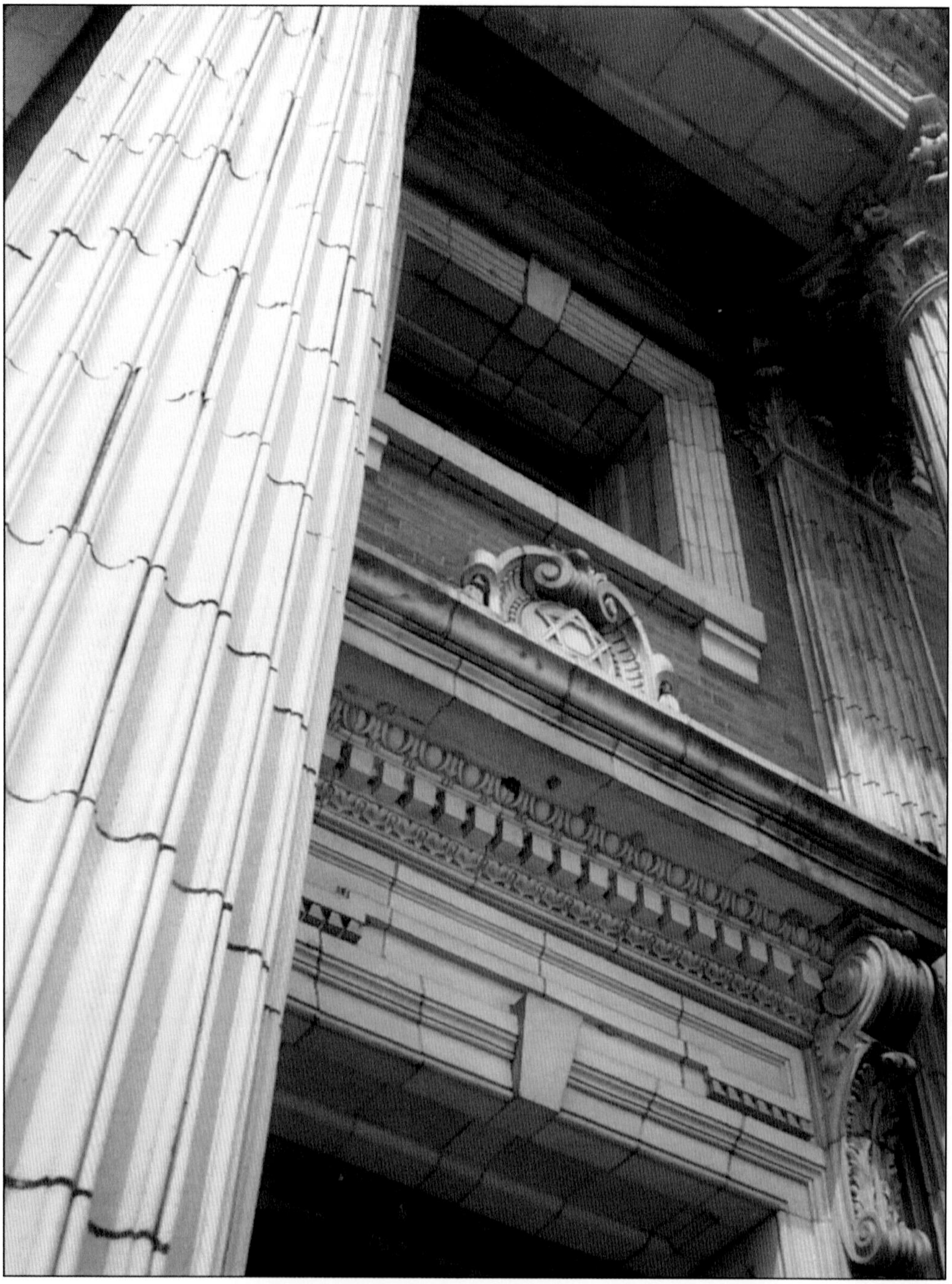

The grand main entrance of the old B'nai Zion Temple at 802 Cotton Street, completed in 1915, reflects the status of the Shreveport Jewish community at the time. Indeed, the temple was one of the city's most impressive religious buildings and remains a landmark today, though vacant. In 1994 it was placed on the National Register of Historic Places.

IMAGES of America

THE JEWISH COMMUNITY OF SHREVEPORT

Eric J. Brock

ARCADIA PUBLISHING

ISBN 978-0-7385-1488-8

Published by Arcadia Publishing
Charleston, South Carolina

Printed in the United States of America

Library of Congress Catalog Card Number: 2002112834

For all general information contact Arcadia Publishing at:
Telephone 843-853-2070
Fax 843-853-0044
E-mail sales@arcadiapublishing.com
For customer service and orders:
Toll-Free 1-888-313-2665

Visit us on the Internet at www.arcadiapublishing.com

Contents

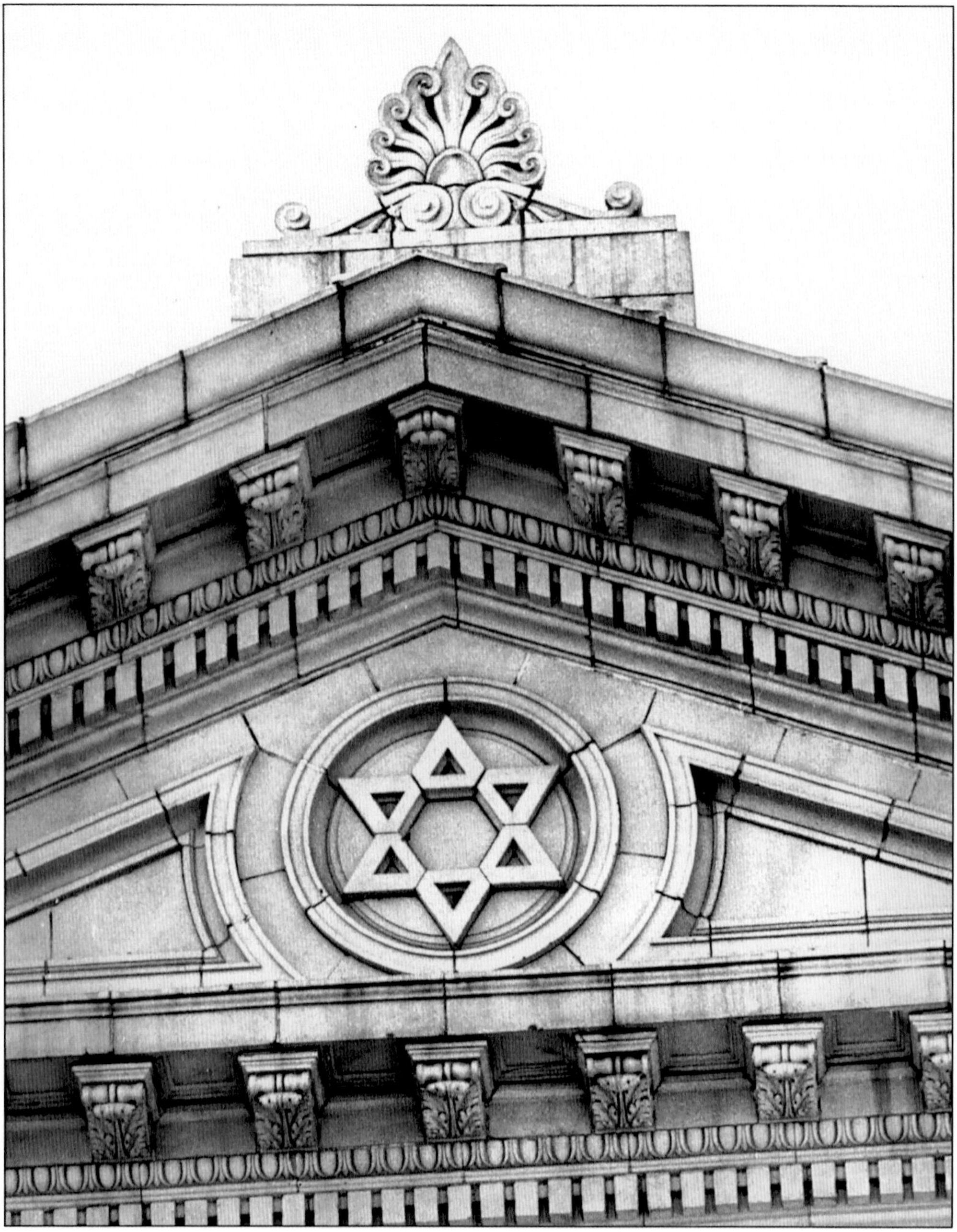

A close-up view shows the terra cotta *magen David*, which ornaments the frieze of the old B'nai Zion on Cotton and Common Streets, 1914–1915.

INTRODUCTION

The Jewish community of Shreveport, though small, is as old as the city itself. In fact, Jacob Bodenheimer, who is believed to have been the first Jewish settler in what is now the Shreveport area, made his home in what is now Bossier Parish several years before Shreveport was founded.

Bodenheimer came to the area as a teenager from Germany in the 1820s. His was the classic tale of a Jewish peddler who did well in his new home, rising to become a civic and business leader. As a teenager, he came to New Orleans by ship. He then traveled the state as a peddler, selling wares of various sorts to planters and farmers. In time he settled on land in the northwest portion of the state, just then opening up to settlement. He briefly returned to New Orleans where he married a young woman of that city, also of German birth, named Eliza Weil.

Jacob and Eliza came to reside permanently in Northwest Louisiana, as did eventually some of her brothers and other relatives. The couple made their home at Bellevue where they ran a tavern and Bodenheimer served as mayor. In time, he became a farmer and cotton planter. By the time of his death in 1865, Bodenheimer was one of the wealthiest and most influential men in Bossier Parish and was one of the founding pillars of the Shreveport Jewish community.

While Jacob Bodenheimer is the first Jew known to have settled in the Shreveport area, within two decades many Jewish families had come here. Before 1840, history records some eight identifiable Jewish names as residents of the city. By 1850, that number had multiplied several times.

Most of the first Jewish settlers were peddlers who became merchants, though some, like Bodenheimer, also became planters and farmers. Almost all of Shreveport's first Jewish settlers were natives of Germany and Alsace. Additionally, a few were native born and quite a few others came from France. Not until after the Civil War was there a significant immigration of Jews from Eastern Europe, especially from Poland and Russia.

The early Jewish community of Shreveport grew quickly. While in the 1830s there could not have been more than a dozen Jews here, there were some 25 families making up Congregation Har El in 1860. Of the men from Shreveport documented as serving in the Confederate army during the Civil War, 77 were Jewish.

In pre-Civil War years, religious services were held in private homes. Initially the community was entirely traditional—what we today would call Orthodox, even being described by 19th-century community leader Simon Levy Jr. as having been "ultra-orthodox" in many respects. The first known Jewish religious services appear to have taken place in the mid-1840s in the home of Abraham and Sarah Winter at the northeast corner of Fannin and Edwards Streets. We then find the congregation meeting at the home of a Mr. Hyams, though which Hyams is uncertain for there were several people in the community by this name. But it was at this same Hyams home that the congregation, first called Har El ("Mountain of God"), was organized in December 1859.

Prior to securing a rabbi early in 1860, services were conducted by Abraham Winter and Asher Weinstock who alternately performed the functions of reader. In 1860, the services of a rabbi, Julius Lewin, were secured but short-lived. Equally short-lived was the tenure of his successor, Rabbi Ferdinand L. Sarner. During the Civil War, religious services were again conducted by laymen from the congregation, though by then a more permanent facility had been found—the ballroom of the Planter's Hotel at Spring and Texas Streets. A few years later, just after war's end, a house was purchased in the 300 block of Fannin Street. This old frame residence was remodeled into the congregation's first synagogue home and was used until 1869 when the first permanent synagogue specifically built for that use was erected on the same site.

On April 2, 1866, the congregation was reorganized under the name B'nai Zion Congregation (meaning "Children of Zion"). Nevertheless, it was commonly called "Hebrew Zion Congregation." Sometimes it was also referred to as "Zion Congregation." The following year the synagogue began its shift to the Reform movement, adopting the Reform prayer book *Minhag America*. Dissatisfaction with the changes led several members to break away in 1875, forming an Orthodox synagogue called Congregation Emanu-El. But the new *shul* was short-lived and in 1877 remerged with B'nai Zion.

For most of the 19th century, the Jewish community and the B'nai Zion Congregation were the same. Not until 1902 would Shreveport's second permanent Jewish congregation, the Orthodox Agudath Achim ("Band of Brothers") synagogue, be formed. Until the 1970s, Agudath Achim remained an Orthodox congregation but since then has been affiliated with the Conservative movement. At the beginning of the 21st century, the Orthodox presence in Shreveport is negligible but the Reform and Conservative movements are strongly represented.

In its early days the community produced numerous civic leaders—not only merchants but politicians as well. While the frequency of Jews serving in elected office continued unabated into the early 20th century, there have been relatively few in recent times. Likewise has been the disappearance of Jewish-owned stores and shops as more and more children of merchants have chosen their own professions over the careers of their parents. The relocation of many younger Jews to larger cities has also caused a decline in the size of Shreveport's Jewish community, though many have returned and remained, hopefully guaranteeing a future for Shreveport Jewry.

The Jewish community of Shreveport began with a handful of pioneers and increased steadily until reaching its peak during World War II, when the war effort brought an influx of Jewish servicemen and their families to the city, most of them connected with nearby Barksdale Army Air Field. Although a considerable decline in numbers has occurred since the 1950s, the community remains a strong and vibrant part of the overall civic, business, and social life of the city. Jewish Shreveporters are particularly well-represented in their patronage of the arts, education, charity, and a host of worthy causes.

This book celebrates the rich heritage of the Shreveport Jewish community. Some 200 images, many previously unpublished, chronicle the growth and life of Shreveport Jewry from Jacob Bodenheimer's settlement to the present day. Certainly not everything, nor everyone, that should be mentioned could be in this short space. It is hoped that the book you hold will paint a portrait of the Shreveport Jewish community that is worthy of its past, its present, and indeed, of its future.

One

Present at the Creation 1827–1869

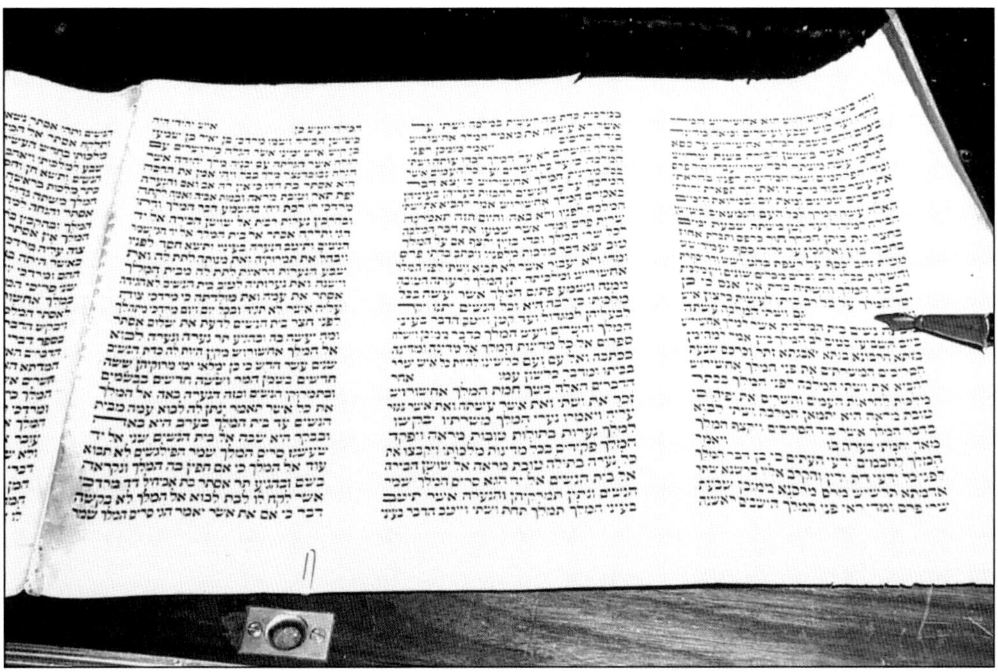

The Torah is the cornerstone of Judaism, and the written Torah scroll is the cornerstone of a Jewish congregation. The first Torah in Shreveport was acquired by the fledgling community around 1845 and signaled the formal establishment of the Jewish community. The first Torah scroll in Shreveport was of Italian origin, dating from about the year 1250. It is still owned and used by B'nai Zion Temple to this day. In 1870, congregation member and early Shreveport jeweler Peter F.L. Frank fashioned a sterling silver *yad* (pointer) for this Torah, which is also still used by B'nai Zion today.

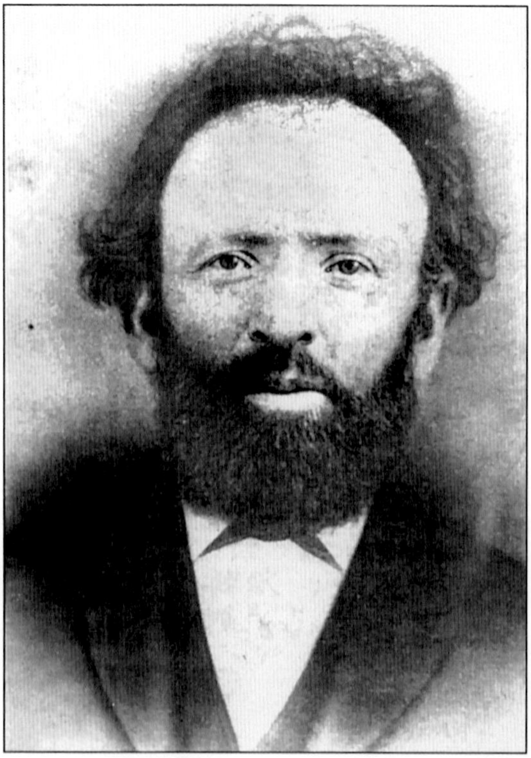

Jacob Bodenheimer (1808–1865), a native of Niederhochstadt, Germany, is believed to have been the first Jewish settler in Northwest Louisiana. In 1822, at age 14, he left home for America, landing in New Orleans and working his way northward. He arrived in what would later become Bossier Parish (then part of Claiborne Parish) about 1827. About 1841, he married Eliza Weil (1823–1906) of New Orleans. A founding member of the Shreveport Jewish community, Bodenheimer and his descendants have been an integral part of the life of that community ever since. Jacob Bodenheimer was killed in March 1865, when a wagon loaded with hay accidentally overturned on him.

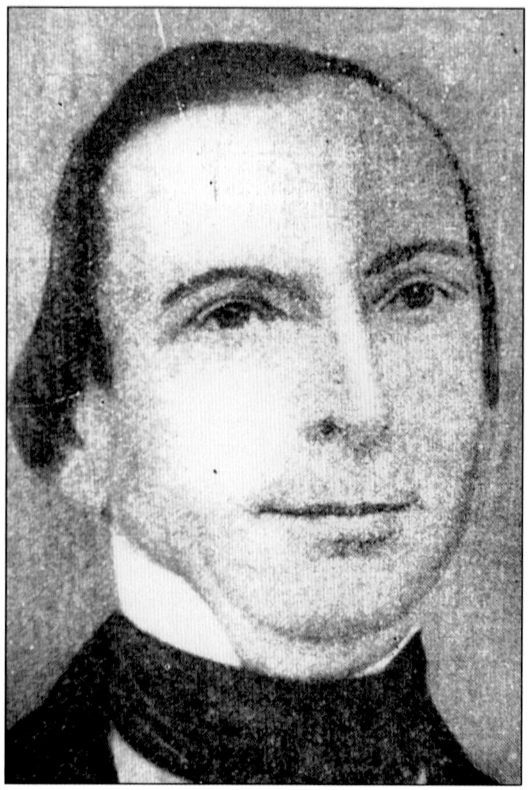

Abraham Winter (1813–1876) was a founding member of the Jewish community and a pioneer settler in Shreveport. Some of the first services held in the city took place at the Winter home at the northeast corner of Fannin and Marshall Streets in the 1840s. Abraham and his brother-in-law Asher Weinstock were the first readers of the community and were instrumental in acquiring its first Torah. Abraham Winter was also founder of the city's first department store, the Winter Company, in 1849. It remained in business until 1935.

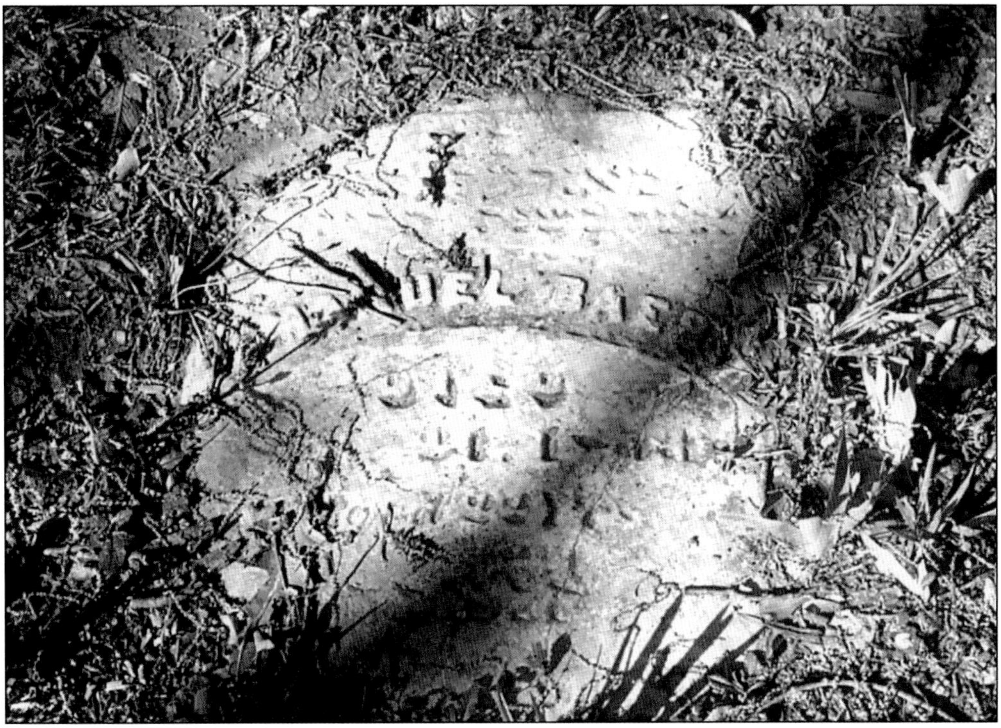

The earliest Jewish gravestone in Shreveport is that of Emanuel Baer, who died at age 22 on September 21, 1853 in the yellow fever epidemic that swept Louisiana that summer and fall. Little is known of Baer or of Mollie Mayer Wolf, the wife of Aaron Wolf, who died at the age of 19 in October 1854. Her grave is not far from Baer's. Both perished before the establishment of a Jewish cemetery and are buried in the non-sectarian section of Shreveport's old Oakland Cemetery.

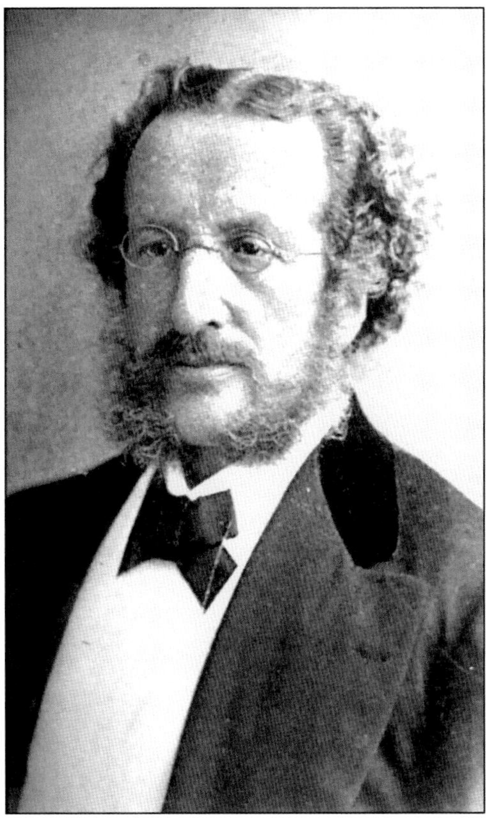

Rabbi Ferdinand Leopold Sarner (1820–1878), a native of Lissen, Germany, was the second rabbi of Congregation Har El (later re-named B'nai Zion), founded in 1859. The first rabbi, Julius Lewin, served the congregation from 1860 to 1861 and was followed by Sarner. Rabbi Sarner left in 1863 because of pro-Union sympathies and relocated in New York where he became a Union Army chaplain. Wounded at Gettysburg, he became rabbi in Syracuse following the war but later returned to the South to serve a congregation in Memphis, where he died of yellow fever in the Mississippi River Valley epidemic of 1878.

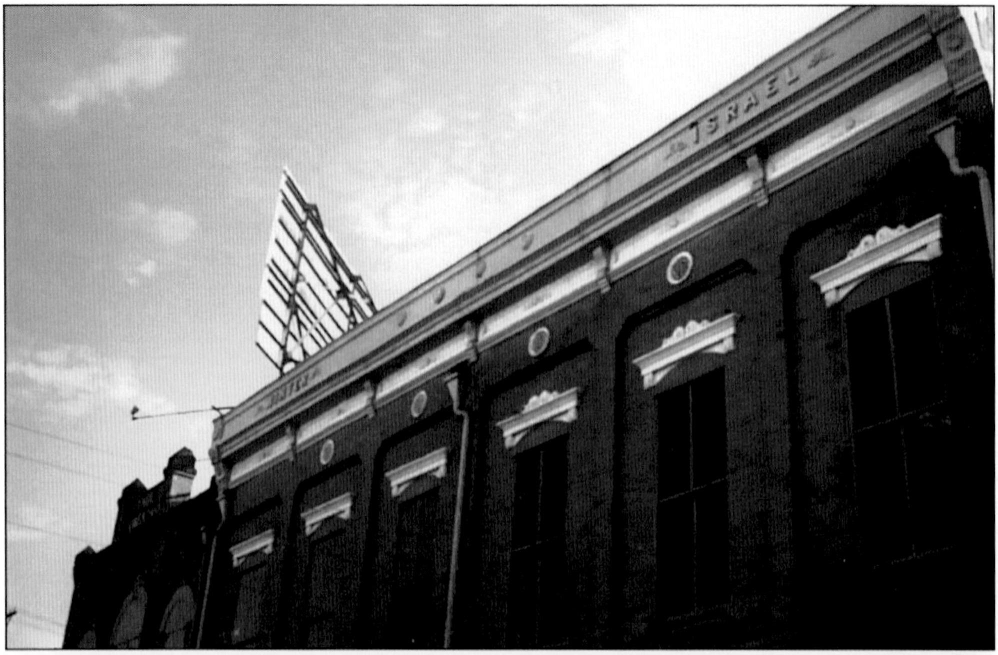

The Winter Company, Shreveport's first department store, was founded as Winter and Weinstock Dry Goods in 1849. In 1882, as the Winter and Israel Company, the store's owners built a new building in the 100 block of Texas Street. On its cast-iron cornice was the name "Winter-Israel," and though the name changed again—this time simply to the Winter Company—and relocated to the 600 block of Texas, the cornice remained, greeting travelers crossing the Red River into Shreveport for 118 years. A downtown landmark and a keystone of the Shreveport Downtown Historic District, the building collapsed in April 2000, following a tornado. With it went the last tangible vestige of the early Jewish community's remarkable mercantile life.

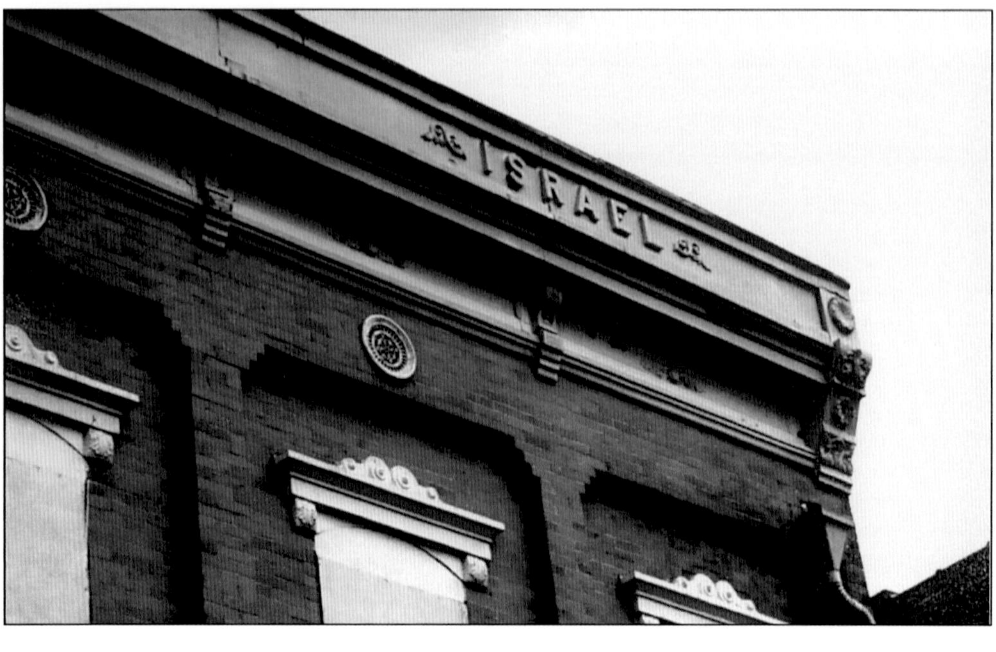

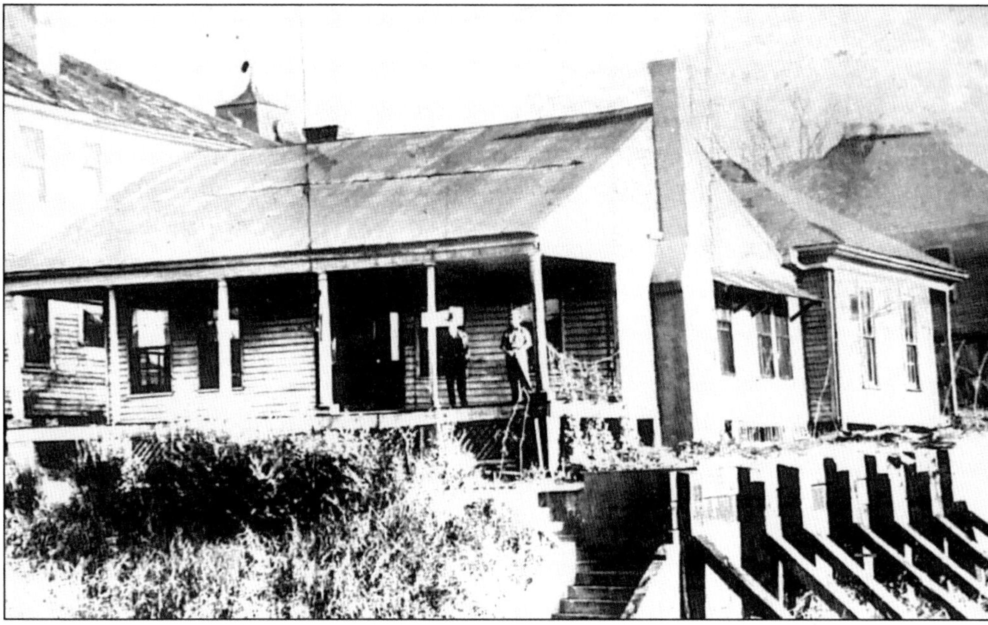

Seen above in 1933, shortly before its demolition, is the residence of Henry Levy (1815–1876), a founding member of the Shreveport Jewish community. It was the last remaining site of early Jewish services, most of which alternated between the Winter, Weinstock, Hyams, and Levy homes, as well as several local hotels, until the acquisition of a structure to serve as a proper synagogue in 1859. The Levy residence, at 219 Cotton Street, corner with Market, was also one of the oldest buildings in the city at the time of its 1933 demolition, following a catastrophic fire. Shown below is Weinstock Street in Allendale, named for Asher Weinstock (1811–1885), a founding member of the Jewish community. Other Shreveport streets named for Jews include Holzman (for Mayor Ben Holzman) and March (for restaurateur David March) in Allendale, Bernstein (for Mayor Ernest Bernstein) in Hollywood, Levy (for Mayor Samuel Levy and his brother, businessman and philanthropist Simon Levy Jr.) in West End, and Levin Lane (for developer Woodrow Levin) in Broadmoor.

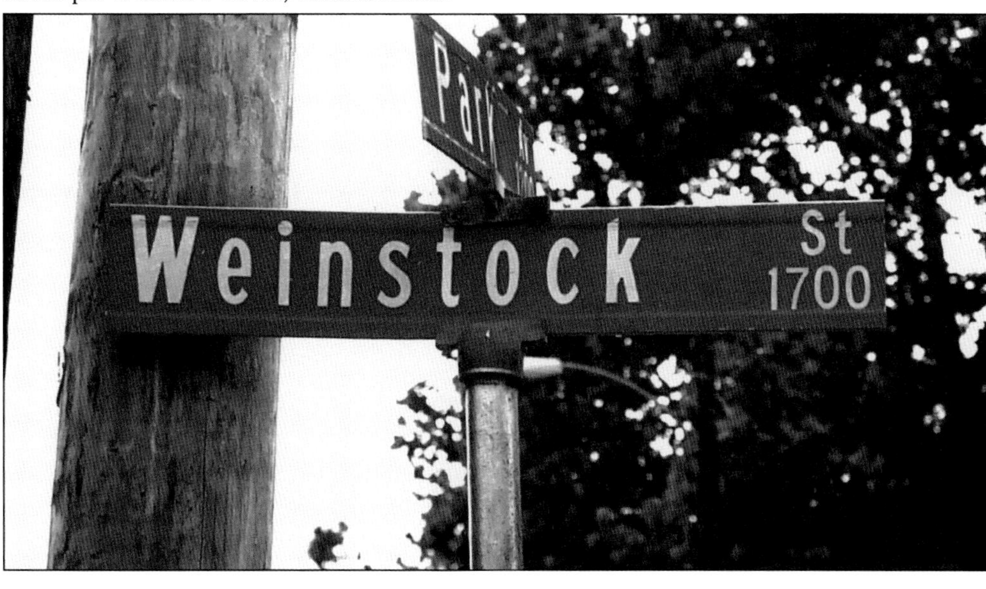

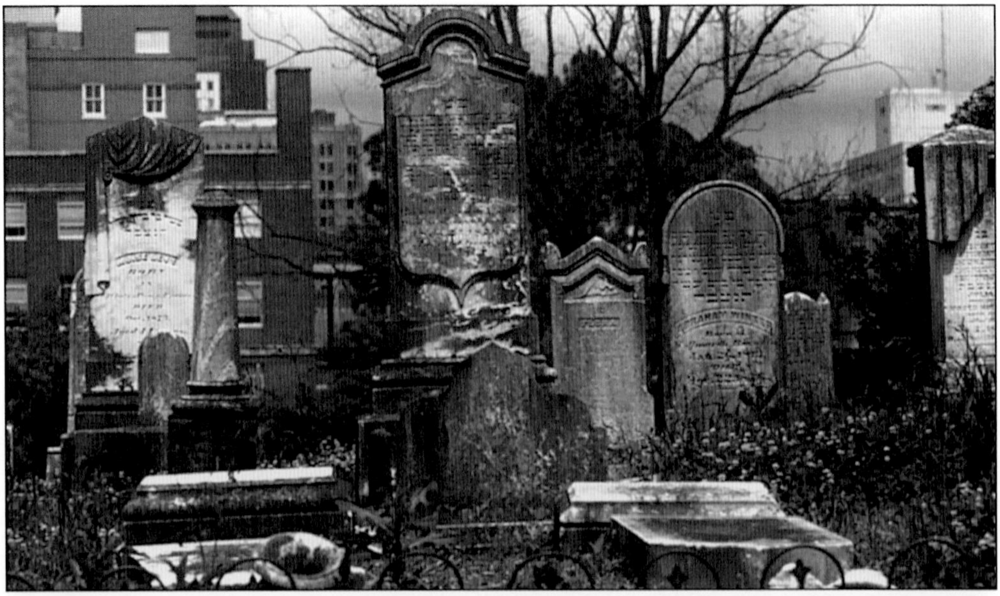

The Hebrew Mutual Benevolent Association (HMBA) was formed in December 1857, in order to secure property for a Jewish cemetery and afterward to provide burial services and community services. The organization served both as *chevra kadisha* and as the equivalent of a modern Jewish welfare federation for the community. Shortly after its formation, the HMBA decided to purchase an acre of land at the northeast corner of Sprague and Mary Streets, opposite Oakland cemetery. For some reason, however, this property was never used and was sold within a few months. On July 17, 1858, the HMBA purchased a quarter-acre of Oakland Cemetery at Sprague and Baker Streets from the City for $160. Thus was born what came to be known as Hebrew Rest Cemetery Number One or simply, the Jewish section of Oakland Cemetery. Just six days after the purchase, merchant Simon Marks, one of the founders of HMBA, became the first to be buried in the new cemetery, only the fifth Jewish burial ground established in Louisiana. Above and below are two views of the cemetery today.

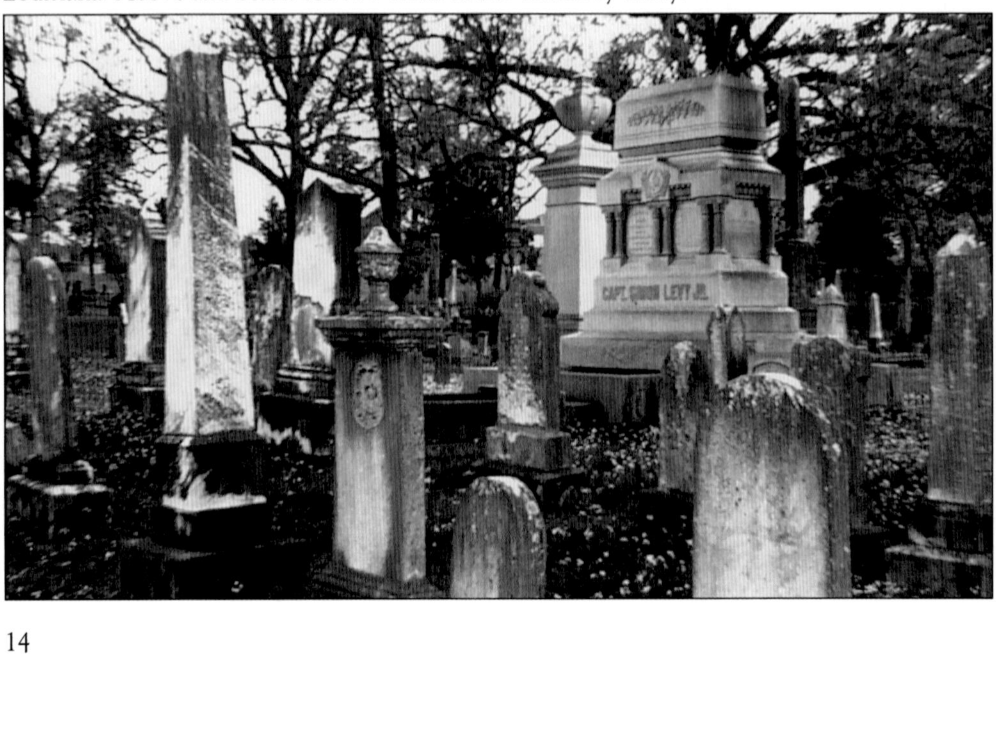

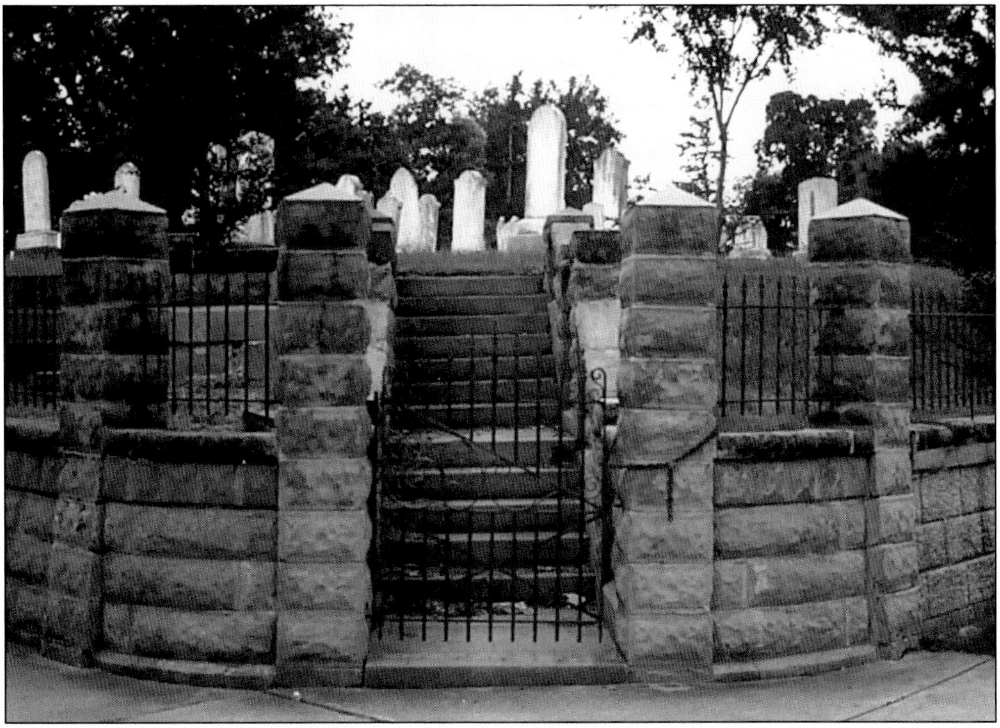

This is the main gate of Hebrew Rest Number One at Sprague and Baker Streets. (Baker Street was eliminated in 1982 and its site became a parking lot and small park.) This gate was built in 1905 and serves as the main entrance to the cemetery, located in the northeast quadrant of Oakland Cemetery.

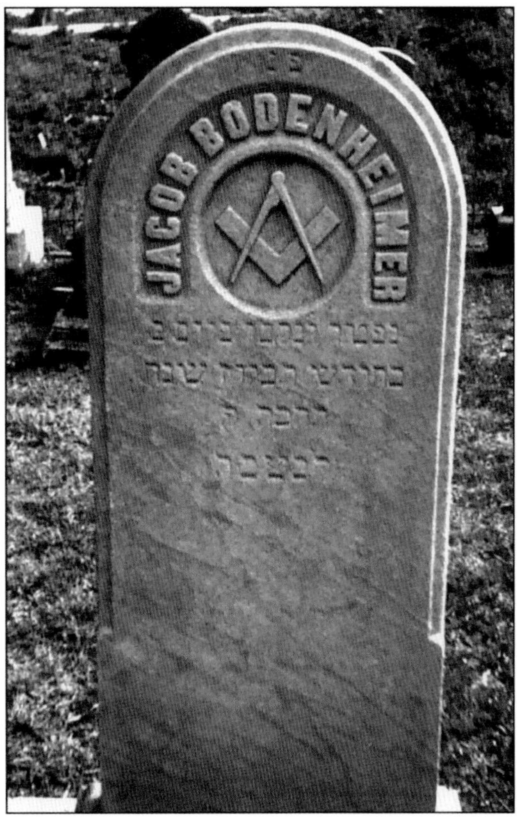

The gravestone of Jacob Bodenheimer bears the square and compass emblem of freemasonry. His widow, who later became Mrs. Jacob Citron, is buried nearby.

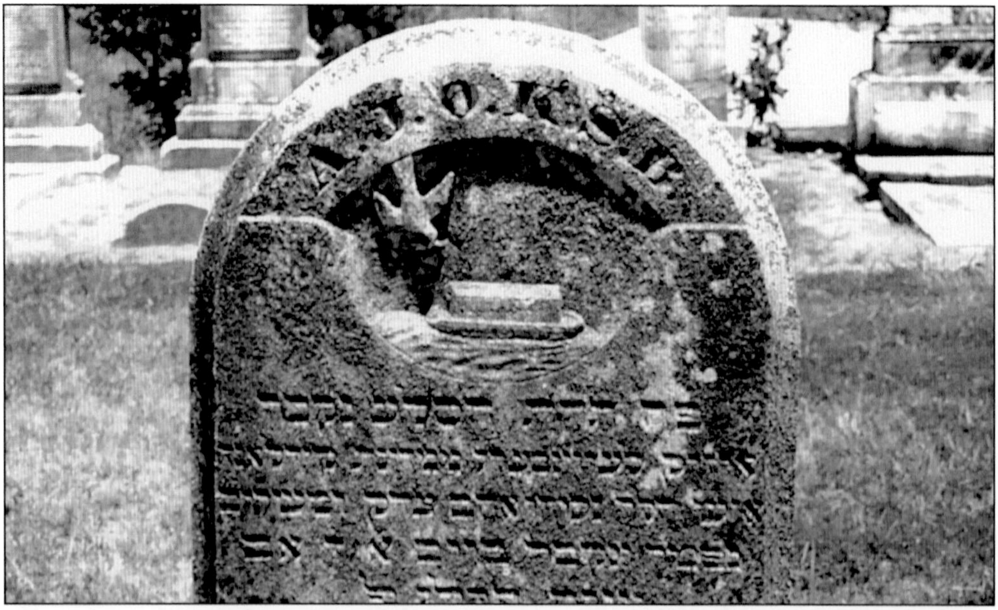

The old stones at Hebrew Rest Number One bear many fascinating motifs and symbols. Interestingly, the *magen David*, so common on modern Jewish gravestones, is not found here at all. Above is the grave of Isaac Lewinberg (d. 1873) depicting the dove descending to Noah's Ark. At the top are the letters AJOKSB denoting his membership in the Ancient Jewish Order of Kesher Shel Barzel, a fraternal society with a lodge (Jordan Lodge No. 102) at Shreveport. Below is the original menorah and cherubim symbol of the Independent Order of B'nai B'rith, which still exists. It appears several times at the cemetery. Here it is seen on the gravestone of Alex B. Weil (1842–1873), a Confederate veteran, wounded at Sharpsburg and captured at Gettysburg. Weil was the first president of the Louisiana Lodge No. 107 of B'nai B'rith.

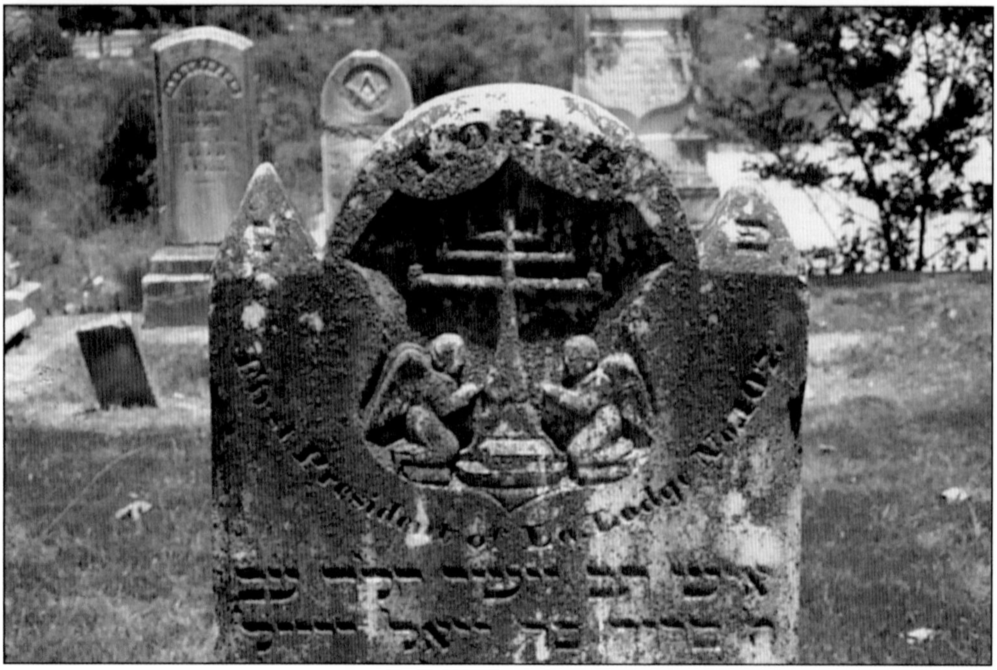

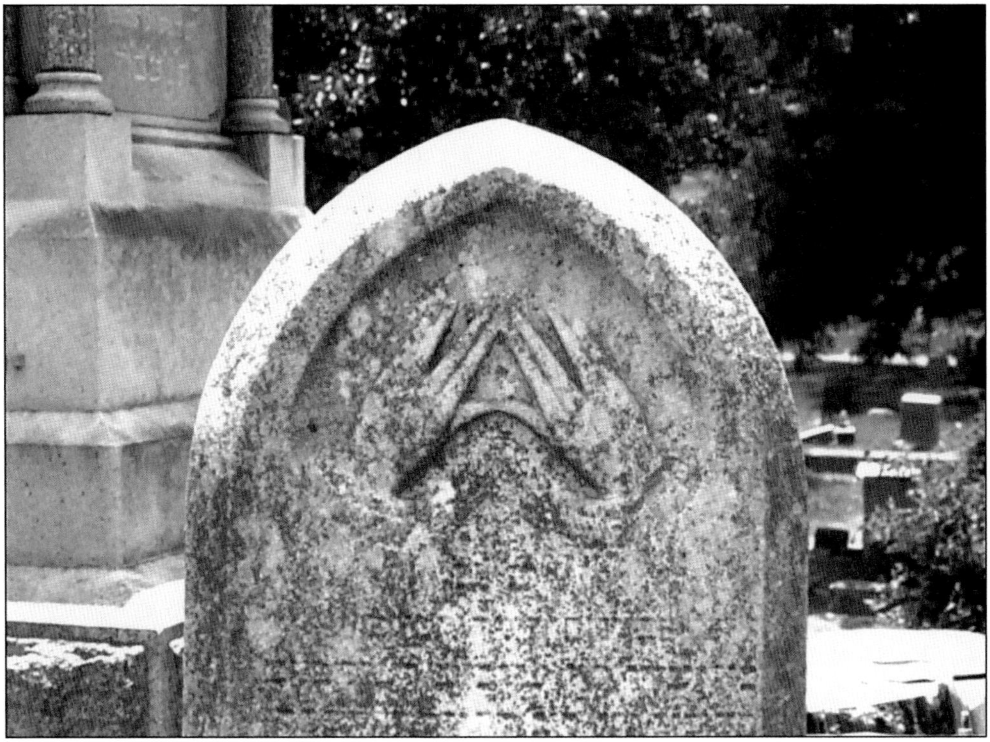

The gravestone of Asher Weinstock depicts a pair of hands in the posture of the traditional priestly blessing. This denotes the fact that Weinstock was a *kohen* or member of the tribe of Aaron, the hereditary priests of ancient Judaism. Weinstock's monument is the only one at Hebrew Rest Number One to bear this symbol.

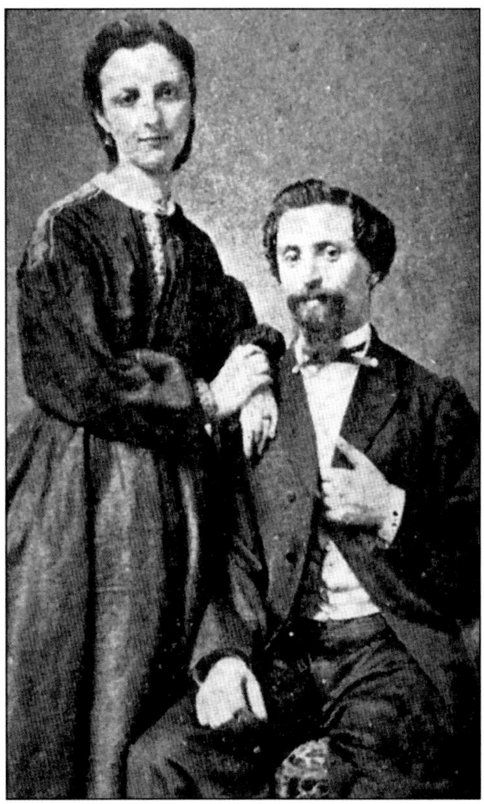

Pioneer merchant Isaac Kahn (1839–1873) and his wife Fannie Cahn Kahn (1846–1890) are pictured here in about 1870. Isaac and his brothers, Julius and Raphael, came to Shreveport from Savannah, Georgia and began what was promising to be one of the most successful general merchandise firms in the city when yellow fever claimed the lives of Isaac and Julius. Raphael later went into the liquor business. Two sons of Fannie and Isaac became notable civic leaders, Leon I. Kahn, city councilman and superintendent of public utilities (and several times candidate for mayor), and Arthur T. Kahn, vice president of Commercial National Bank and president of Shreveport National Bank.

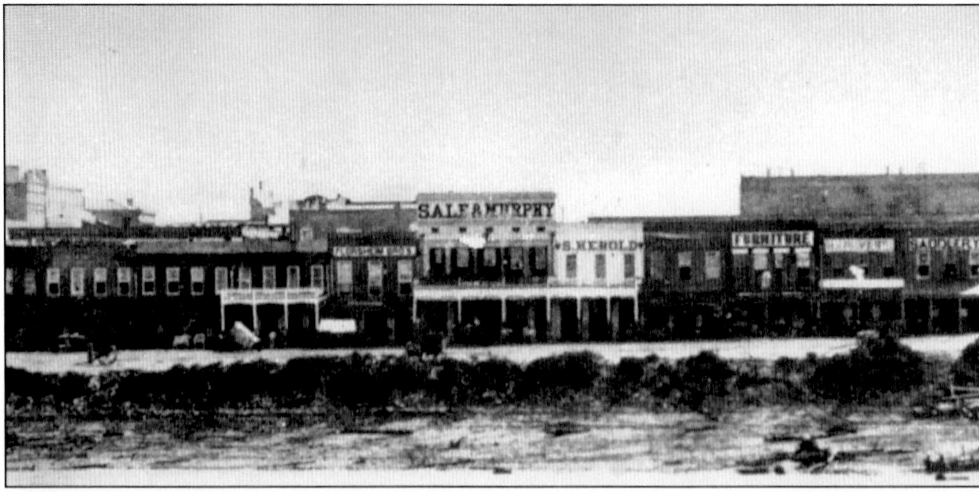

These are two views of the riverfront in the 19th century. Approximately two-thirds of all merchants in the city in the years during and immediately following the Civil War were Jewish. Among those on Commerce Street, which faced the river and served as the wharf for steamboat traffic to and from New Orleans and East Texas, were Leopold Bahr, Abraham Dreyfuss, Florsheim Brothers, Simon Herold, Herman Herold, Charles Leadman, Henry Shulsinger, Isaac Abramson, and Henry Weinstock. On nearby Texas Street were Aaron Kahn, Joseph Bergman, Michael Cohen, Jacob Citron, Asher Weinstock, Abraham Winter, Morris Levy, Felix Weiler, Ludwig and Samuel Sokolosky, Emmanuel Phelps, Isaac Simmons, Raphael Silverstein, Benjamin Holzman, Benjamin Silvernickel, Edward and Benjamin Jacobs, Samuel Warshauer, Henry Ripinsky, Edward Eberstadt, Mark Israel, Kahn Brothers, Max Kaempfer, Julius Jacobs, Louis Liebman, Paul Lowenthal, David Moch, A. Rosenwald, and many others. Some of these family names are still well known in Shreveport today; others have vanished from the community.

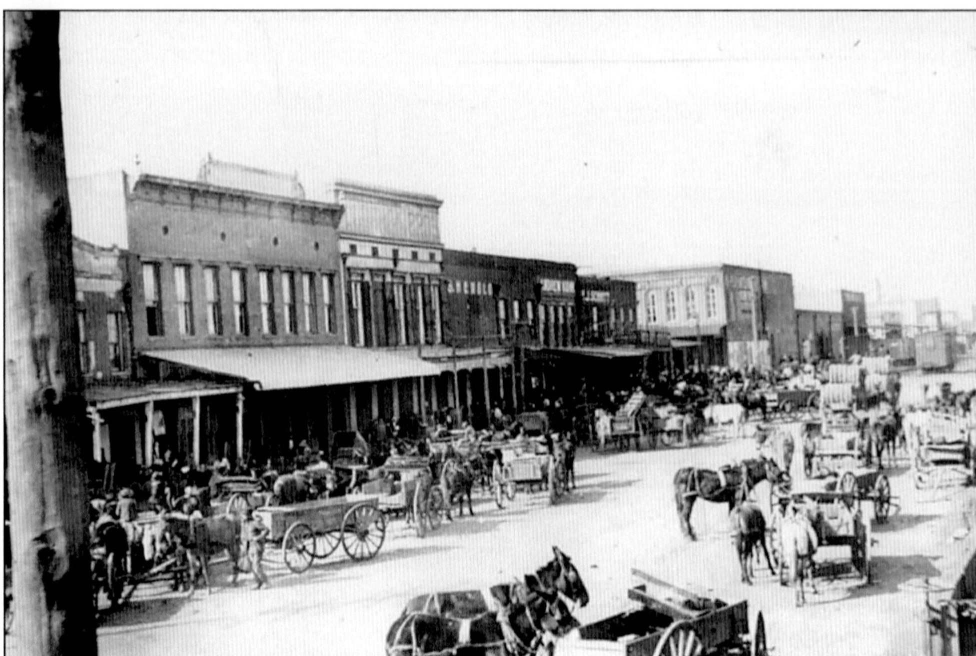

Simon Herold (1835–1909) was born in Germany and immigrated to the United States in 1854. Although he settled in Mississippi, he was opposed to slavery and went north when war erupted, joining the 42nd Ohio Infantry. After the war, he returned to the South, entering the mercantile business with his brother, Herman. Although Shreveport's Jewish community had been fiercely pro-Confederate, Herold was accepted and came to be one of its most respected leaders. From 1876 to 1878, he served as president of B'nai Zion Temple. He is buried with his second wife, Rosa Simmons Herold (1854–1914) at Hebrew Rest Cemetery Number Two (better known as simply Hebrew Rest) on Texas Avenue. His first wife, Sophie Kaufman Herold (1846–1875), is buried at Hebrew Rest Number One.

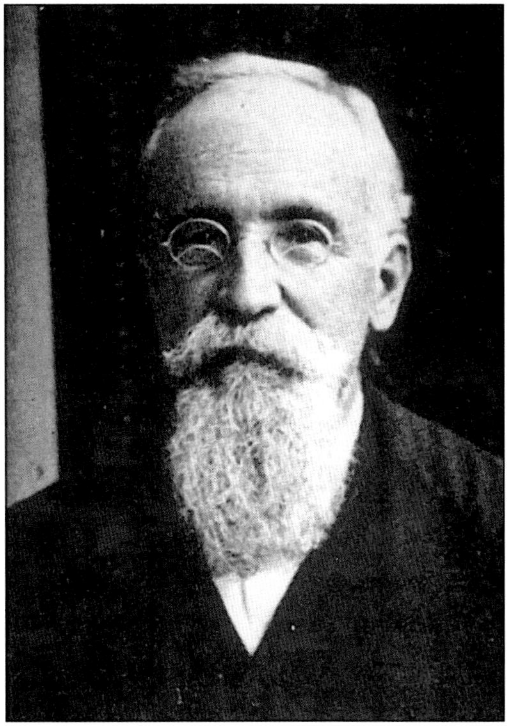

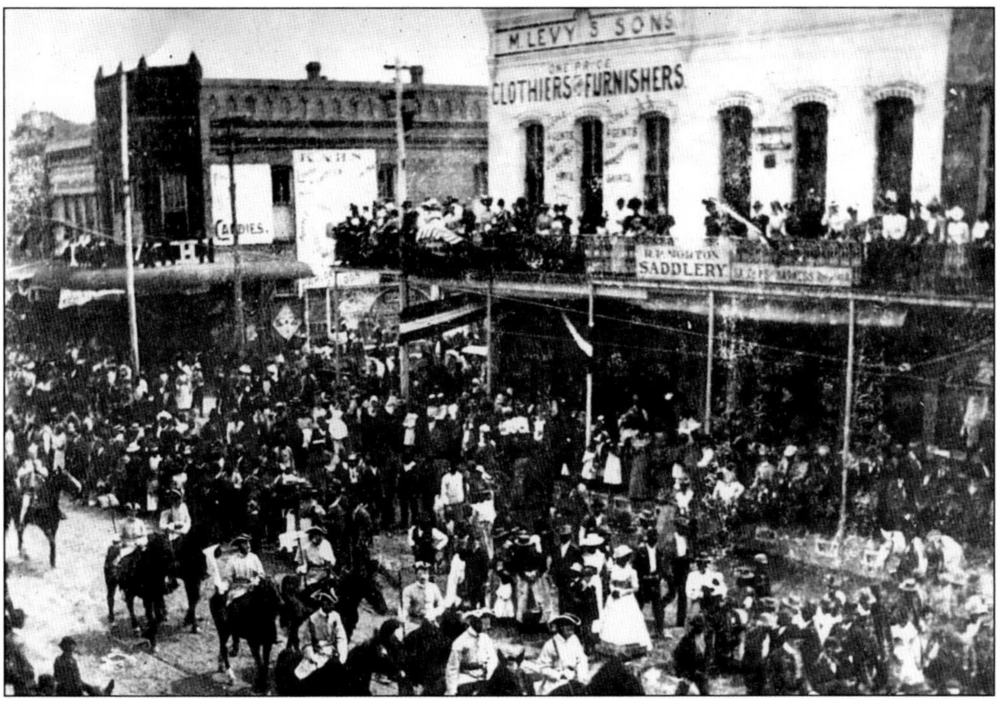

M. Levy's Sons clothing store was founded in 1857 by Morris Levy (d. 1898) and grew to become one of Shreveport's longest lived department stores. Seen here with a 19th-century Mardi Gras parade passing by, the original store at the southwest corner of Texas and Spring Streets remained in use until 1888. M. Levy's Sons remained in continual operation until 1980.

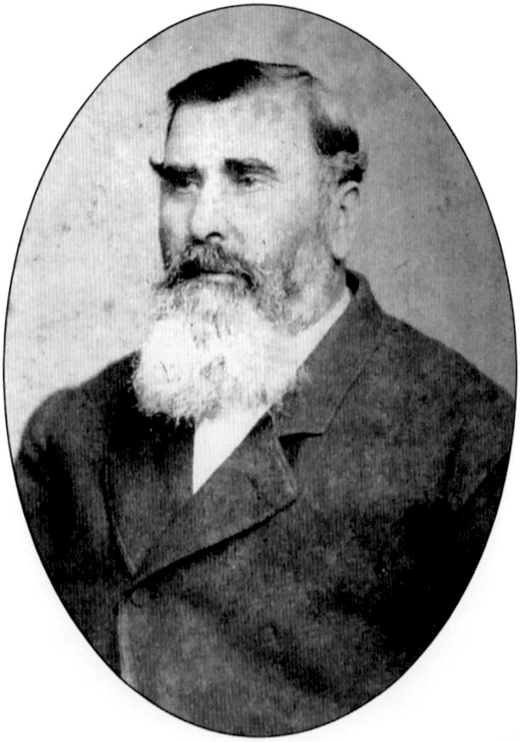

Henry Dreyfuss (1818–1886) a native of Wörth, Alsace, established H. Dreyfuss and Sons, dry goods and clothiers before the Civil War. During the war he was an organizer of the Shreveport Home Guards, a military unit comprised of men beyond service age who volunteered to defend Shreveport, the Confederate capitol of Louisiana, from Union attack.

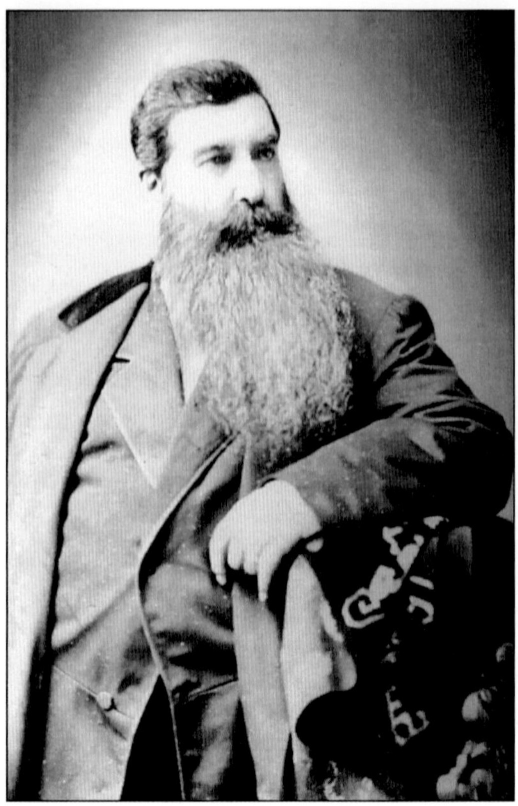

Edward Jacobs (1822–1896), born Ephraim Jacobi in Freinwalde, Pomerania, immigrated to New Orleans in 1842 and became a peddler. Two years later, he moved to Shreveport where he established a dry goods business, later bringing two of his brothers, Benjamin and Julius, to Shreveport as well. By the time of the Civil War, the Jacobs store was one of the city's largest firms. Jacobs vowed that if the Confederacy lost the war he would never shave or trim his beard again, and his postwar whiskers became his trademark. In 1877, he and his brother Ben established the Banking House of E. and B. Jacobs, which became the First National Bank in 1886. (Today it is Bank One.) Because his wife was not Jewish, Edward and his family are buried at Oakland Cemetery outside the boundary of Hebrew Rest Number One, but in a lot situated directly against the edge of the Jewish cemetery. Ben, who gave the land for Hebrew Rest Number Two, is buried nearby.

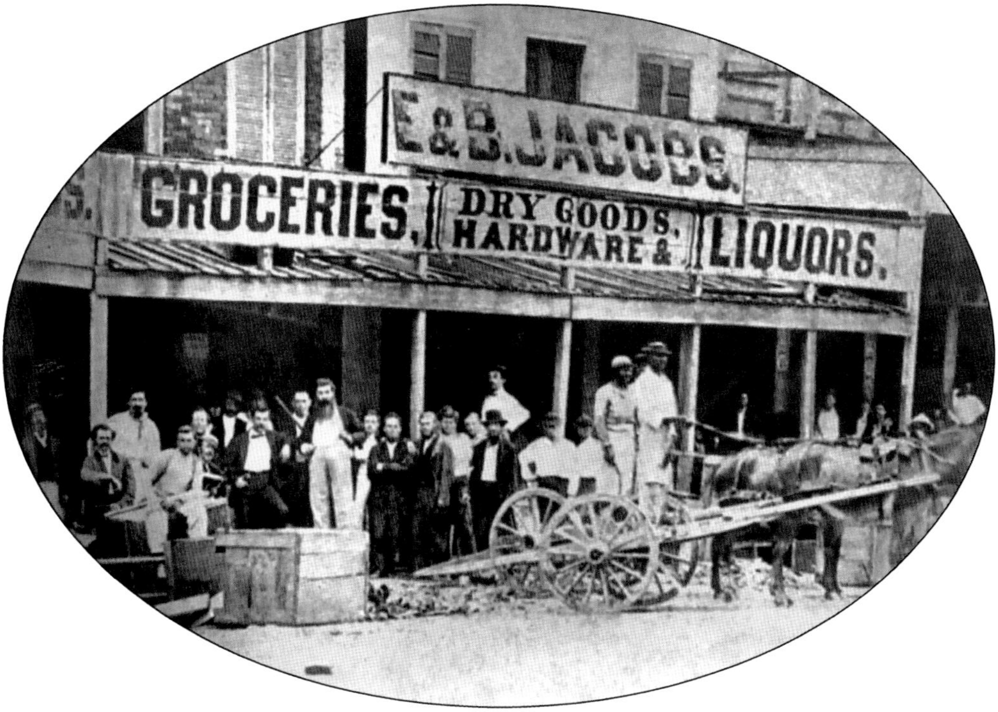

Above is the original Jacobs store in the 100 block of Texas Street, as it appeared in 1868. Edward and Benjamin stand together behind the large crate at left. An interior view of the new building of the Jacobs Brothers' store is pictured below in the 1870s. In March 1881 the four-story structure, located one door east of the south-west corner of Texas Street and Green's Alley, burned in a dramatic fire that took the life of Michel Bompet, 48, a French-Jewish immigrant who had been a manager there for a number of years.

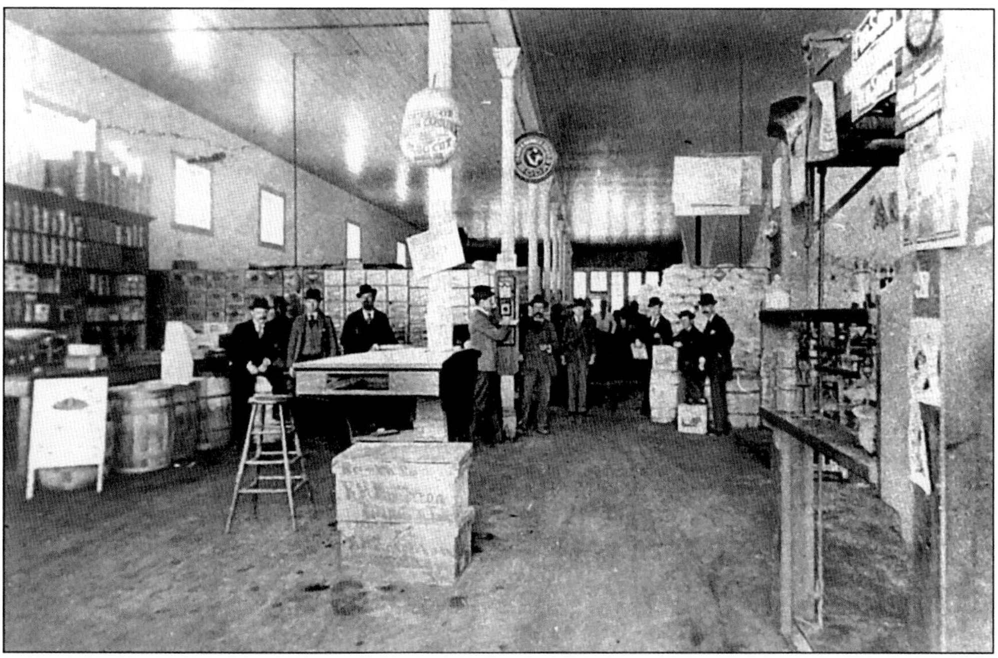

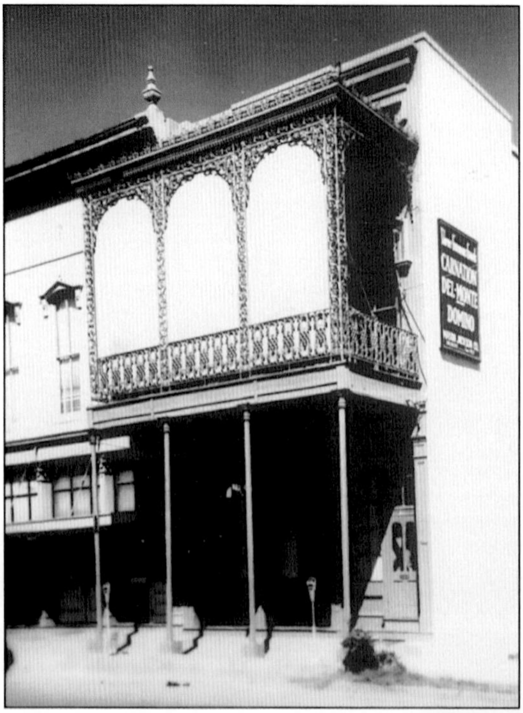

This building at 525 Spring Street was built in 1865 as Tally's Bank. Tally's was short-lived, however, and in 1876 was sold to Julius Asher (1818–1881), a pioneer Jewish merchant who decided to try his hand at banking, thus becoming Asher's Bank. Asher's Bank was even shorter-lived, for only a year later Asher sold his firm to Edward and Benjamin Jacobs and it became the Banking House of E. and B. Jacobs. When Benjamin left the bank to focus on the dry goods business, Edward's son, Walter Byron Jacobs (1855–1904) became partners with his father. In 1886, the firm's name was changed to the First National Bank after receiving the first national banking act charter in Shreveport. The bank remained in this building until 1903. It is now the Spring Street Museum.

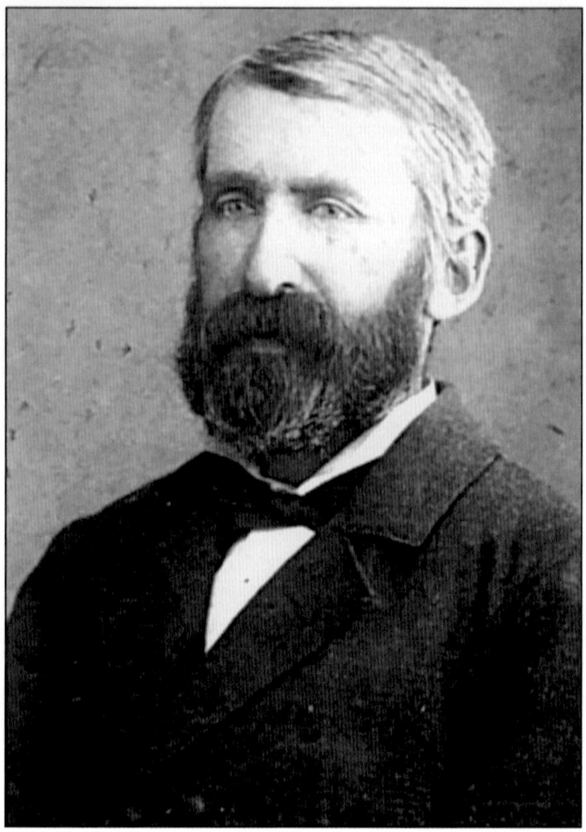

Another pioneer merchant was Marx Bloch, a native of Ingweiller, Alsace. Like so many others, Bloch perished in the yellow fever epidemic of 1873, which took the lives of almost one-fifth of the city's population. The Jewish community was particularly hard-hit by the epidemic because so many local Jews were merchants who feared abandoning their stores if they fled the city as so much of the population did.

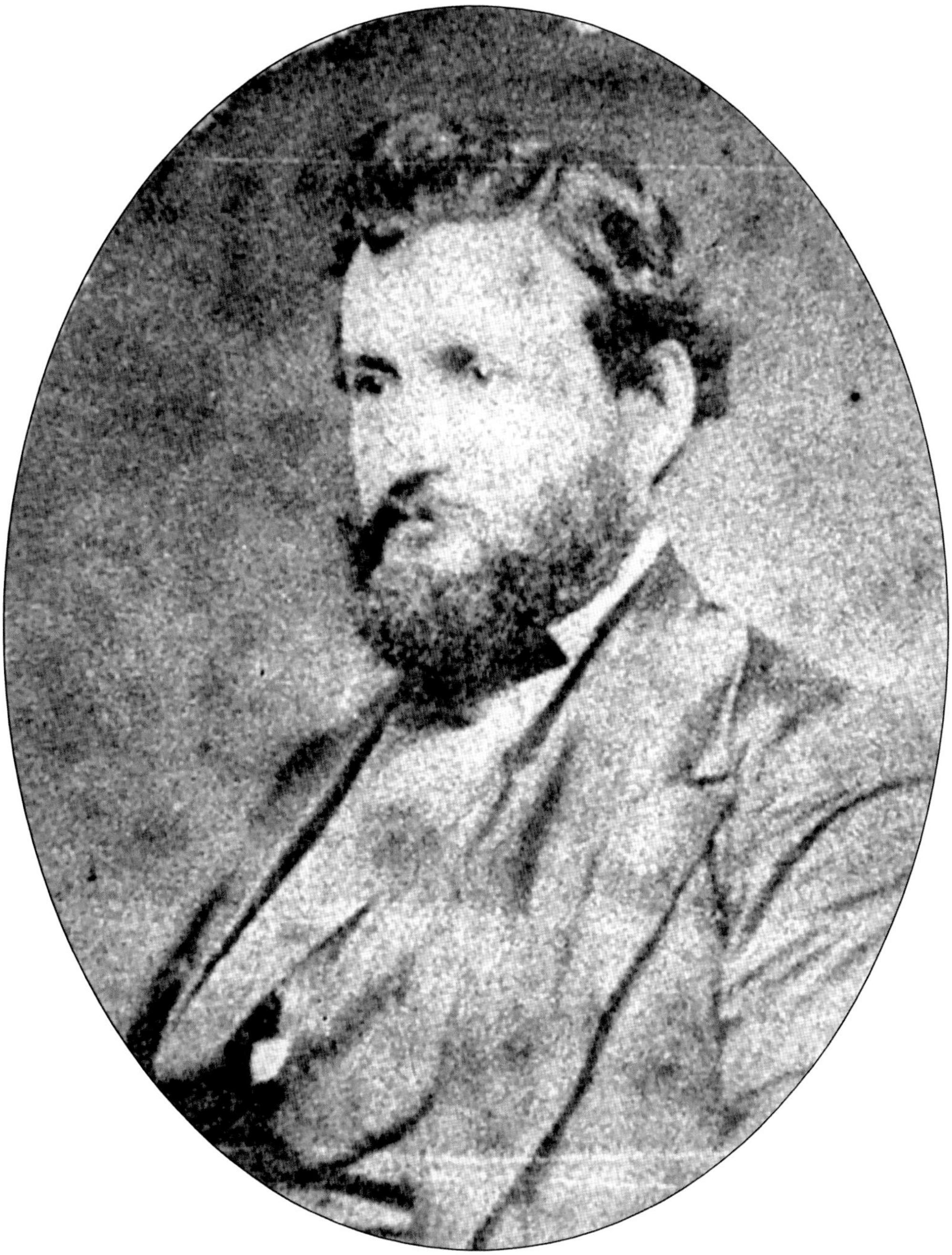

Only three Louisiana Jews attained the rank of colonel in the Confederate army. One of these was Leon D. Marks (1829–1863) of Shreveport. A lawyer before the war, Marks is believed to have been the first of his faith to practice law in Shreveport. Additionally, he published a weekly newspaper, the *Caddo News*, during part of the 1850s. Colonel Marks died at his home in September 1863 of injuries received during the defense of Vicksburg three months earlier. He is buried with his wife's family at Oakland Cemetery. Today a Shreveport encampment (chapter) of the Sons of Confederate Veterans is named in his honor.

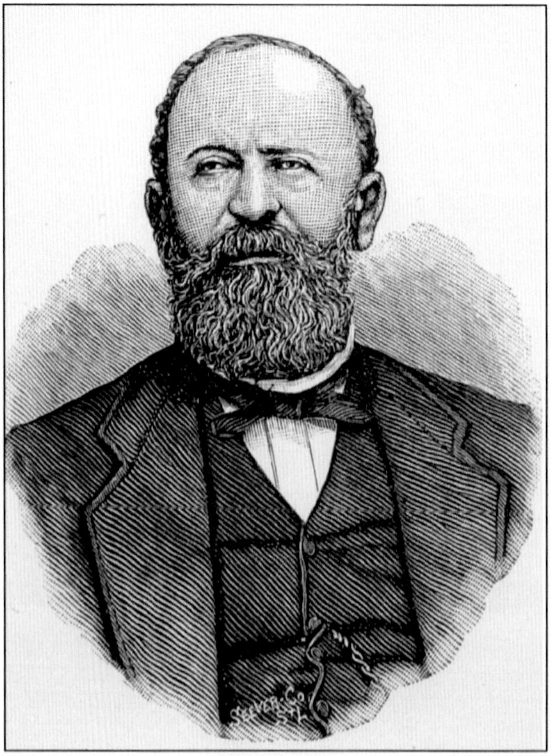

Abraham Sour (1824–1887), a native of Leona, Germany, settled in Shreveport in the 1850s, initially operating a small farm south of town in what is now the St. Vincent area of the city. During the Civil War, Sour served as a veterinary surgeon attached to Company A, 8th Louisiana Cavalry. He afterward served on the staff of Gen. Edmund Kirby Smith, commander of the Trans-Mississippi Department of the Confederate Army, which was headquartered at Shreveport. After the war, until his death, Sour was a hardware and crockery merchant with a store located at 127 Texas Street. The 1888 edition of *White's General Directory for the City of Shreveport*, forerunner to today's *Polk Directories*, was dedicated to Sour's memory, an unprecedented and never-repeated honor.

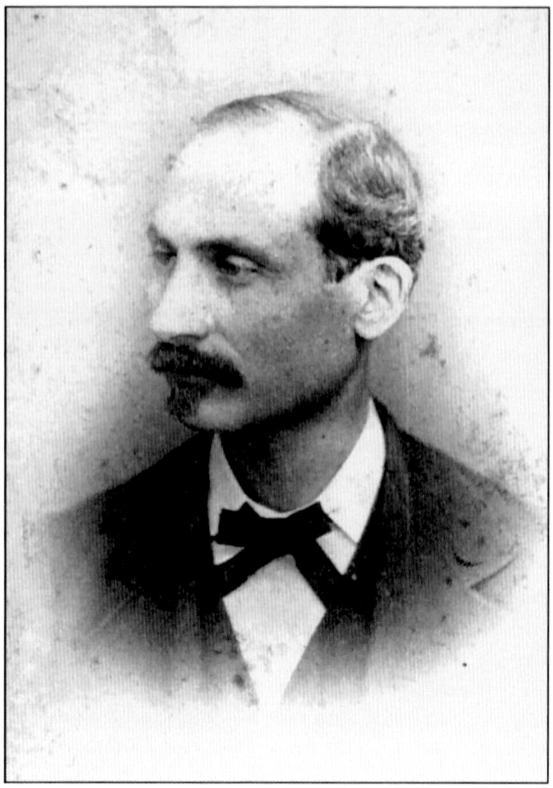

Emanuel Phelps (1840–1931), a native of Wreshen, Germany, was a Confederate veteran and shoemaker who came to Shreveport from New Orleans just after the Civil War and in 1869 established Phelps's Shoe Store. Generations of Shreveporters grew up with the slogan "Phelps' shoes are good shoes" and the Phelps brand came to be known across the nation. Phelps's Shoes remained in business until 1985.

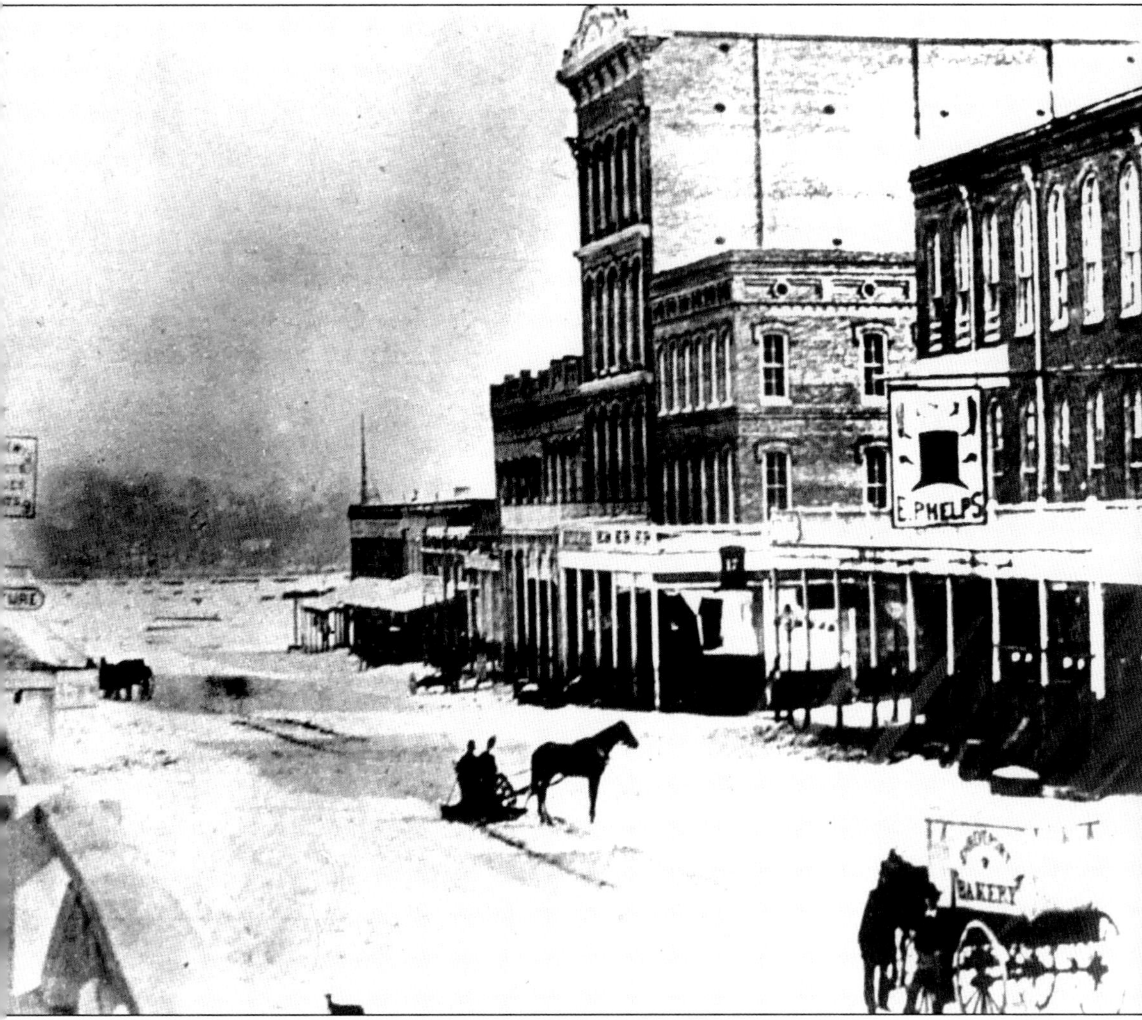

Snow covers Texas Street in the late 19th century. Prominent at right is Emanuel Phelps's store. Across Green's Alley, to its left, is the three-story building of Abraham Sour, next to which is the four-story building of E. and B. Jacobs. The Jacobs and Sour buildings were destroyed by fire in 1881 and replaced by the Winter-Israel Building shown on page 12.

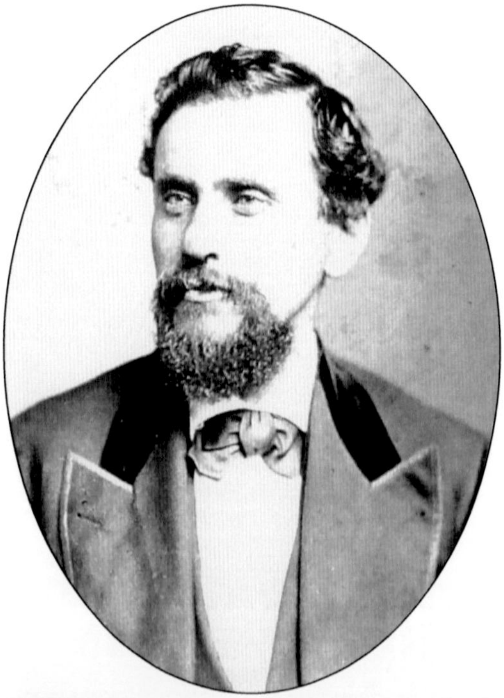

Capt. Simon Levy Jr. (1839–1898), a native of Niedersbach, Alsace, immigrated to America in 1855 with his older brother Samuel, coming to Shreveport where they engaged in the grocery business until the outbreak of war. Both enlisted in the Confederate army and Simon rose to the rank of captain. In 1866, Simon married Harriette Bodenheimer (1850–1878), daughter of Jacob Bodenheimer, the area's first Jewish settler. From 1866 to 1875 and again from 1879 to 1892, Levy was president of B'nai Zion Temple. He also operated the Banking House of S. Levy and Company, which in 1892 merged into Commercial National Bank, of which Levy became president. Additionally, he was vice president of KCS Railroad and a founder of the Louisiana Charity Hospital System.

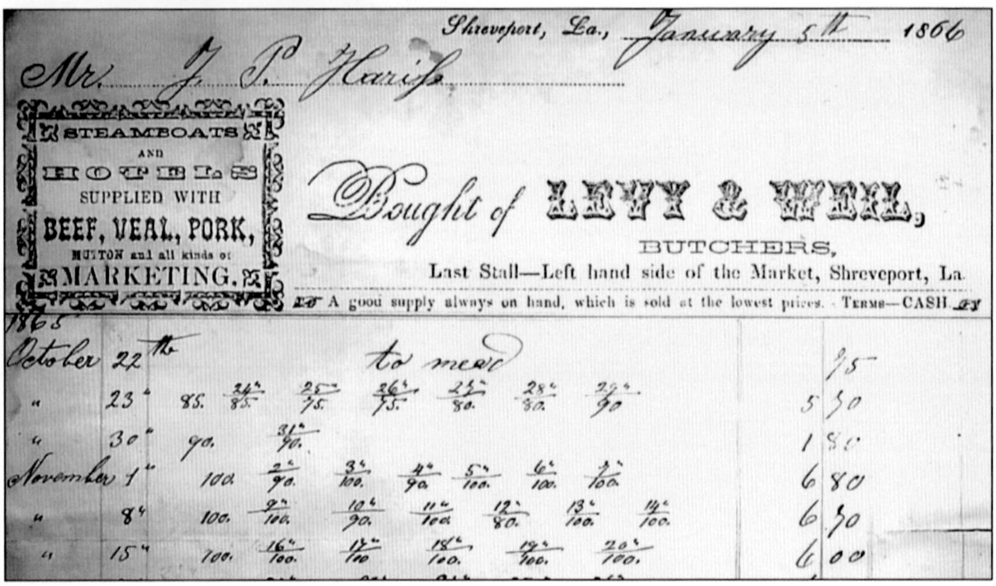

Shreveport, La., January 5th 1866

Mr. J. P. Harris

STEAMBOATS AND HOTELS SUPPLIED WITH BEEF, VEAL, PORK, MUTTON and all kinds of MARKETING.

Bought of LEVY & WEIL, BUTCHERS,

Last Stall—Left hand side of the Market, Shreveport, La.

A good supply always on hand, which is sold at the lowest prices. Terms—CASH.

1865

October 22th to meat 75

" 23 5 50

" 30 1 80

November 1 6 80

" 8 6 70

" 15 6 00

This receipt is from the butcher shop of Levy and Weil, which operated in a stall of the large City Market located in the middle of Market Street between Texas and Travis Streets. (In 1871, the Market was moved to the northwest corner of Milam and Louisiana Streets.) Simon Levy Jr. and his wife's cousin, Samuel Weil (1834–1897), a Confederate veteran, operated this business immediately after the Civil War. In the 1870s, Levy went into the grocery business with his brother-in-law, Lazarus Bodenheimer and then opened a saloon before getting into the banking business. Levy was a leader of the effort to change the early synagogue's practice to Reform. Note that he and Weil dealt in pork as well as other meat. Though Jews of European birth, they were thoroughly assimilated and their butcher shop was not kosher.

Two

Growth and Development 1869–1900

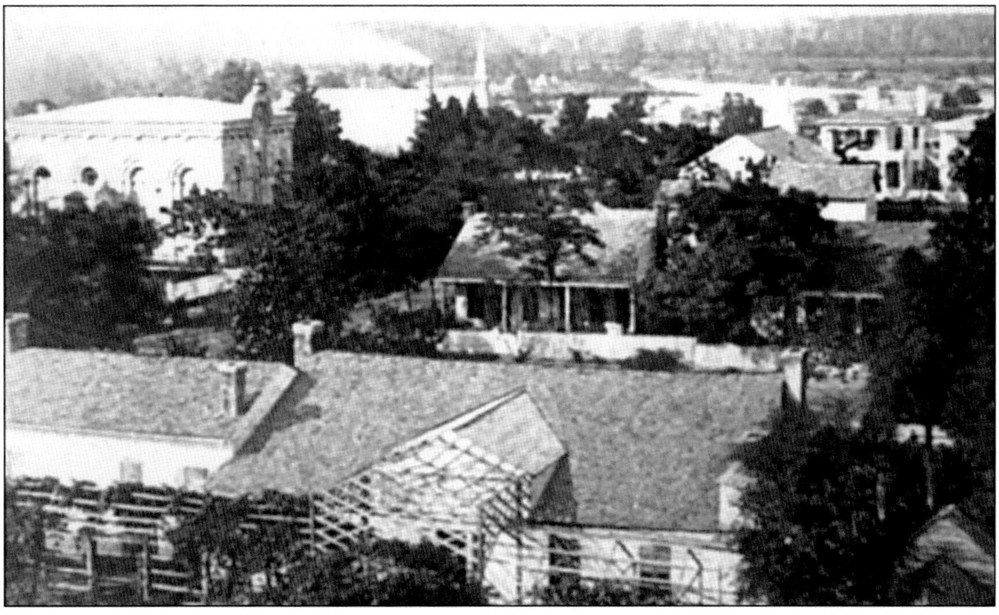

This is an 1870 view of part of the area around the intersection of Edwards and Fannin Streets. At upper left is the newly consecrated B'nai Zion Temple. Also known as Hebrew Zion, the synagogue, located at 320 Fannin Street, replaced a frame house that once stood on the same site and had been used as a synagogue since 1859. When the new temple was built, the old frame structure was moved to the rear of the lot where it became "The German School," a private school founded on the design of the German "gymnasium" system. As most of the community was of German or Alsatian background, it was only natural that parents wanted to educate their children in the manner of their homeland. Many German Christians also patronized the school, which was operated by the temple through the 1890s. In addition to the temple, this photograph shows the residences of Emanuel Phelps (one-story house with porch at center) and Simon Levy (two-story house with upper and lower porches).

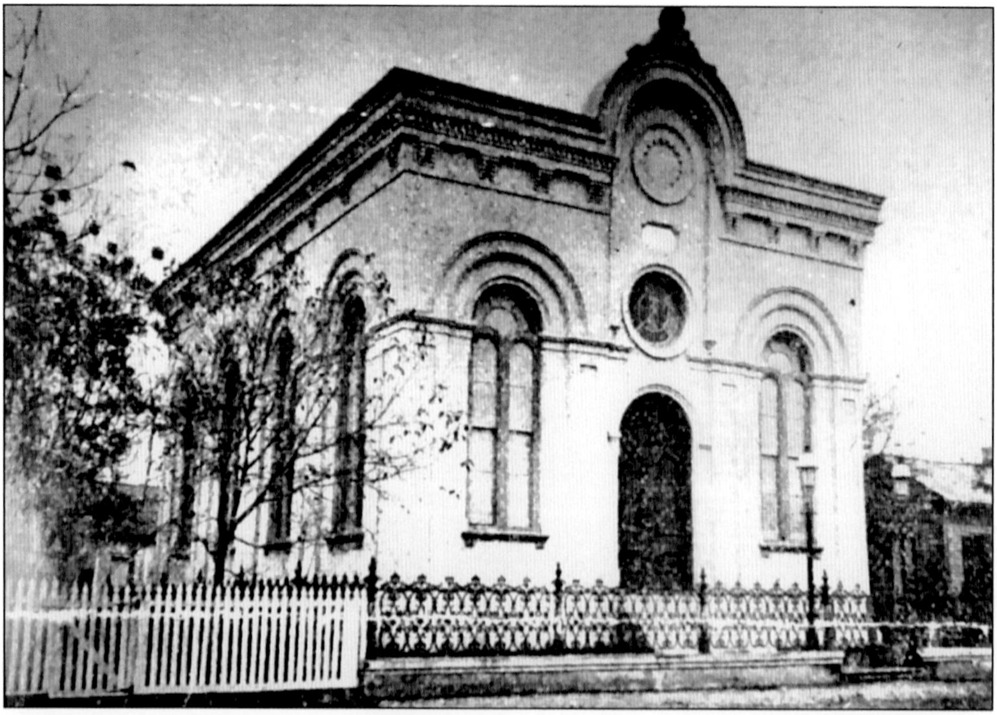

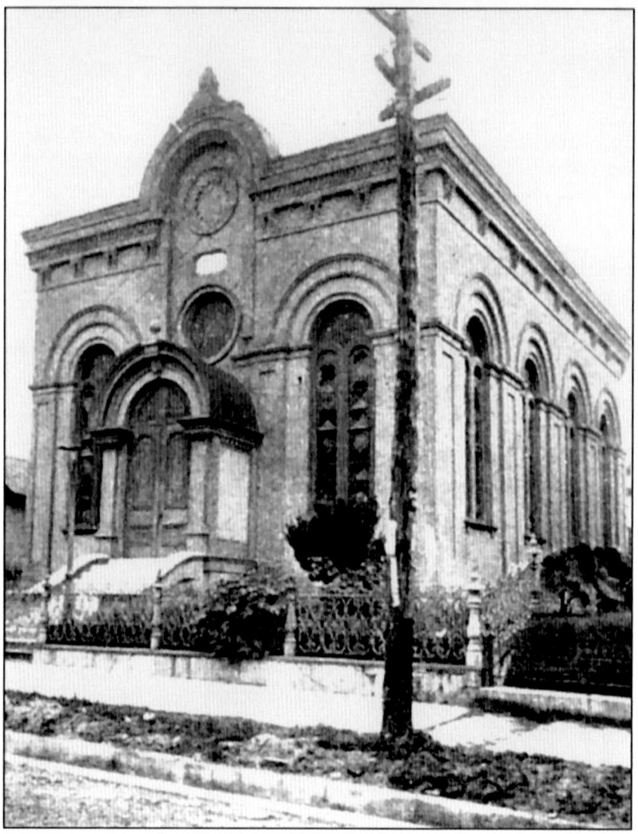

On this and the following page are four images of the first permanent synagogue in Shreveport, B'nai Zion Temple, located at 320 Fannin Street. It was designed by New Orleans architect Benjamin W. Harrod. The cornerstone was laid on July 27, 1869, and the building was dedicated as a house of worship on May 27, 1870. Capt. Simon Levy Jr. was congregational president and Dr. Max Samfield was rabbi at the time. The new temple was completed at a total cost of $27,000. The image above is of the temple soon after completion. To the left is an image from around 1890 showing the enlarged main entrance constructed after the building was damaged by fire in 1881. Many early temple records were lost in that same blaze.

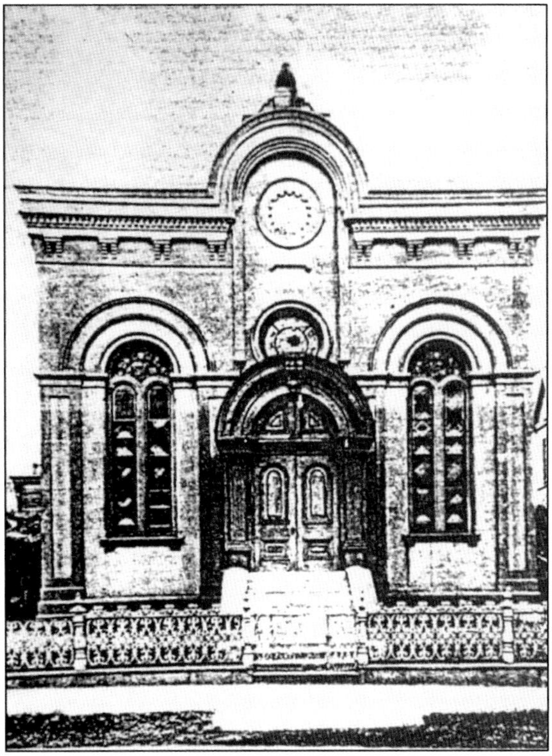

At right is a view of the temple in the 1890s. It is shown below around 1912. By 1906, the congregation had begun to outgrow the Fannin Street temple and the idea of building a larger synagogue was discussed. Two lots were purchased at the corner of Cotton and Common Streets but nothing more was done with regard to a new temple until 1914. Meanwhile, the Fannin Street temple was the center of the Jewish community. Above its doorway, in Hebrew letters, were the words *Kahal Kodesh B'nai Zion*—Holy Assembly of the Children of Zion.

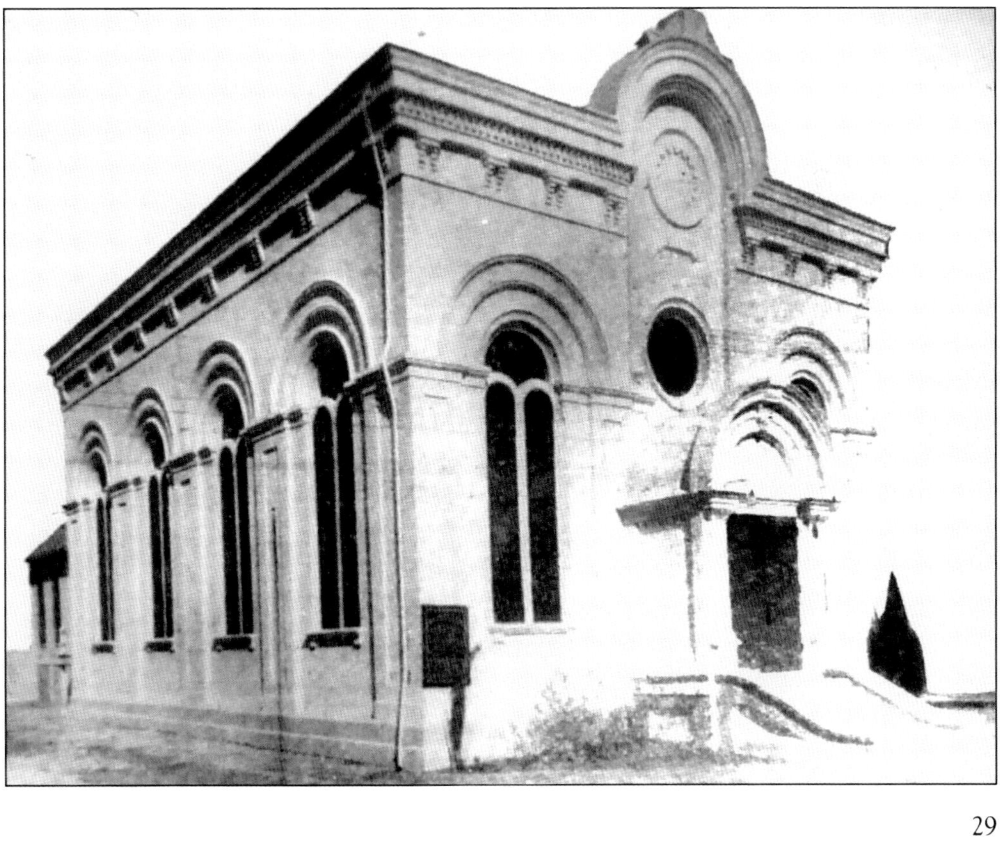

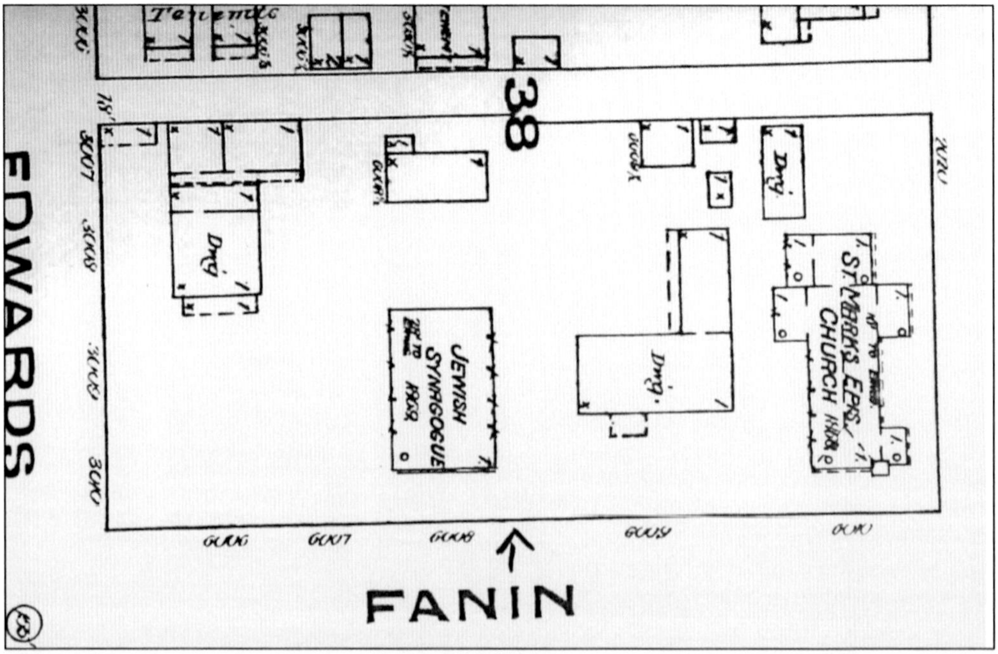

The Sanborn fire insurance maps are a remarkable resource and show every building in the city for the year the map was published. Above is the Sanborn map of 1885 showing B'nai Zion Temple with the old frame building behind it. Below is the 1897 map noting that a cistern has been added and the frame building used by the "German School" turned around on the lot. Note also that the name of the temple is given as "B'nai Zion."

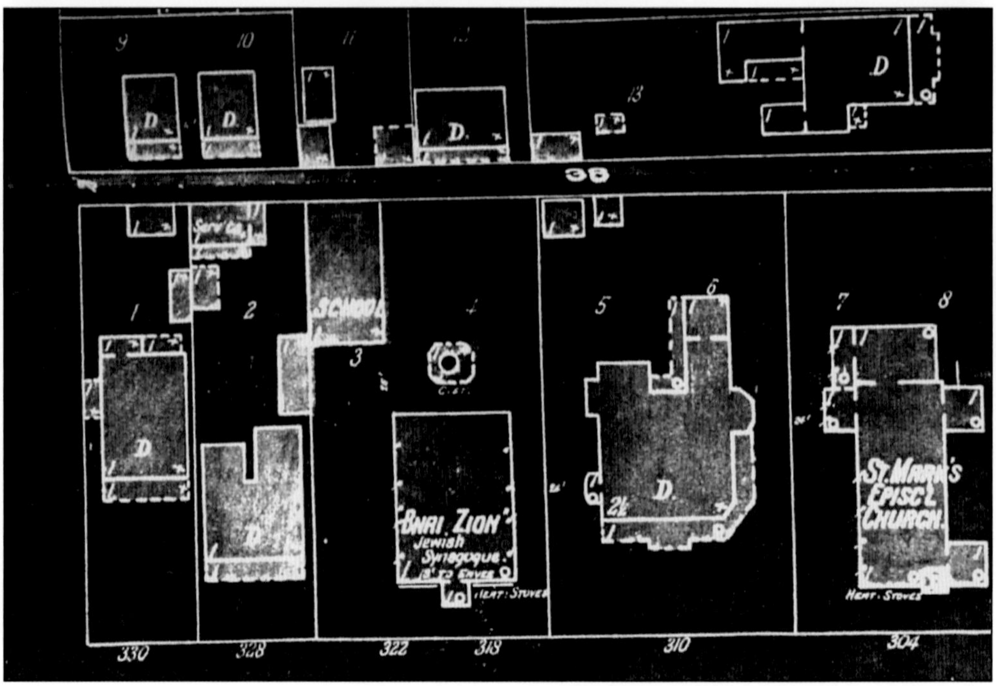

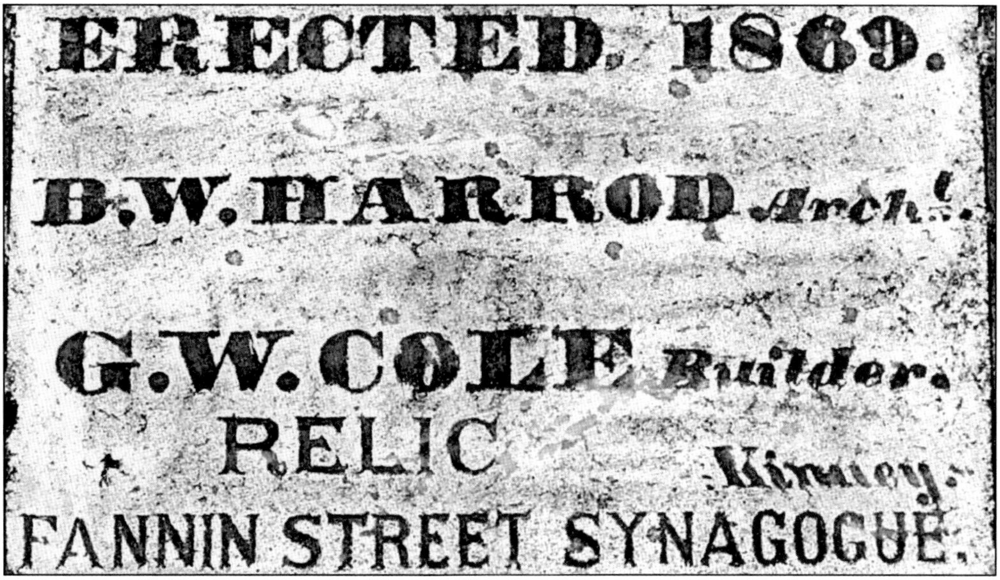

This is the cornerstone of B'nai Zion's 1869 temple. Note that it reads simply "Fannin Street Synagogue." Six years later, in 1875, a traditionalist (Orthodox) segment of the congregation broke away from B'nai Zion to form a new congregation, Emanu-El. The Reform part of the community came to be known as "Hebrew Zion," though both congregations met at the B'nai Zion synagogue. In 1877, the two merged but the name Hebrew Zion—or simply "Zion Congregation"—stuck and came to be used interchangeably with the name B'nai Zion. Not until 1915 and the move to a new temple would the name B'nai Zion again be used solely to represent the Reform congregation of Shreveport.

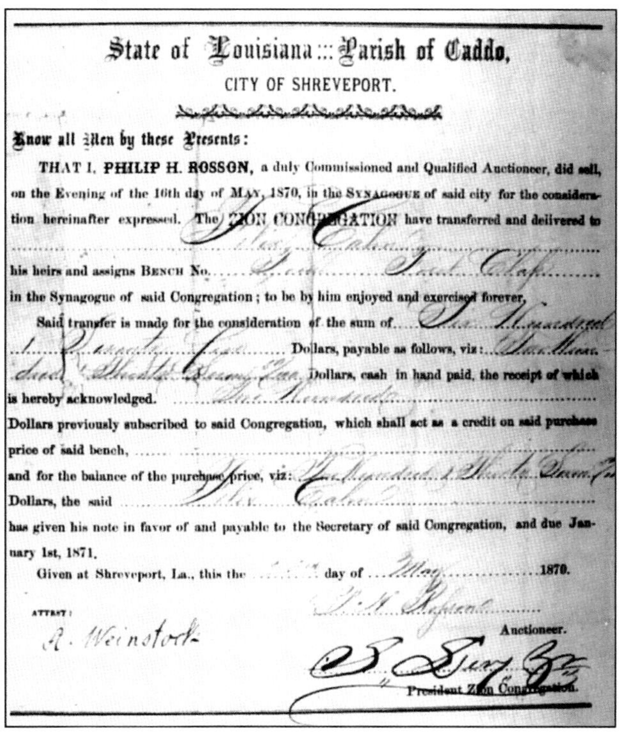

State of Louisiana ::: Parish of Caddo,

CITY OF SHREVEPORT.

Know all Men by these Presents:

THAT I, PHILIP H. ROSSON, a duly Commissioned and Qualified Auctioneer, did sell, on the Evening of the 16th day of MAY, 1870, in the SYNAGOGUE of said city for the consideration hereinafter expressed. The ZION CONGREGATION have transferred and delivered to Felix Cahn his heirs and assigns BENCH No. ... in the Synagogue of said Congregation; to be by him enjoyed and exercised forever.

Said transfer is made for the consideration of the sum of ... Dollars, payable as follows, viz: ... Dollars, cash in hand paid, the receipt of which is hereby acknowledged. ... Dollars previously subscribed to said Congregation, which shall act as a credit on said purchase price of said bench, ... and for the balance of the purchase price, viz: ... Dollars, the said Felix Cahn has given his note in favor of and payable to the Secretary of said Congregation, and due January 1st, 1871.

Given at Shreveport, La., this the ... day of May 1870.

ATTEST: A. Weinstock

Auctioneer.

President Zion Congregation.

As was the custom in many Christian churches of the day, pews were sold at the old B'nai Zion Temple on Fannin Street. At left is a contract for the sale of a pew to Felix Cahn dated 1870 and signed by Simon Levy Jr. and Asher Weinstock. The pew was located fourth from the *bimah* and sold for $75.

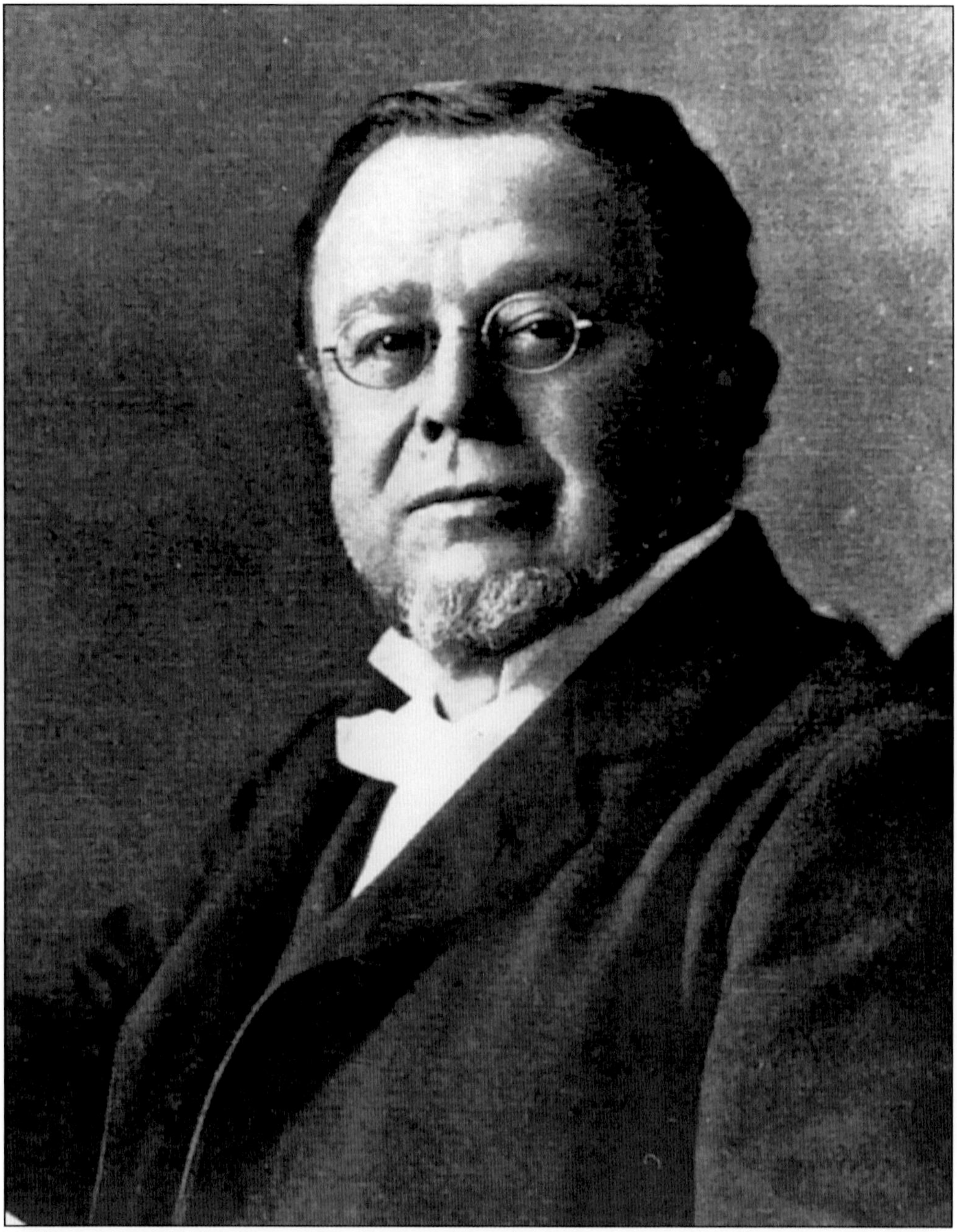

Rabbi Max Samfield (1846–1915), a native of Markstift, Germany, was educated and ordained a Reform rabbi in his native country. In 1867, he came to the United States at the invitation of B'nai Zion Congregation in Shreveport to become the synagogue's first Reform rabbi. It was during his rabbinate that the term "temple" came to be used with reference to B'nai Zion. In addition to serving as rabbi, Samfield was principal of the German School. He remained at B'nai Zion only four years, accepting an invitation to become rabbi of Temple B'nai Israel in Memphis, Tennessee in 1871, where he remained for the rest of his life. In October 1815, Rabbi Samfield was scheduled to participate in the dedication services of B'nai Zion's new temple on Cotton Street, but he died only a few days before his scheduled return to Shreveport.

The cover of the *Constitution and By-Laws of Hebrew Zion Congregation* is shown here, first published in 1866 and amended by the edition shown in 1888. This is the basis of today's by-laws of B'nai Zion Temple. Note that in 1888 the congregation was still using the name "Hebrew Zion," though it was formally chartered under the name "B'nai Zion."

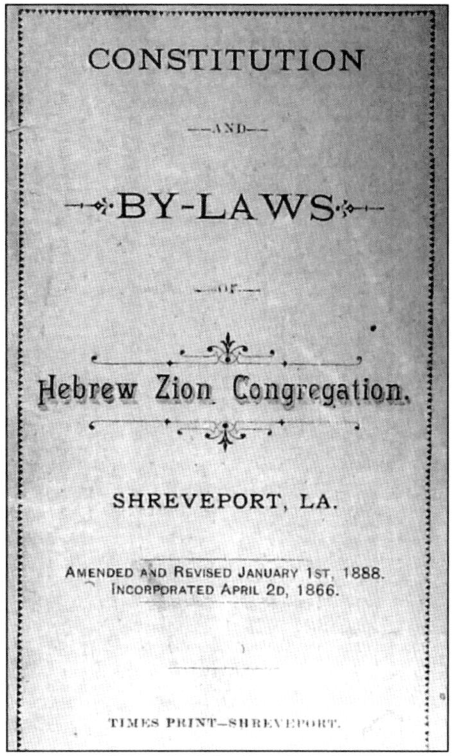
CONSTITUTION

—AND—

BY-LAWS

—OF—

Hebrew Zion Congregation,

SHREVEPORT, LA.

AMENDED AND REVISED JANUARY 1ST, 1888.
INCORPORATED APRIL 2D, 1866.

TIMES PRINT—SHREVEPORT.

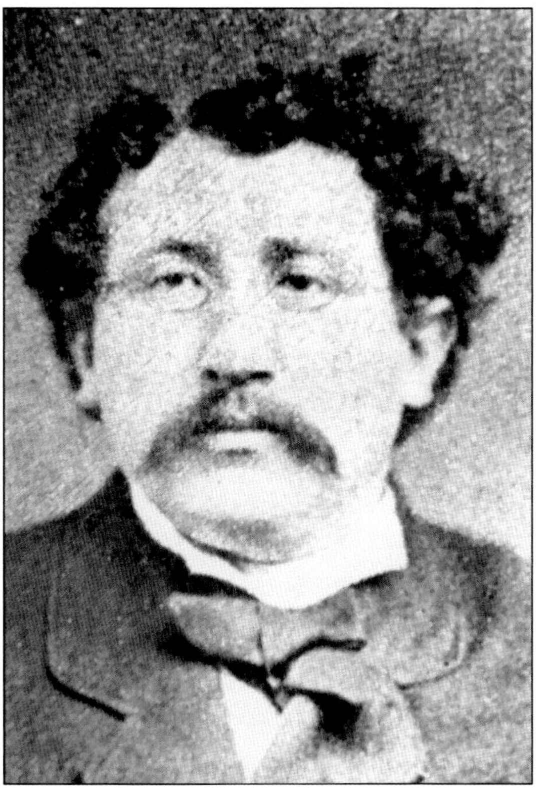

From 1871 to 1875, Rabbi Meyer Greenblatt (1849–1885), served B'nai Zion Temple, leading the congregation through one of its most trying episodes, the yellow fever epidemic of August–November 1873. Although he urged members of the Jewish community to relocate to nearby Marshall, Texas until the epidemic passed, few did so. Nevertheless, Rabbi Greenblatt held High Holy Day Services in Marshall that year. In all, B'nai Zion lost 48 members to the epidemic, proportionally more than any church in the then-small city of Shreveport. In 1875, Rabbi Greenblatt moved to Pine Bluff, Arkansas where he died of typhoid 10 years later.

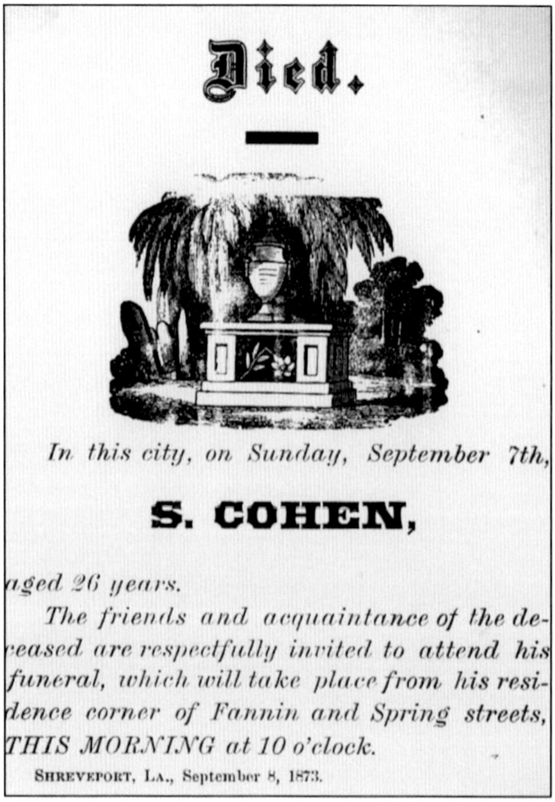

Died.

In this city, on Sunday, September 7th,

S. COHEN,

aged 26 years.

The friends and acquaintance of the deceased are respectfully invited to attend his funeral, which will take place from his residence corner of Fannin and Spring streets, THIS MORNING at 10 o'clock.

SHREVEPORT, LA., September 8, 1873.

Black-bordered paper death announcements, which could be posted on walls and telegraph poles, were typical in Louisiana and much of the South during the mid- and late 19th century. Unfortunately, during epidemics such as that which struck Shreveport in 1873, these announcements were seen daily by the dozens. A few still survive and many of these mourn the deaths of members of the Jewish community.

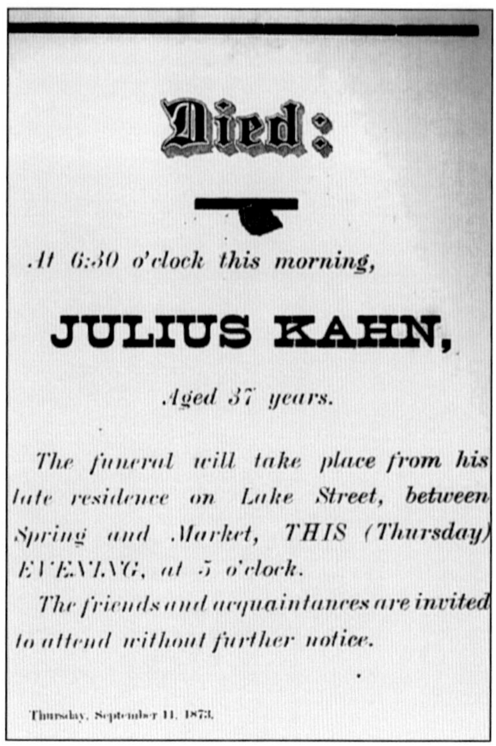

Died:

At 6:30 o'clock this morning,

JULIUS KAHN,

Aged 37 years.

The funeral will take place from his late residence on Lake Street, between Spring and Market, THIS (Thursday) EVENING, at 5 o'clock.

The friends and acquaintances are invited to attend without further notice.

Thursday, September 11, 1873.

Shown on this page are announcements of the deaths of Simon Cohen (1847–1873), a native of Neckla, in the Duchy of Posen, Prussia, and Julius Kahn (1836–1873). Kahn, a native of Waldenheim, Alsace came to Shreveport from Savannah, Georgia, with his brothers before the Civil War (see page 17). During the war, he was a private in Company E of the 3rd Louisiana Cavalry, Confederate Army. Both Cohen and Kahn are buried at Hebrew Rest Cemetery Number One adjacent to Oakland Cemetery on Sprague Street.

This is the grave of Mayor Samuel Levy (1835–1883) at Hebrew Rest Number One. Serving in the city's highest office in 1873, Levy was faced with two major problems—reconstruction and the yellow fever epidemic. City services had already virtually fallen apart due to government corruption, and Levy's attempts at straightening out the mess he inherited from his predecessors was compounded by the onset of the epidemic. His answer was to pay the city's bills out of his own pocket during the course of the epidemic and hope to be reimbursed later. He died a decade later, still uncompensated.

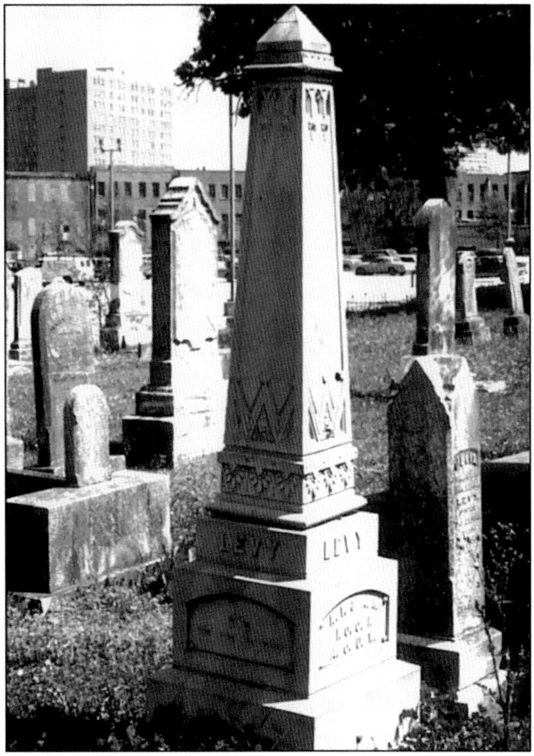

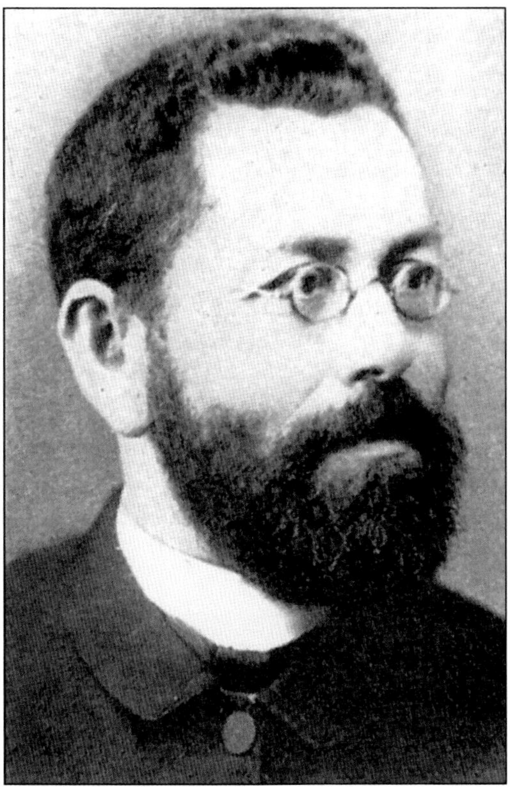

Rabbi Emanuel Hess (1845–1906), a native of Meerholz, Germany, came to B'nai Zion in 1876, a year after the split that created Congregation Emanu-El. During this time, Rabbi Hess shared the *bimah* of the Fannin Street Synagogue with Rabbi Nachman I. Benson, an Arkansan who hoped to reunite the two congregations in the Orthodox tradition. Rabbi Hess hoped to reunite them in the Reform tradition. Working together, the rabbis did persuade their congregations to reunite in 1877, under Reform practice but with a nod toward traditionalism. Rabbi Hess was extremely popular and remained at B'nai Zion until 1888 when he left to assume the rabbinate of Mt. Zion Temple in St. Paul, Minnesota, where he remained until his death.

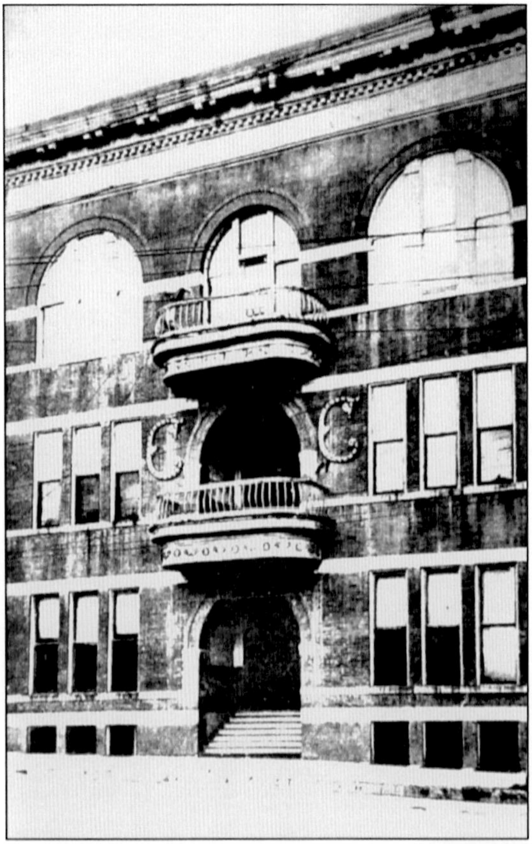

The Columbia Club, a private Jewish social and dining club, was founded in 1893 and continued in operation until 1933 when it became a victim of the Great Depression. Its first president was Simon Levy Jr. and its first manager was David March, for whom an Allendale area street is named. March (1836–1905) was a native of Germany, a Confederate veteran, and a longtime area restaurateur and saloonkeeper. The Columbia Club was first located in a remodeled house in the 200 block of Lake Street but in 1898 moved to 311 Milam, shown here.

The tomb of Rabbi Israel Saenger (1841–1918) and his wife Henriette (1850–1896) are shown below at Hebrew Rest Cemetery Number Two. Dr. Saenger served B'nai Zion from 1889 to 1901 and was rabbi emeritus from 1901 until his death. During his rabbinate the Ladies Home Charitable Association was founded to assist orphaned children (1892) and the Shreveport chapter of the National Council of Jewish Women was formed (1897).

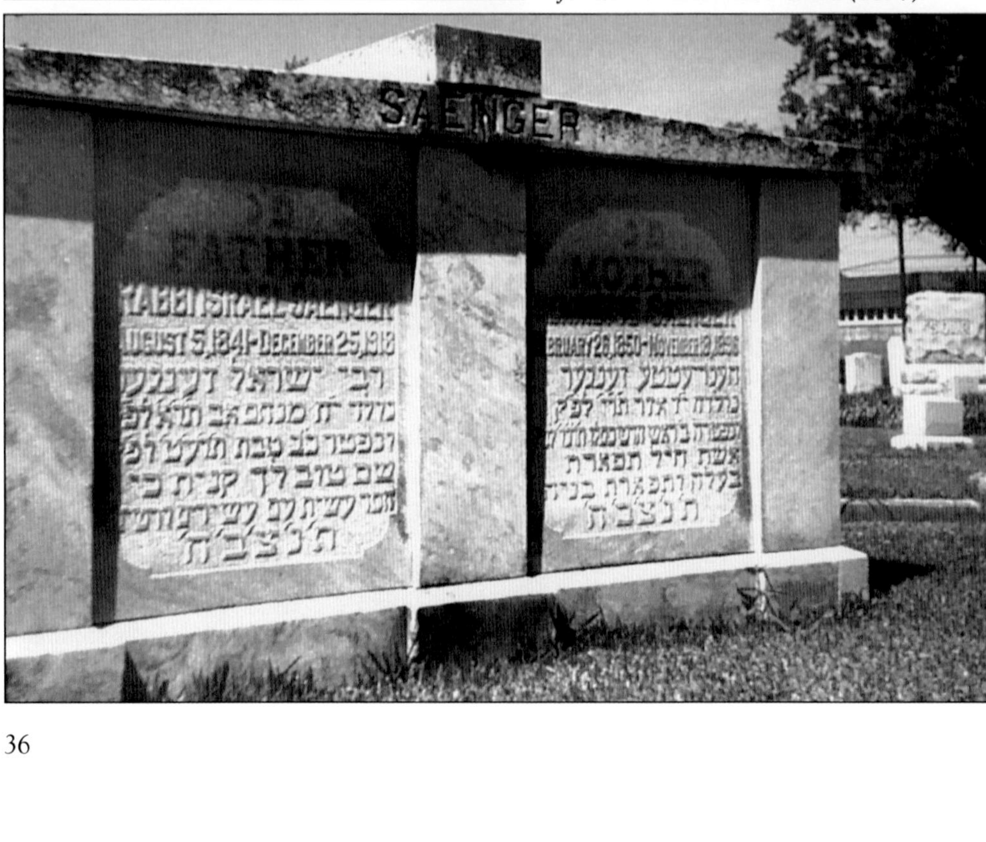

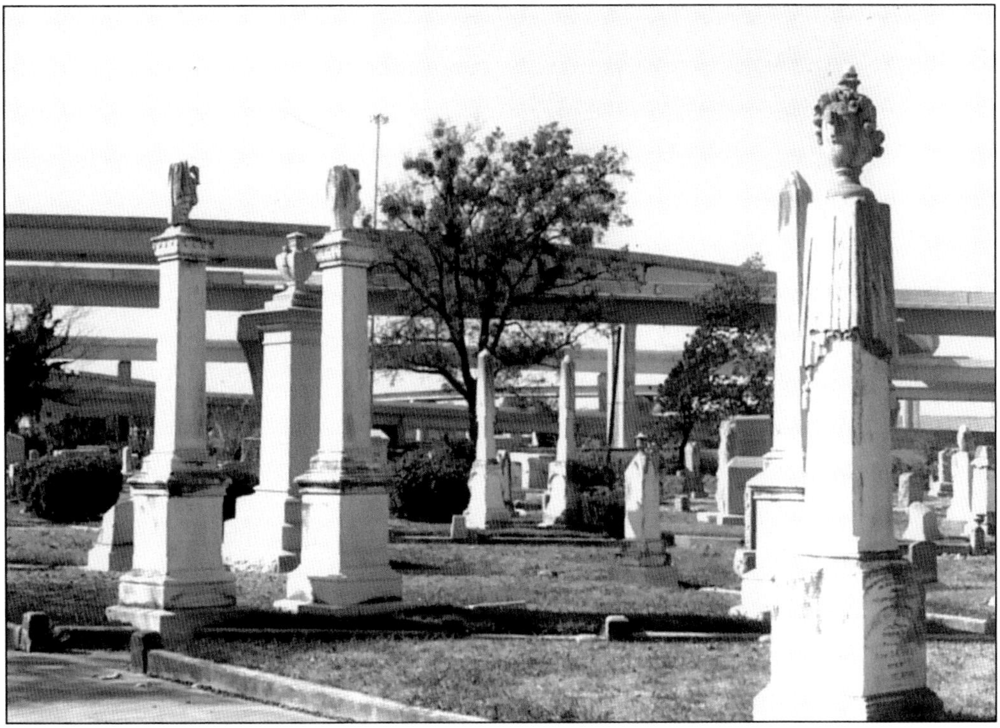

Hebrew Rest Cemetery Number Two, at Texas Avenue and Depot Street, was consecrated in 1886 during the rabbinate of Dr. Hess. Nearly four times the size of the first Hebrew Rest Cemetery, the new cemetery would remain in continual use until 1933. While burials in Hebrew Rest Number One took place in the traditional European Jewish fashion, with individuals buried chronologically in rows without regard to family groups, the new cemetery was divided into family plots in American fashion. Walkways separate each plot from its neighbors. Today Interstate 49 passes the cemetery to the west and Interstate 20 to the north, as may be seen in the photographs on this page.

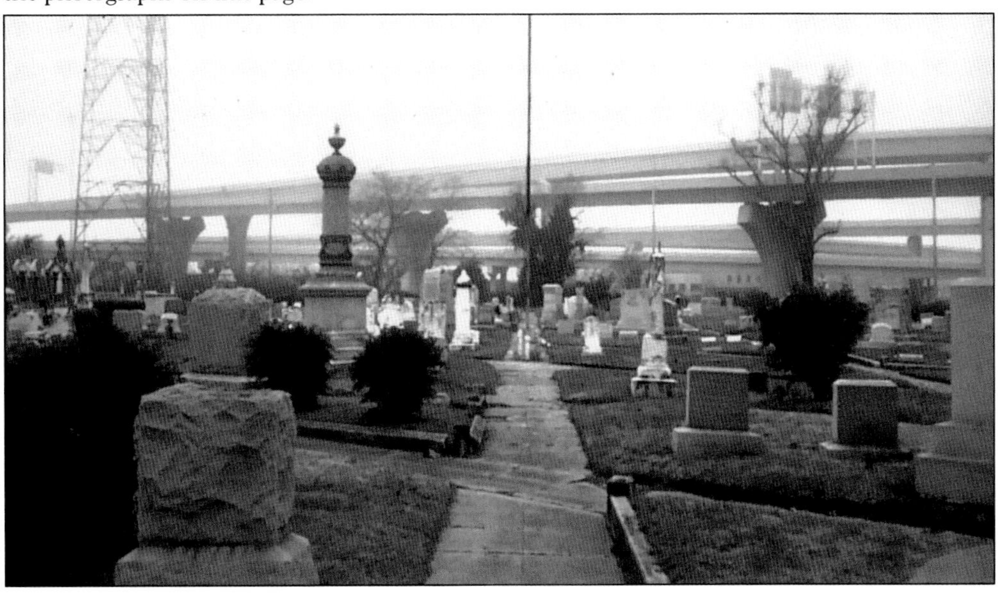

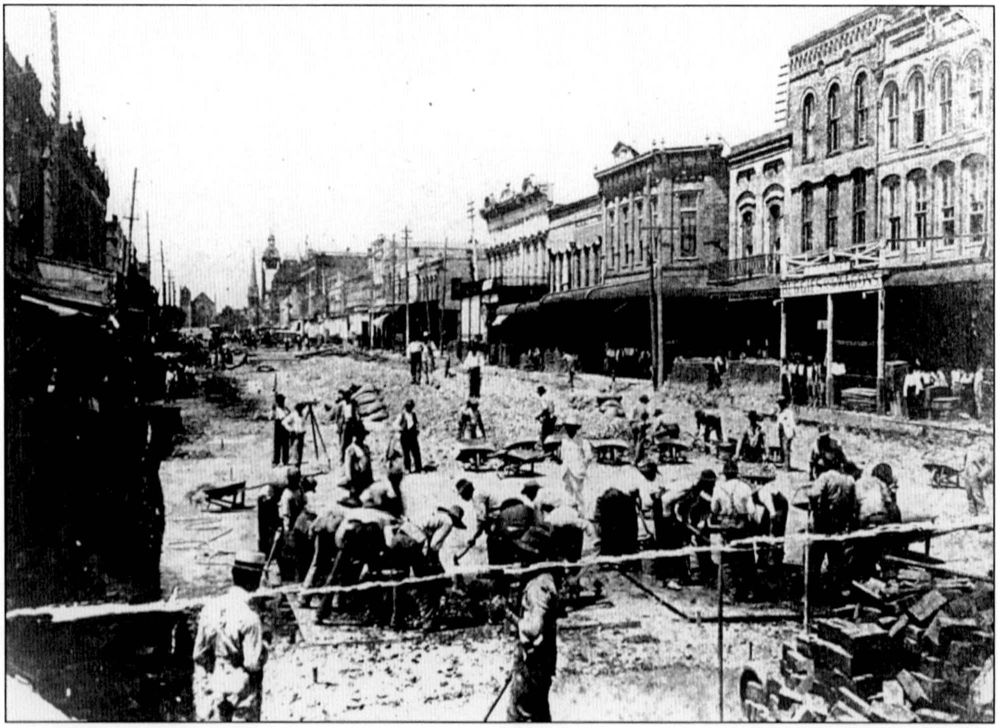

The paving of Texas Street near the river is shown above in the 1890s. At this time, dozens of merchants had their businesses in the 100 block of Texas. Of these, only three were not members of the Jewish community. Below is the building at 120 Texas (also seen near the center of the photograph above), which was home first to S.G. Dreyfus and Company and then to A. Weinstock and Company. It still stands today.

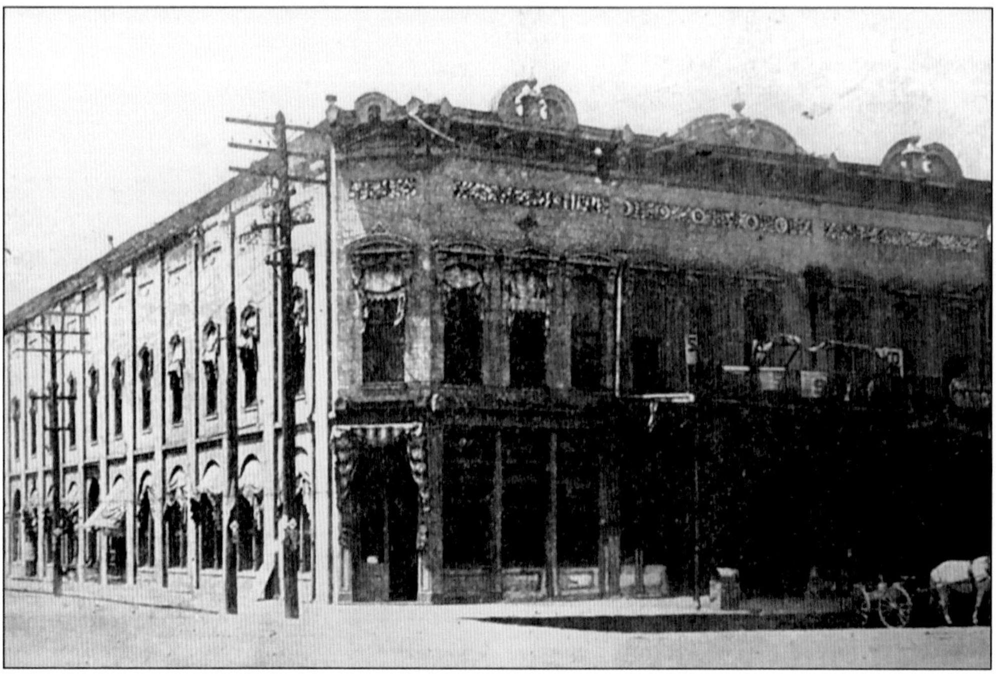

The remarkable gravestone of Nathan Goldkind (1849–1885), a native of Plotsk, Poland, stands facing Baker Street at Hebrew Rest Number One. Goldkind came to Shreveport in the 1870s and was a well-known merchant here. He was also known as a gambler and in 1885 lost his life during a late-night card game in his Common Street store. When his killer's sentence was commuted, his executor, Louis Liebman, had this monument placed so that all could see the murderer's name.

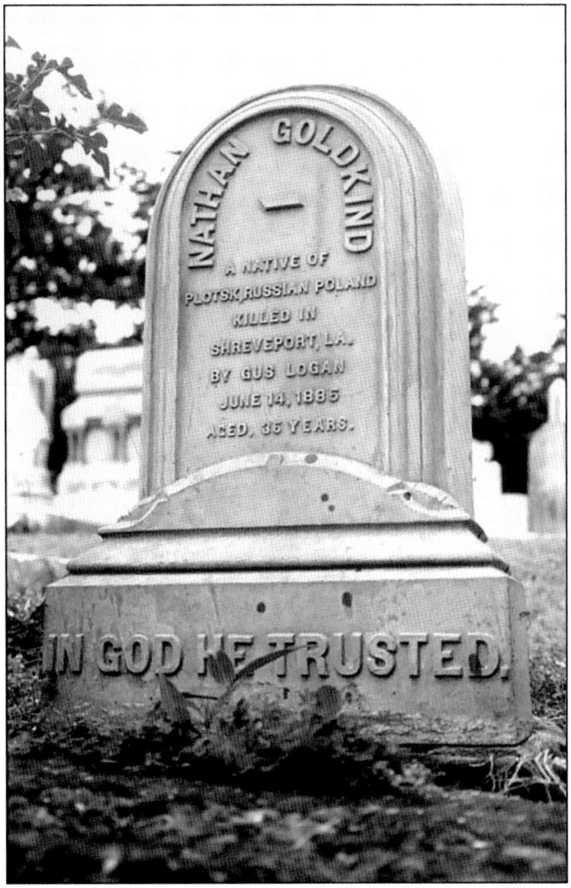

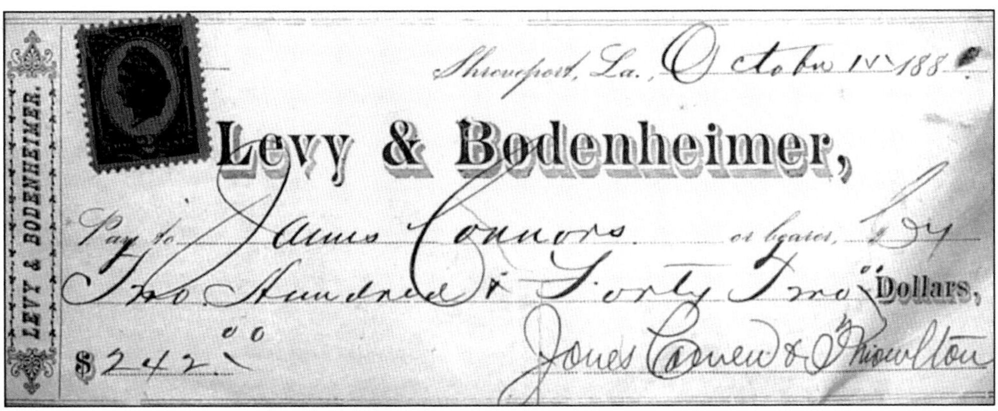

The wholesale grocery firm of Levy and Bodenheimer was operated by Simon Levy Jr. and his brother-in-law, Lazarus Bodenheimer. By the mid-1880s, it was one of the city's principal wholesale grocery firms, in a city that was a major distribution center for the grocery business. Seen here is a receipt from the firm dated 1881.

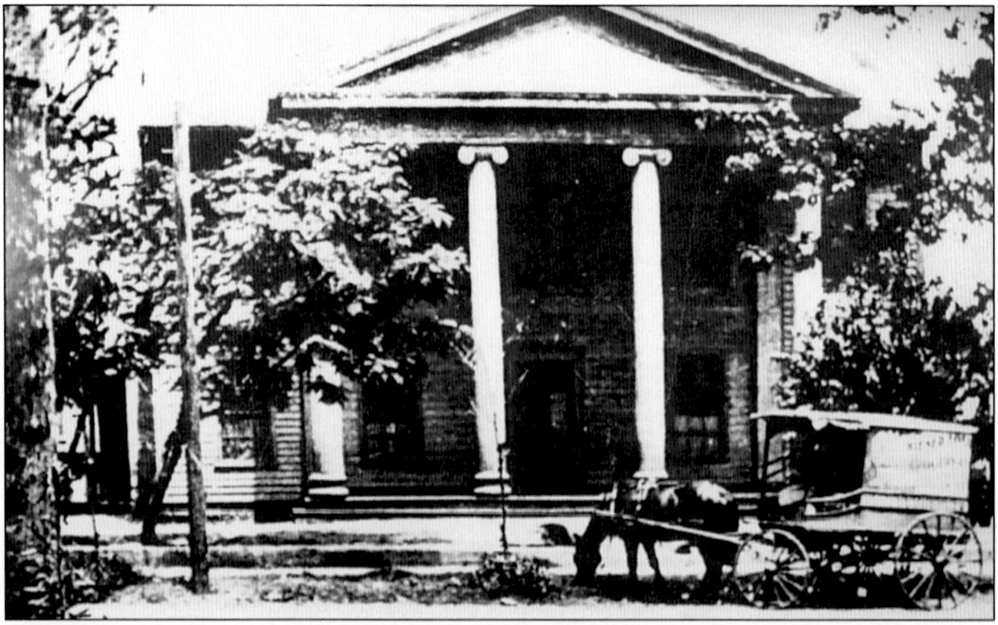

Another important late 19th-century grocery firm was that of Wiener and Loeb, which was founded in 1896 by Samuel Wiener Sr. and Leon B. Loeb. In 1922, Wiener and Loeb became the Big Chain Grocery Company. Above is a Wiener and Loeb grocery wagon hitched in the 300 block of Edwards Street around 1900. The company's early wagons spelled the name "Wiener" on one side and "Weiner" on the other, due to the sign painter's uncertainty about which spelling was correct. Shown below is the Wiener family home on Christian Street, built in 1896. The four Wiener sons, Jacques, Earl, William, and Samuel are said to have always hung their monogrammed towels in a certain order so the word "JEWS" was spelled out.

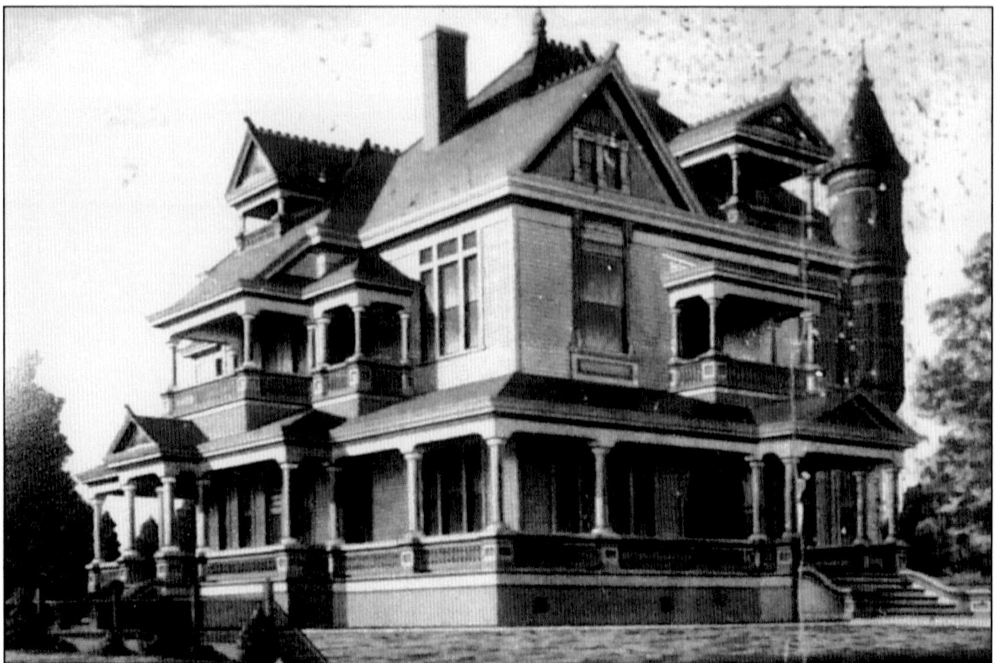

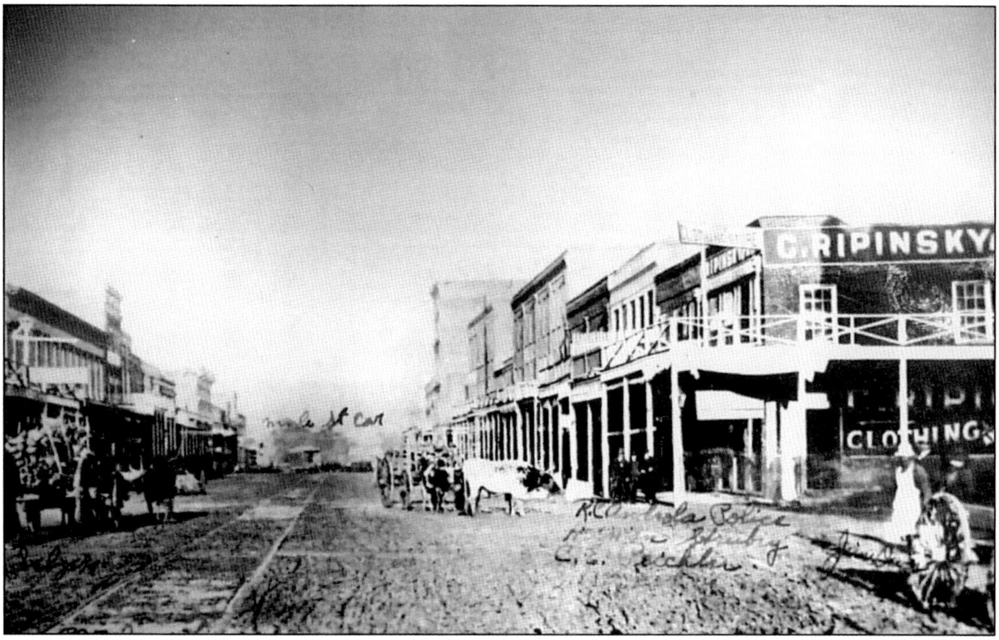

This is Texas Street as it appeared in the 1870s and early 1880s, prior to being paved. The view is east from the intersection with Market Street. At the corner is the firm of C. Ripinsky and Brother, an early clothing and department store operated by Charles and Morris Ripinsky and later by Charles's son Gabe.

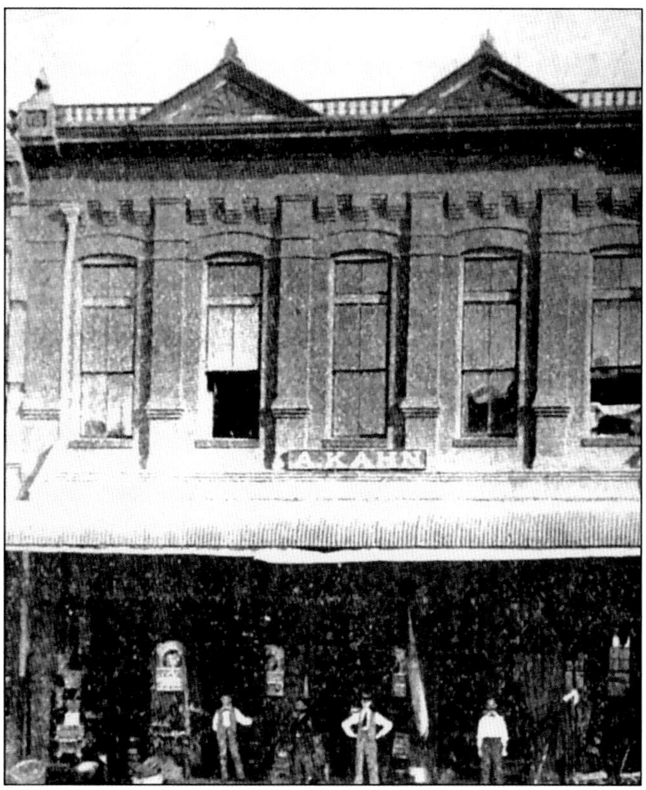

The firm of Aaron Kahn and Company sold tinware, crockery, and hardware from their store in the 100 block of Texas Street, built in 1874. The company later moved to the 200 block, but the original building, which boasted a row of notable cast-iron columns (virtually invisible in this 1890 photograph due to the shade of the metal awning), stood until 2001.

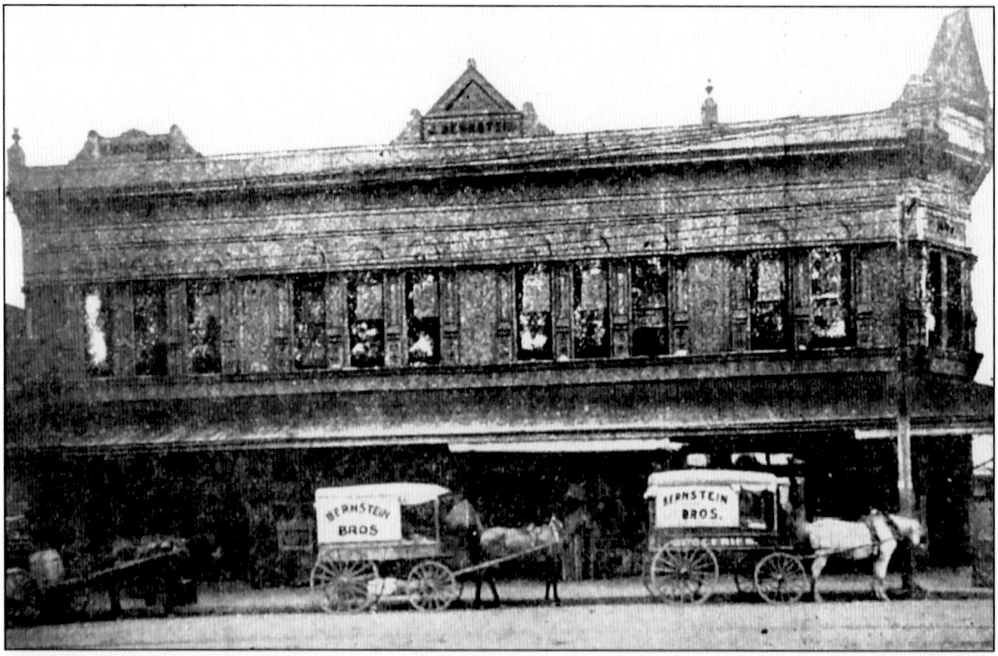

The Jacob Bernstein Building, shown above, at the corner of Texas Avenue and Murphy Street, housed the grocery, drug, and general store of Jacob's sons, Ernest, Julius, and Michel. Another son, Alexander, was court crier for the federal court of the Western District of Louisiana. He was later a United States Marshal. Ernest Bernstein came to be mayor of Shreveport and vice president of Commercial National Bank. He was an early vocal and influential supporter of future governor and United States senator Huey P. Long. The image below shows the huge cotton yard of Herman Loeb and Company near the riverfront. One of the area's principal cotton dealers in an age when Shreveport was the nation's third largest inland cotton port, Loeb also dealt in hides, wool, and furs with tanneries, the warehouse, and the cotton yard near the riverfront. The large Jacobs Company cotton yard and compress was nearby.

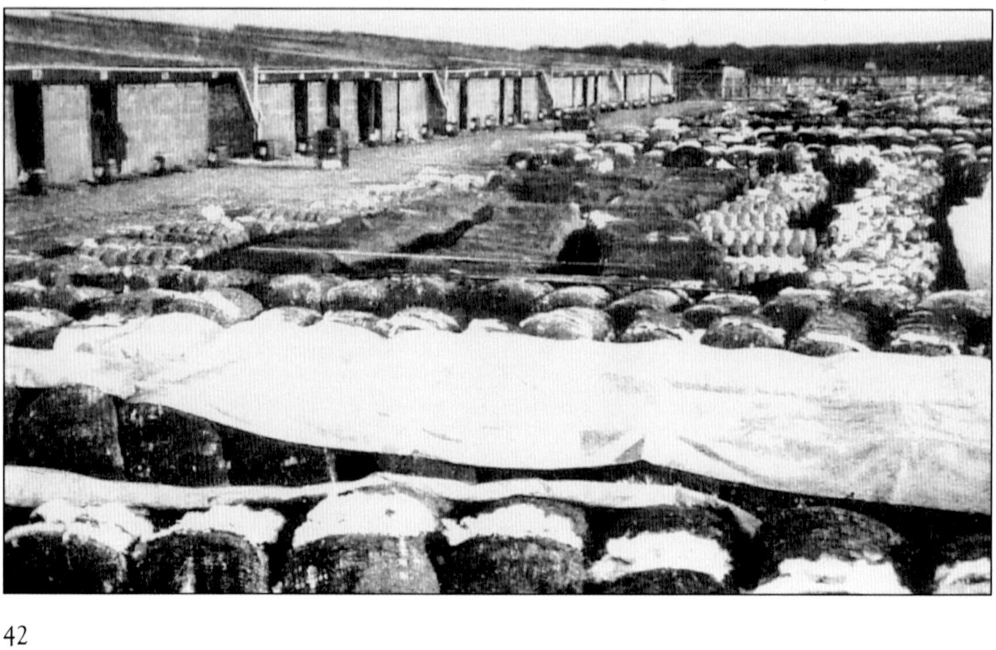

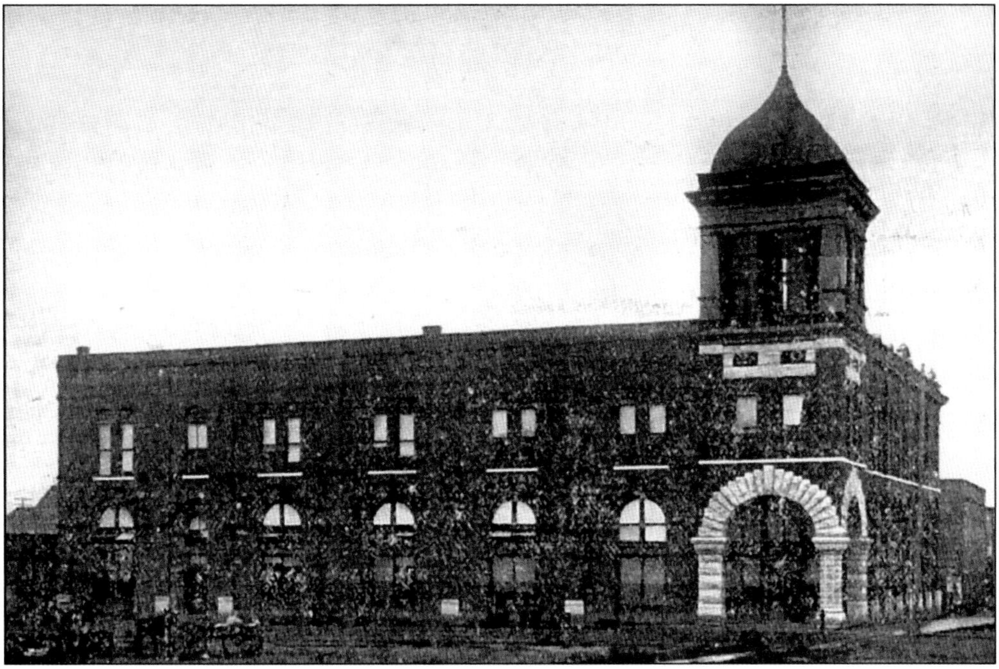

Pictured above is the S.G. Dreyfus Company, one of the city's largest dry goods firms, which was established in 1874 by Samuel G. Dreyfus. In 1889, the firm built this large facility at the southwest corner of Crockett and Spring Streets. Dreyfus remained in operation until 1937 when economic setbacks forced its closure. The name Paul Lowenthal remained on his former building at 109 Texas Street, shown below, until its demolition in 2001. Lowenthal (1851–1913) was a general merchandise dealer and from 1902 to 1912 served on the Shreveport City Council.

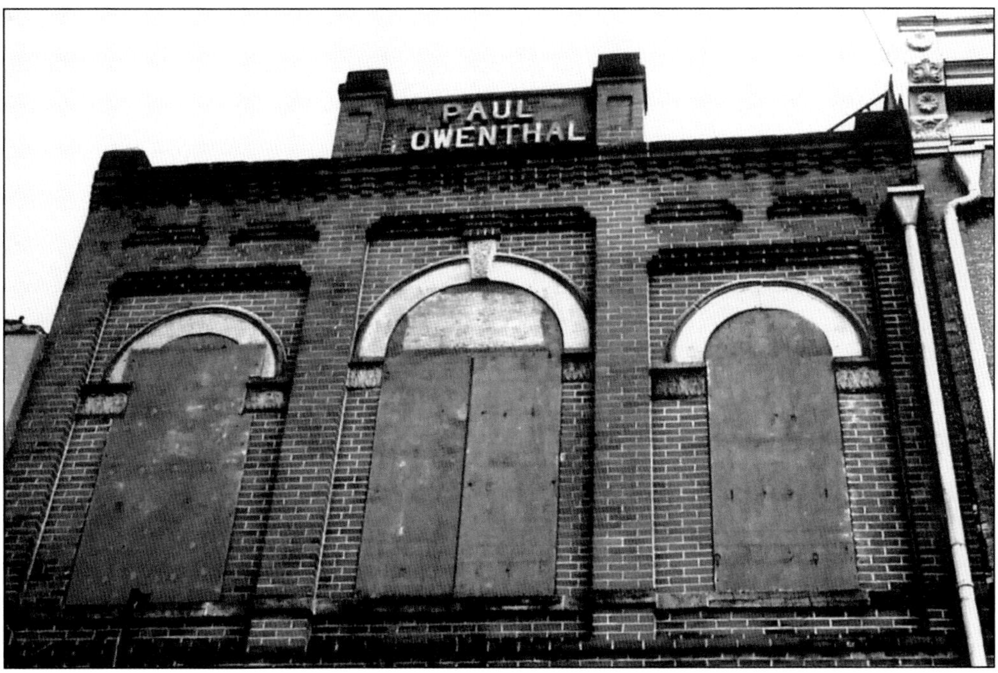

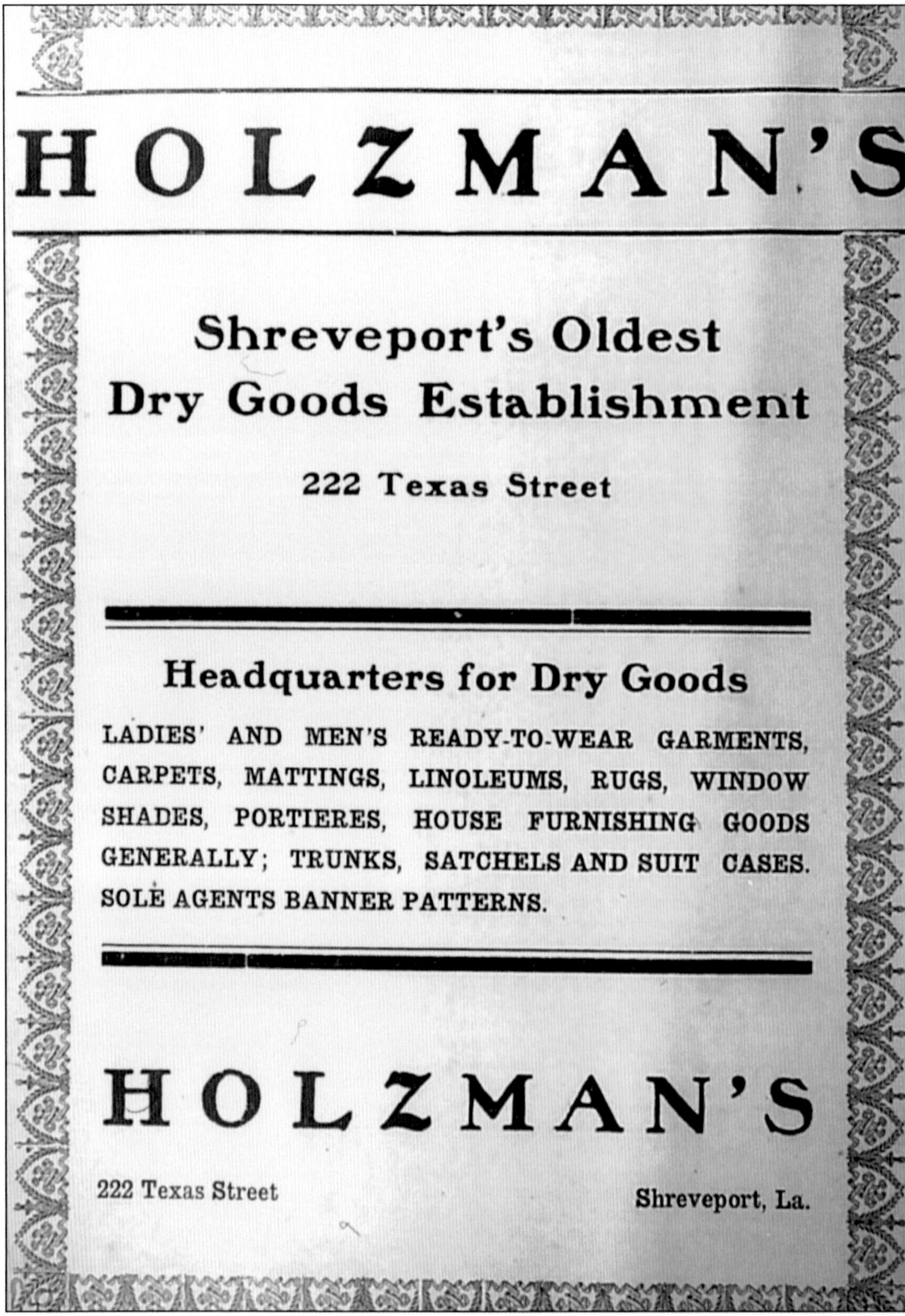

By the end of the 19th century, Holzman's, established in 1865, claimed to be the oldest continually-operating dry goods firm in the city. A city directory advertisement from the period describes the firm's offerings. Several older firms that had begun as dry goods stores were still in operation at the time but had since evolved into department stores.

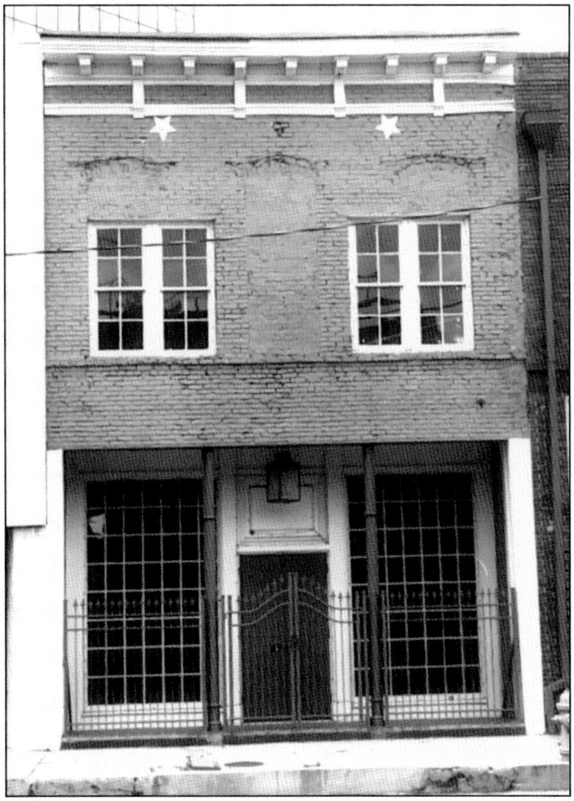

In this small building in the 200 block of Texas Street, Ben Holzman established his dry goods business at the end of the Civil War. The firm later moved to another location in the same block. During the Civil War, Holzman served in the Confederate Navy and was a member of the crew of the CSS *Virginia*, also known as the *Merrimack*.

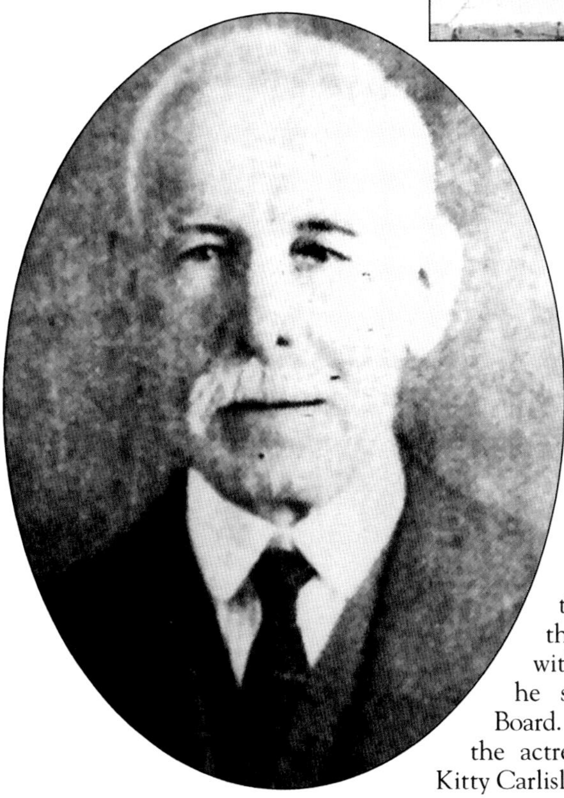

Benjamin Holzman (1844–1922) served on the city council from 1896 to 1899, was elected mayor in 1899, and served through 1902. His administration saw the completion of paving of all streets within the city limits. From 1906 to 1914, he served on the Caddo Parish School Board. Mayor Holzman's granddaughter is the actress and New York City arts promoter Kitty Carlisle Hart, widow of composer Moss Hart.

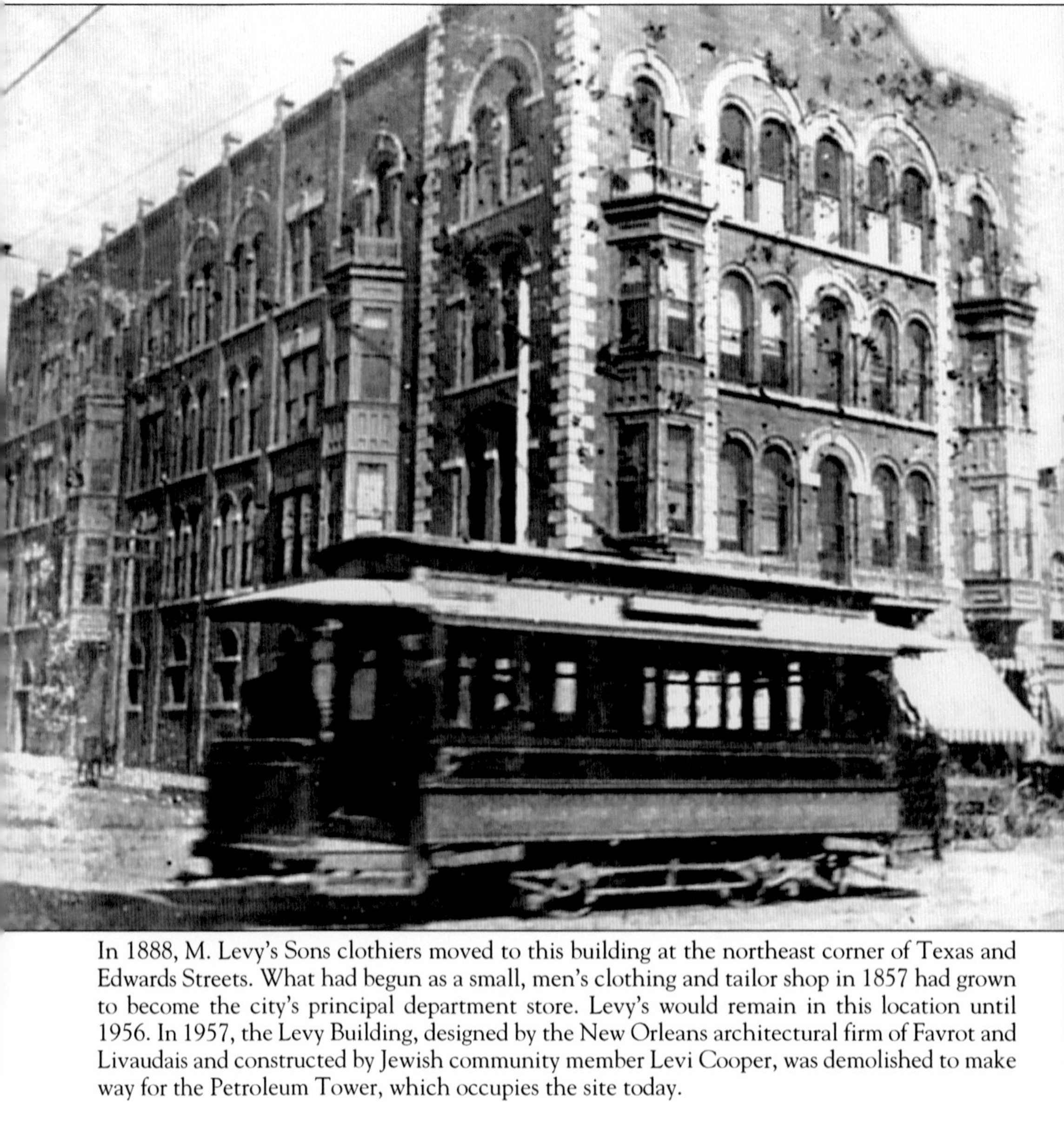

In 1888, M. Levy's Sons clothiers moved to this building at the northeast corner of Texas and Edwards Streets. What had begun as a small, men's clothing and tailor shop in 1857 had grown to become the city's principal department store. Levy's would remain in this location until 1956. In 1957, the Levy Building, designed by the New Orleans architectural firm of Favrot and Livaudais and constructed by Jewish community member Levi Cooper, was demolished to make way for the Petroleum Tower, which occupies the site today.

This is an 1890s M. Levy's advertisement for men's hats. The store was known for handling top-of-the-line goods and the prices of the hats advertised—in an era in which $1 had the buying power of more than $20 today—demonstrates that fact. Levy's was one of the few pioneer Shreveport stores to weather the Depression. Though the company showed negative income for much of the 1930s, its owners were determined to keep the store open. M. Levy's would not close its doors until 1980.

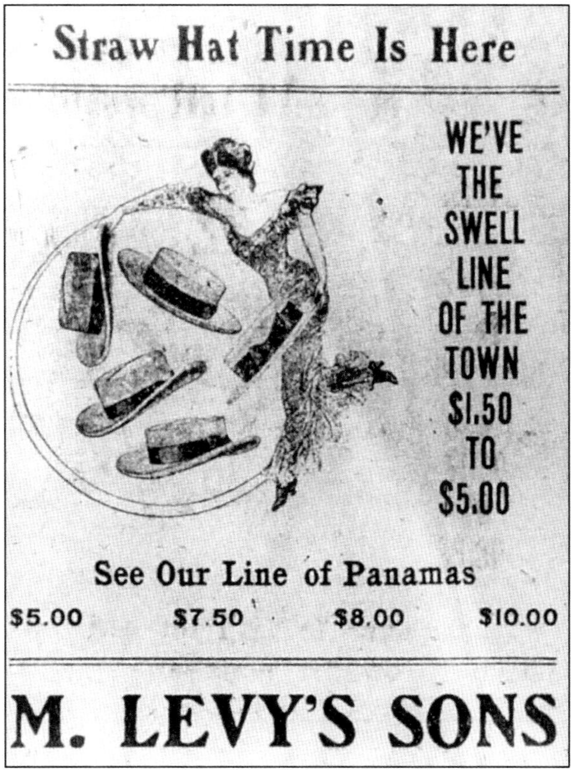

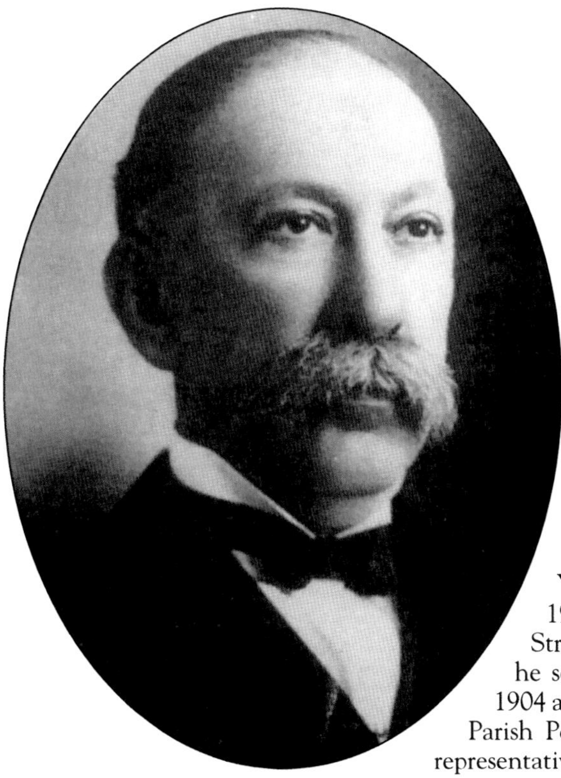

William Winter (1849–1917) was a son of Abraham Winter (see page 10) and a partner in the Winter Company, as well as a Shreveport agent for the New York Life Insurance Company in the late 19th century, with offices at 525 Spring Street (see page 22). From 1890 to 1892, he served on the city council, from 1896 to 1904 and again from 1912 to 1917 on the Caddo Parish Police Jury, and from 1904 to 1908 as a representative in the state legislature.

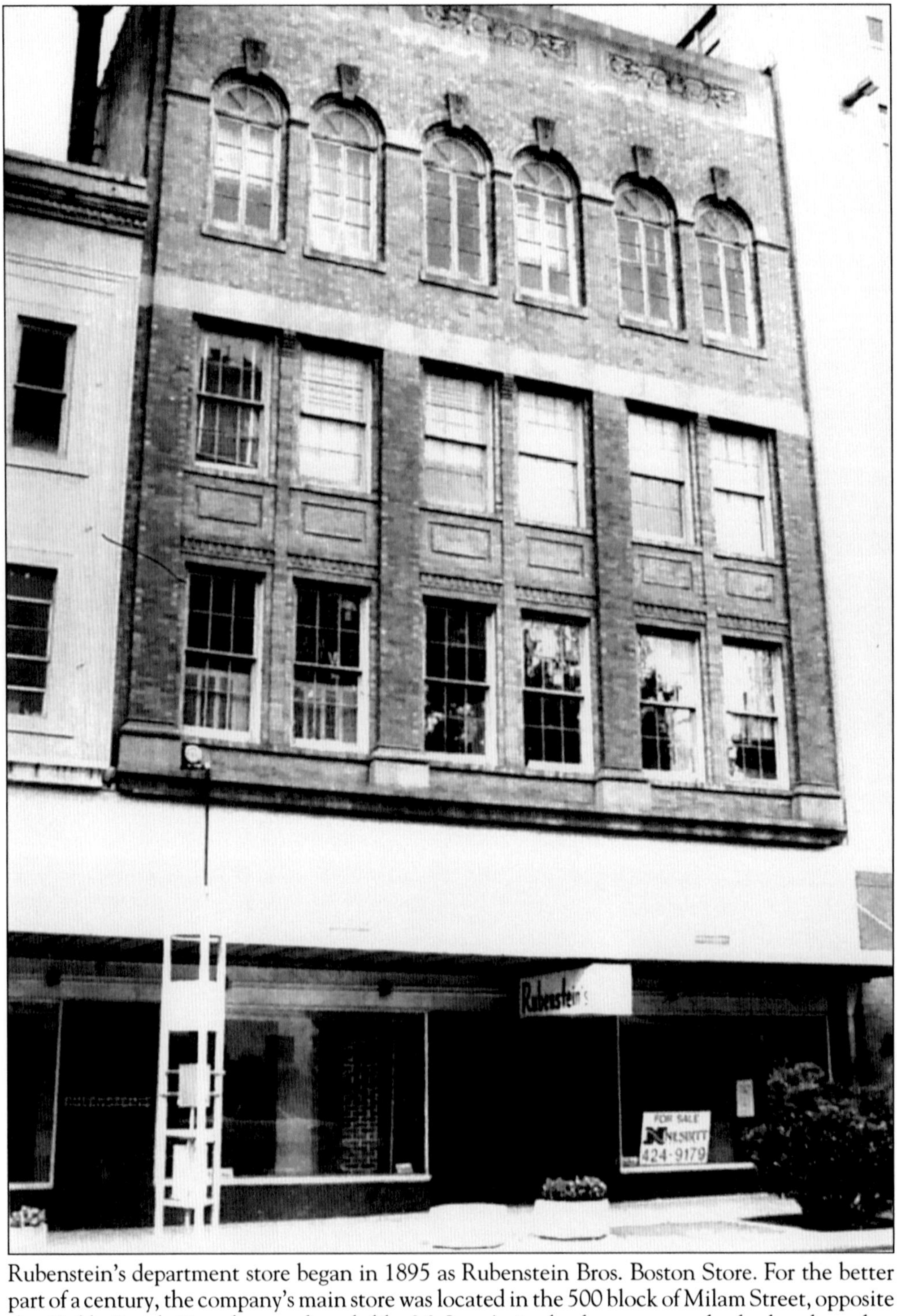

Rubenstein's department store began in 1895 as Rubenstein Bros. Boston Store. For the better part of a century, the company's main store was located in the 500 block of Milam Street, opposite the Caddo Parish Courthouse, though like M. Levy's, it also later operated suburban branches throughout Shreveport and Bossier City. Rubenstein's remained in operation until 1986.

One of the most influential Shreveporters of the late 19th century was educator Samuel Goldstein (1840–1906). Professor Goldstein was the driving force behind the creation of the Caddo Parish public school system, and in the 1890s he proposed the first tax specifically for the construction and support of public schools. Though noted as an educator, Goldstein was also a successful businessman and a partner in the grocery firm of Goldstein, Rose, and Company and later, Goldstein and Mabry, Ltd. He was also a longtime director of the Shreveport Mutual Building Association, later known as First Federal Savings and Loan Company.

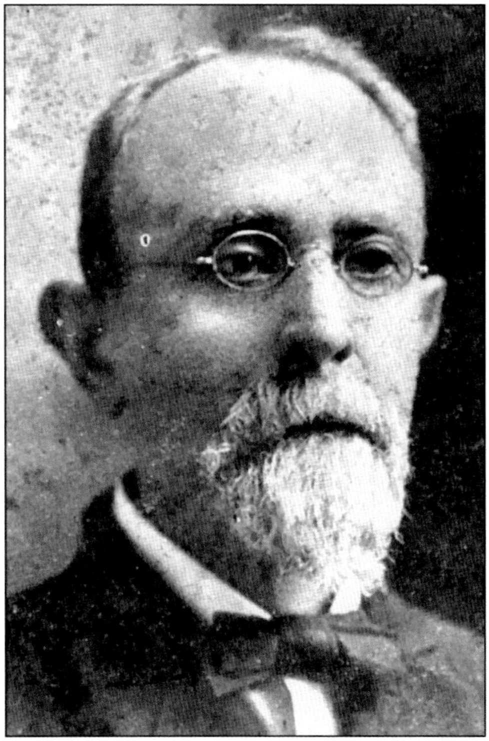

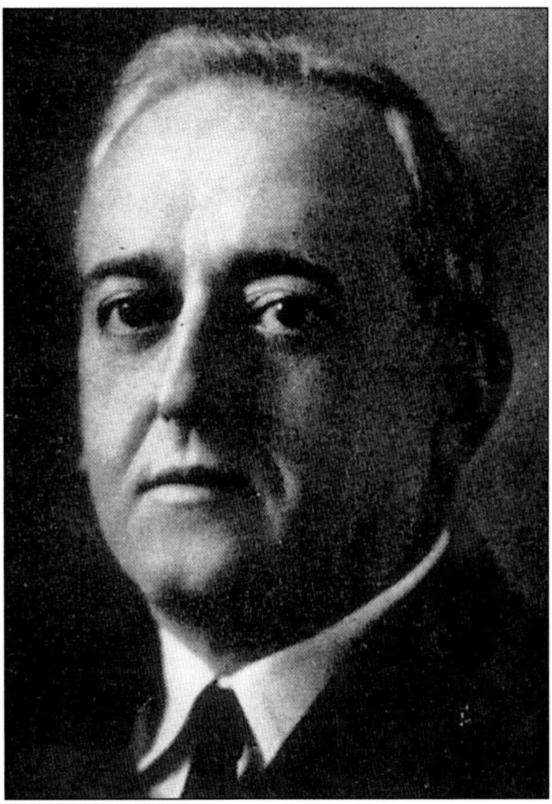

Dr. Louis Abramson (1868–1930), the son of a Baton Rouge area planter, studied medicine at Tulane and came to Shreveport to practice under Dr. Thomas E. Schumpert at his clinic and sanitarium (today's Schumpert Medical Center). Until Schumpert's death in 1908, Dr. Abramson remained associated with the clinic, but that year he opened a new hospital, the North Louisiana Sanitarium, first located on Louisiana Street near Crockett. Today, the North Louisiana Sanitarium—the first local hospital established in the 20th century—is known as Doctor's Hospital. Abramson also figured prominently in establishing the first Shrine Hospital for Crippled Children, founded at Shreveport in 1922 and now located the nation over.

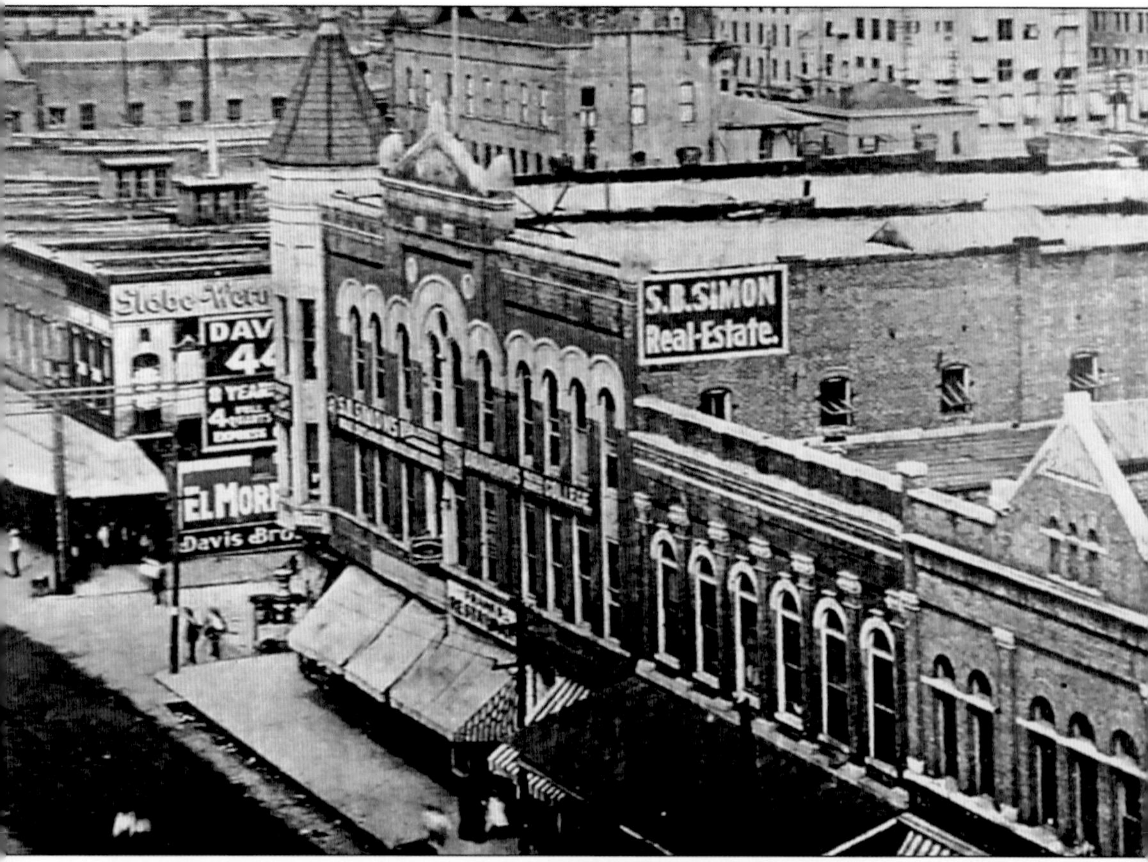

This is the S.B. Simon building at Texas and Edwards Streets as it appeared at the beginning of the 20th century. The Simon Building housed S.B. Simon Real Estate, one of Shreveport's earliest and most successful real estate firms. The firm was established by Seymour B. Simon (1875–1944) when he was only 23 years of age. By the close of the 19th century, the firm owned and occupied the building shown and was handling the majority of real estate transactions in the city. Only a decade earlier, such agencies were virtually unknown and most real estate transactions were made directly between buyer and seller or through an attorney. Many such important changes—in business, social life, and even religion—were in store for the city and for its Jewish community as the new century dawned.

Three

The Early 20th Century 1900–1950

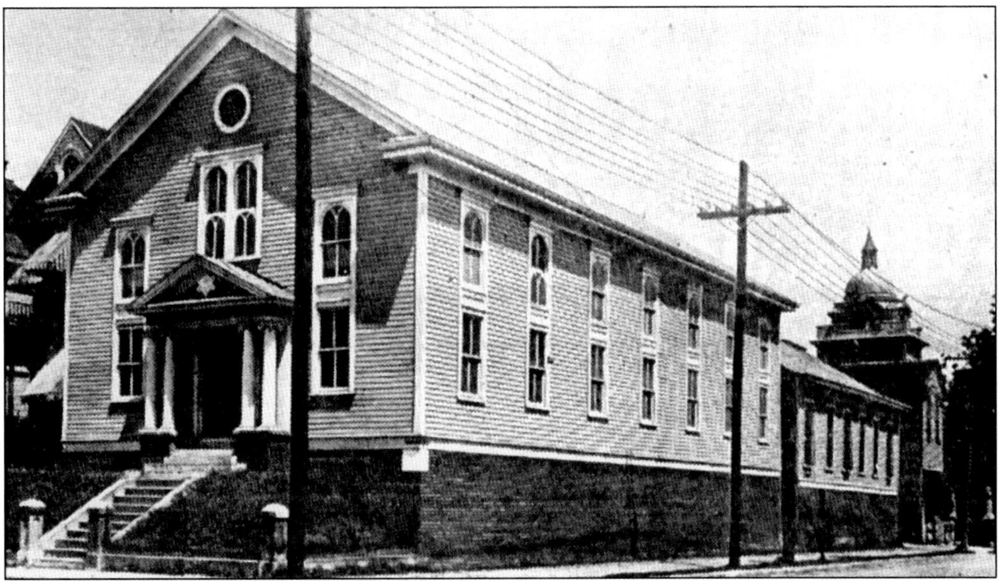

The Hebrew Relief Society of Shreveport, chartered on April 6, 1887, strove to provide assistance for newly arrived immigrants, as well as for indigent Jews and travelers in need. The organization was much needed, for during the 1880s and 1890s, a small but steady influx of Eastern European Jews, mostly Russians and Poles, began to arrive in Shreveport, bringing with them the Orthodox tradition of their homelands. As their numbers grew, the burgeoning Orthodox community began meeting in homes, much as their German and Alsatian predecessors had done a half-century earlier. In 1890, a congregation, Beth El ("House of G-d") was organized, and in 1892, another small congregation, Beth Joseph, was formed. These congregations met in members' homes as well as in the Simon Building and at a hotel called Bogel's Hall. In 1902, the congregations merged to form a new congregation, Agudath Achim ("Band of Brothers"). In 1904, the congregation purchased property at the southeast corner of Fannin and McNeill Streets and a year later dedicated its first synagogue, shown above.

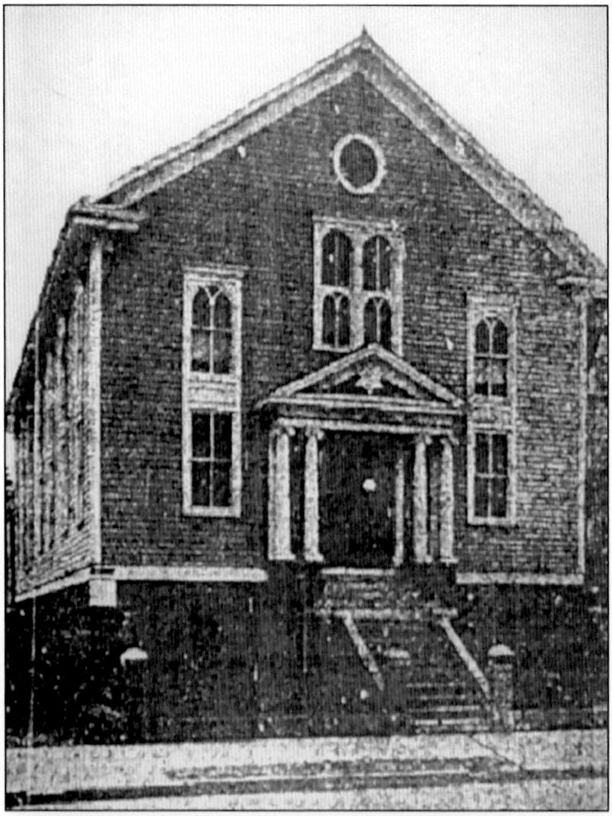

This is an early view of Agudath Achim Synagogue on Fannin Street. The building was dedicated on September 8, 1905 with the installation of the Torah scroll. Participants in the dedication included officers of B'nai Zion Temple and its rabbi, Moses P. Jacobson, Mayor Andrew Querbes of Shreveport, Rabbis Joseph Getzler and Harriss Wolenske, and others. Below is the cornerstone of the first *shul*, as Agudath Achim is known in the community. The old cornerstone is today embedded in the wall of the present Agudath Achim Synagogue on Village Green Drive.

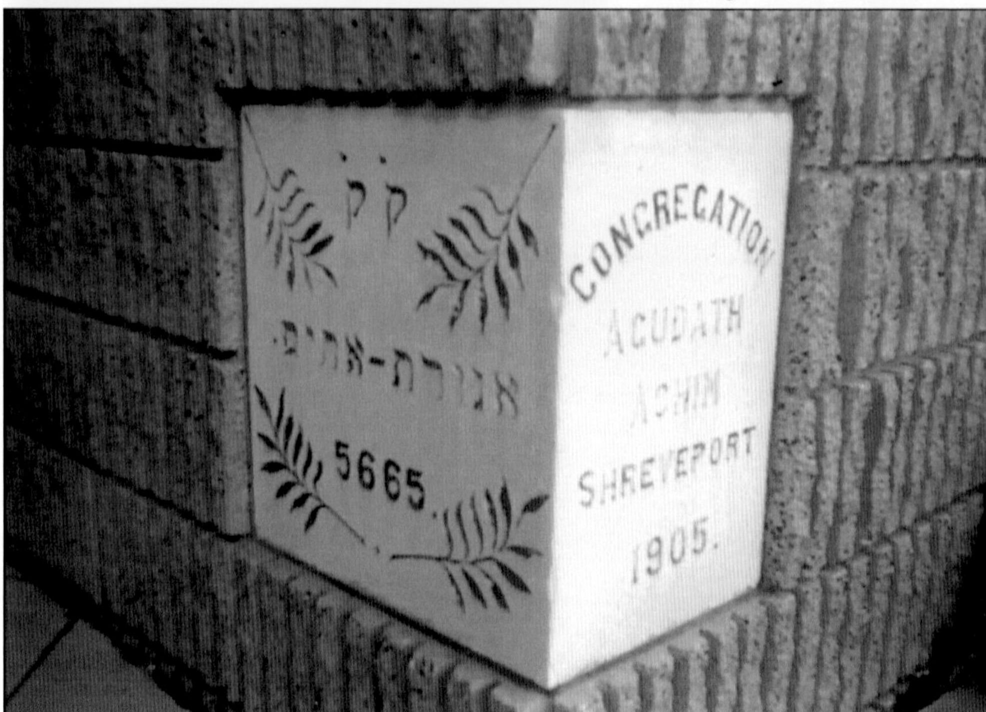

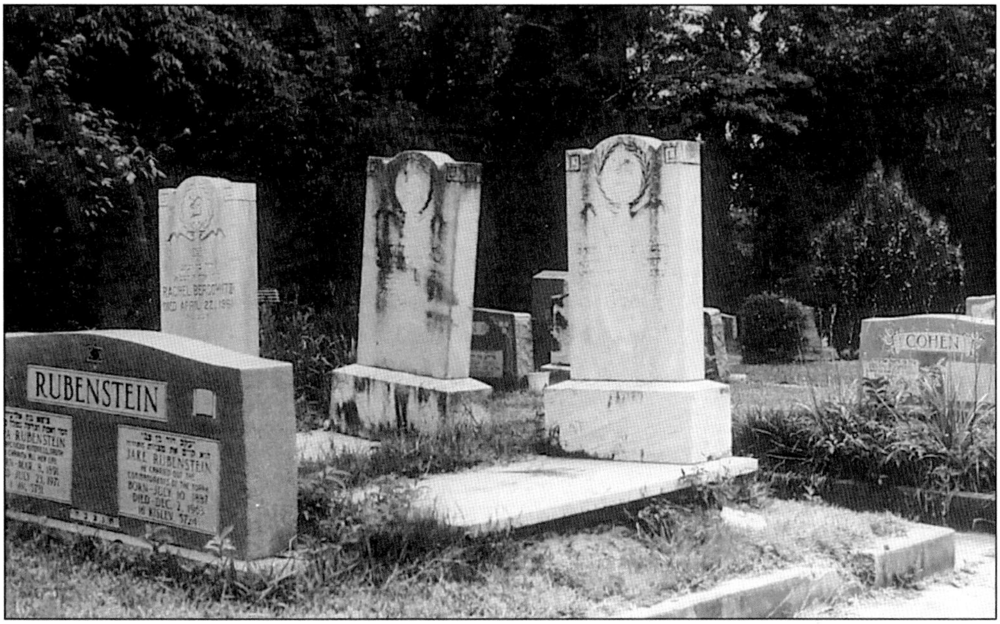

In 1901, Congregation Beth El formed a burial society, Chessed Shel Emeth, which purchased half a city block on Dove at Yale Streets in the West End area for $150. In 1902, the cemetery came under the jurisdiction of the newly formed Congregation Agudath Achim and, although formally named Chessed Shel Emeth Cemetery or afterward "Orthodox Hebrew Rest," it has since come to be known simply as Agudath Achim Cemetery. This was the third Jewish cemetery established in Shreveport.

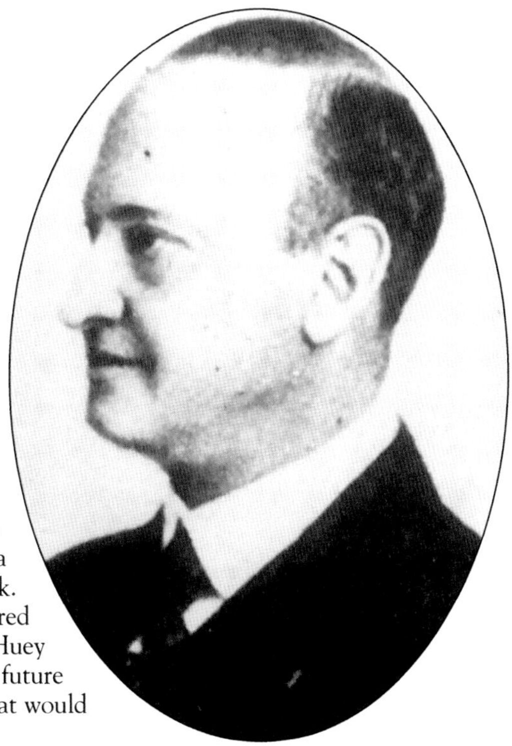

Ernest Ralph Bernstein (1868–1932), a partner in the firm of Bernstein Brothers (see page 42), was elected mayor in 1905 and was sworn in at the beginning of 1906. He served a single two-year term and afterward was an officer of the Commercial National Bank (CNB). In 1922, while vice president of CNB, Bernstein was fired by the board of directors for alleged malfeasance relating to a loan he had made to the failed Texlahoma Oil Company. Bernstein sued the bank. Despite the fact that the bank was considered untouchable, Bernstein and his attorney, Huey P. Long, won. It was the beginning of the future Governor Long's career and of a friendship that would last until Bernstein's death.

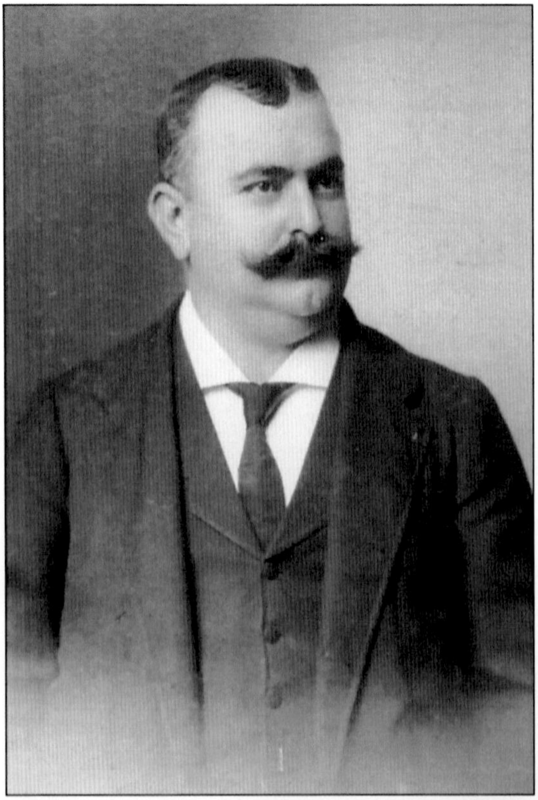

Jules Dreyfuss (1854–1909), a son of Henry Dreyfuss (see page 20), first worked for his father's firm and then became an insurance agent. From 1888 to 1892 and again from 1904 to 1909, he served on the Caddo Parish Police Jury. At the time of his death, Dreyfuss was president of the Shreveport Mutual Building Association. Below is the scene at his grave at Hebrew Rest Number Two the day of the funeral. Floral offerings came from Dreyfuss's many friends in the business and political communities as well as the Jewish and general communities of Shreveport.

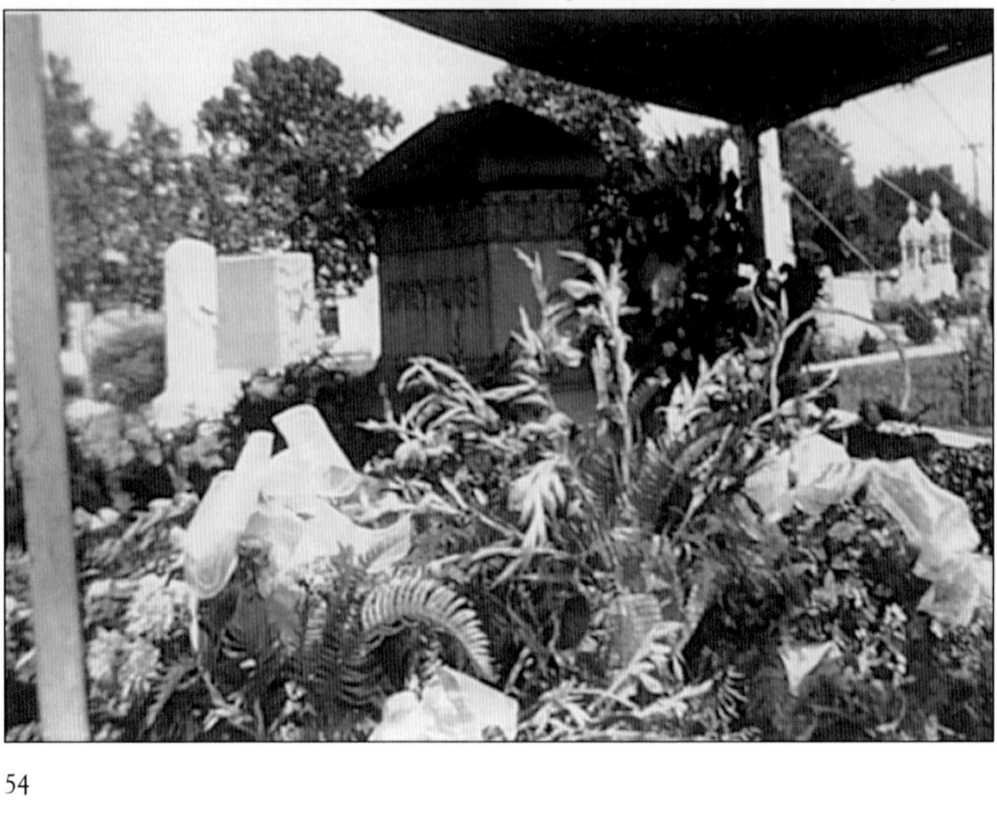

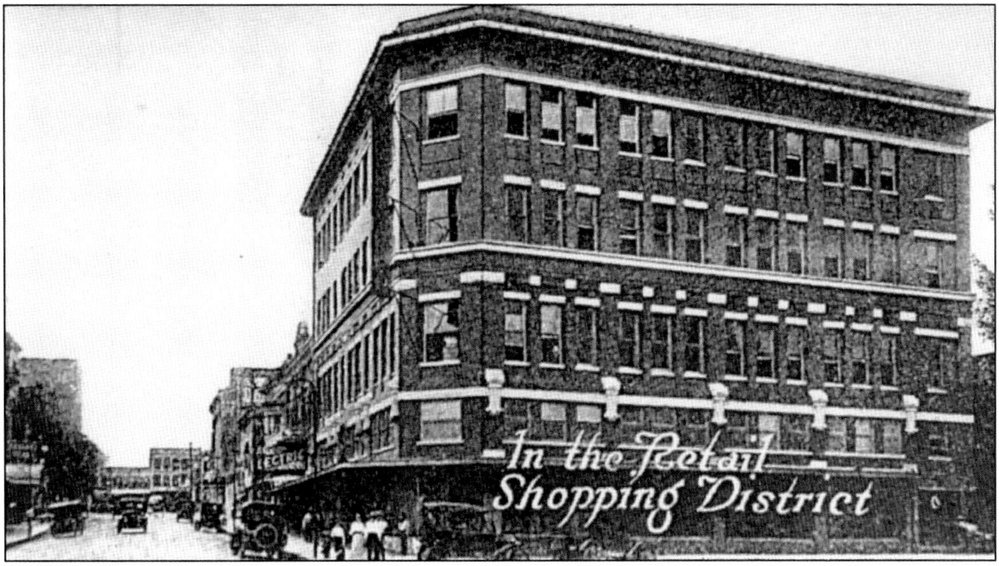

In 1906, Dreyfuss Dry Goods, the firm founded before the Civil War by Henry Dreyfuss (not to be confused with S.G. Dreyfus and Company), built a large new building at the northwest corner of Milam and McNeill Streets to house the growing department store. In 1930, the company became Palais Royal department store, which operated until 1987. Extensively remodeled in 1946, the Milam Street building was demolished in 2002.

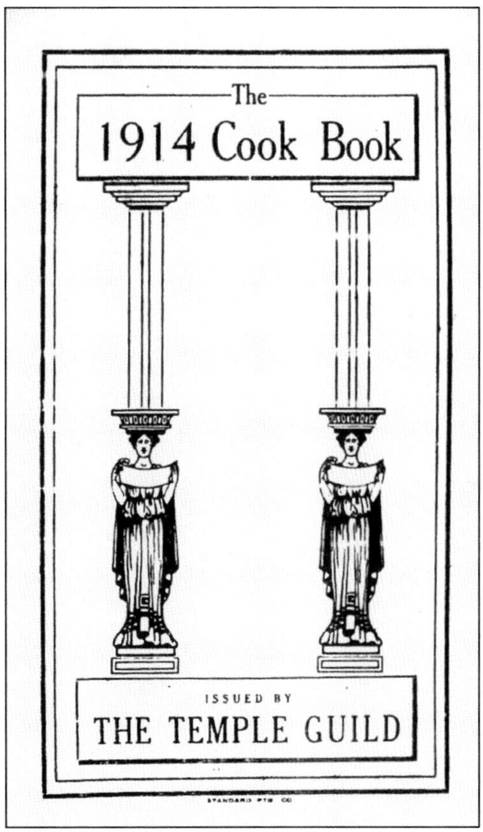

In 1907, the Temple Guild, the women's auxiliary of B'nai Zion Temple, was founded. As a fund-raiser, in 1914 the Guild published the first cookbook prepared by ladies of the Jewish community. That same year the Temple Guild became the Sisterhood. Since then the Sisterhood of B'nai Zion has published four more cookbooks and that of the Agudath Achim Sisterhood, founded in 1916 as the Ladies Auxiliary (successor to the earlier Orthodox Ladies Charity Society), at least two. The Agudath Achim Ladies Auxiliary became the Sisterhood in 1959.

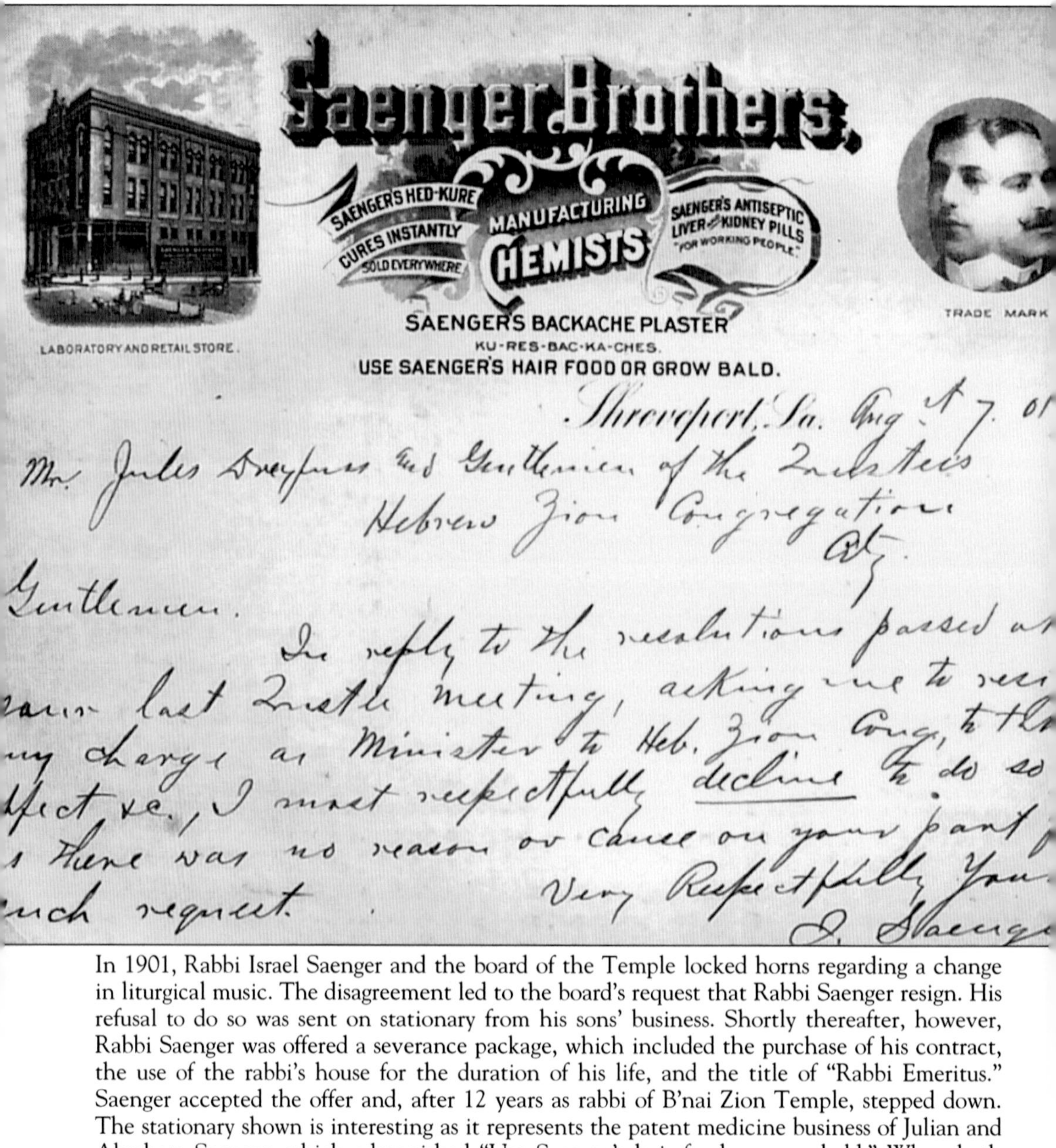

Saenger Brothers,

MANUFACTURING CHEMISTS

SAENGER'S HED-KURE CURES INSTANTLY SOLD EVERYWHERE

SAENGER'S ANTISEPTIC LIVER & KIDNEY PILLS "FOR WORKING PEOPLE."

LABORATORY AND RETAIL STORE.

TRADE MARK

SAENGER'S BACKACHE PLASTER

KU-RES-BAC-KA-CHES.

USE SAENGER'S HAIR FOOD OR GROW BALD.

Shreveport, La. Aug. 7. 01

Mr. Jules Dreyfuss and Gentlemen of the Trustees
Hebrew Zion Congregation
City.

Gentlemen.

In reply to the resolutions passed at your last Trustee meeting, asking me to resign my charge as Minister to Heb. Zion Cong, to that effect, &c., I most respectfully decline to do so as there was no reason or cause on your part for such request.

Very Respectfully Yours
I. Saenger

In 1901, Rabbi Israel Saenger and the board of the Temple locked horns regarding a change in liturgical music. The disagreement led to the board's request that Rabbi Saenger resign. His refusal to do so was sent on stationary from his sons' business. Shortly thereafter, however, Rabbi Saenger was offered a severance package, which included the purchase of his contract, the use of the rabbi's house for the duration of his life, and the title of "Rabbi Emeritus." Saenger accepted the offer and, after 12 years as rabbi of B'nai Zion Temple, stepped down. The stationary shown is interesting as it represents the patent medicine business of Julian and Abraham Saenger, which admonished "Use Saenger's hair food or grow bald." When both brothers (whose merged portrait is shown on the letterhead) did in fact themselves grow bald, the "hair food" line came to an end.

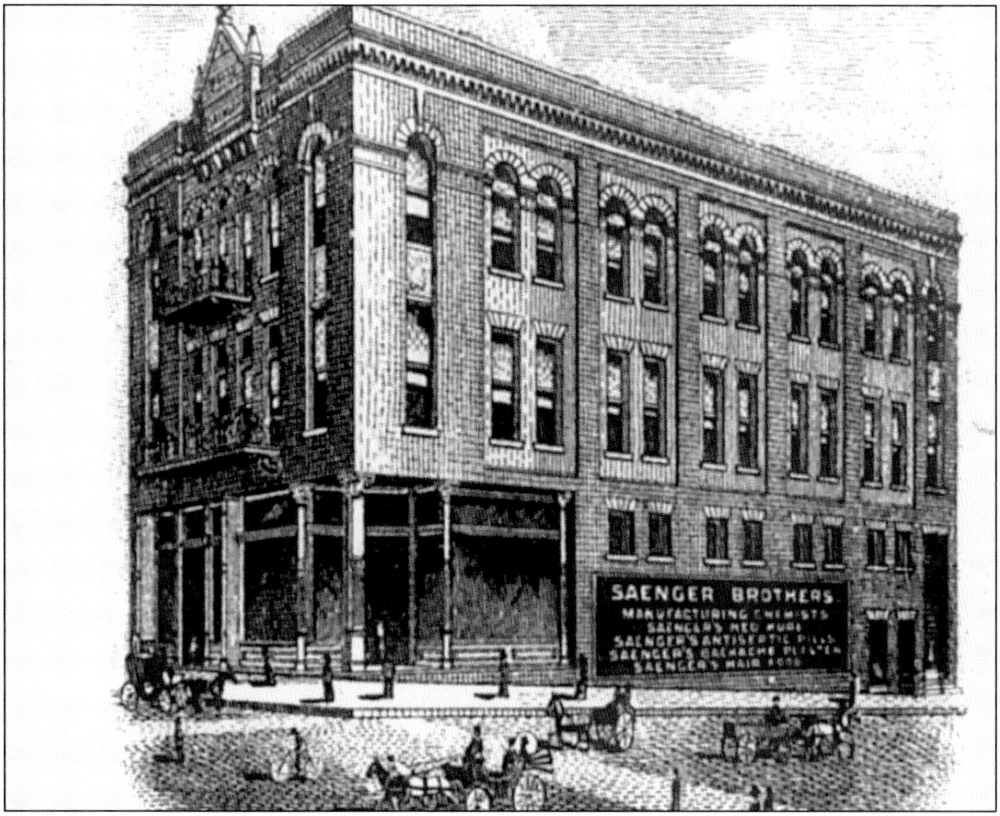

The Saenger Brothers's base of operations was this building (above), constructed in 1900 at the northeast corner of Louisiana and Milam Streets. The building, which still stands, housed the Saenger all-night drug store on its ground floor and the brothers' other enterprises, including a nickelodeon and magic lantern theater above. The upper floors also later housed the Saenger Hotel. Below is a 1906 view of the interior of the Saenger drug store showing its soda fountain, a favorite gathering spot for Shreveport teenagers of the 1900s and 1910s.

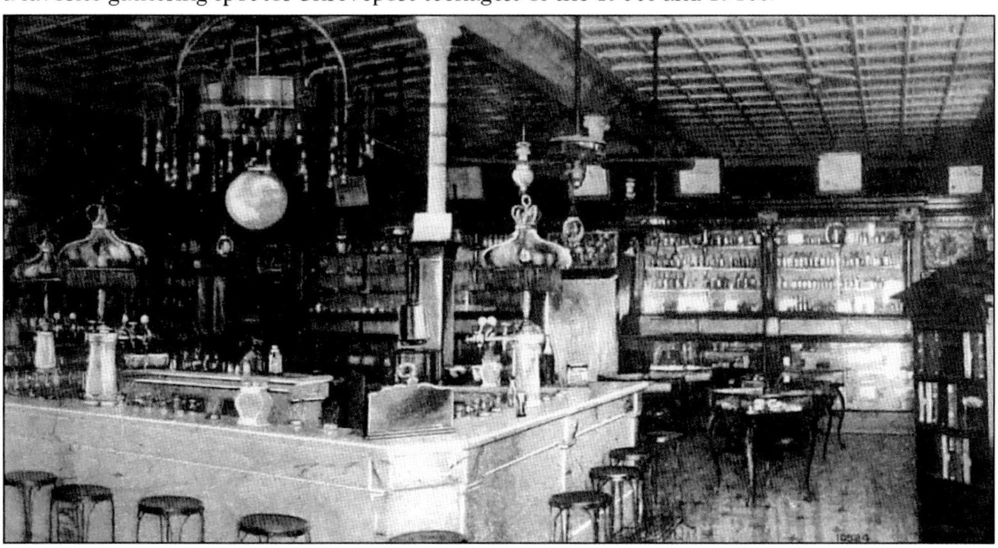

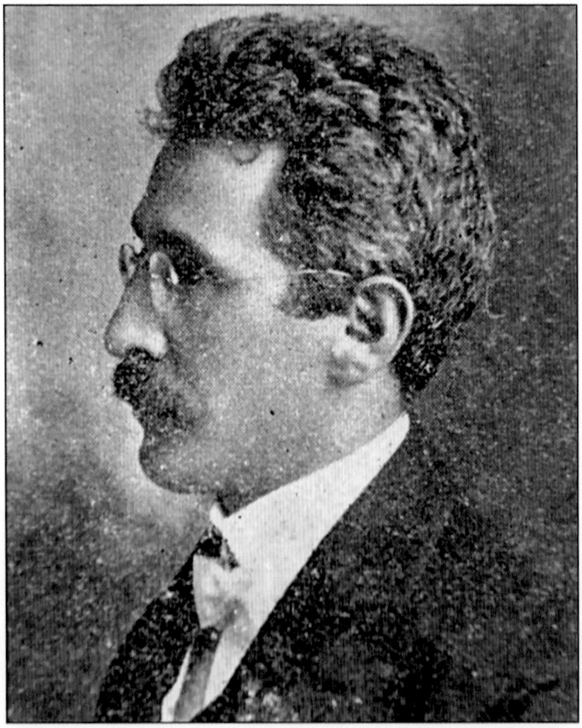

Rabbi Saenger's successor was Rabbi Moses Perez Jacobson, a native of Ft. Wayne, Indiana. He had also been Rabbi Saenger's successor at Temple Beth Israel in Macon, Georgia. In between, he had served congregations at numerous places including San Antonio, Texas; Salt Lake City, Utah; Youngstown, Ohio; and Chicago, Illinois. He also published a newspaper called *The Jewish Chronicle* in Mobile, Alabama, for a time. All this was before he was 37, at which age he came to Shreveport where he would serve B'nai Zion until 1919.

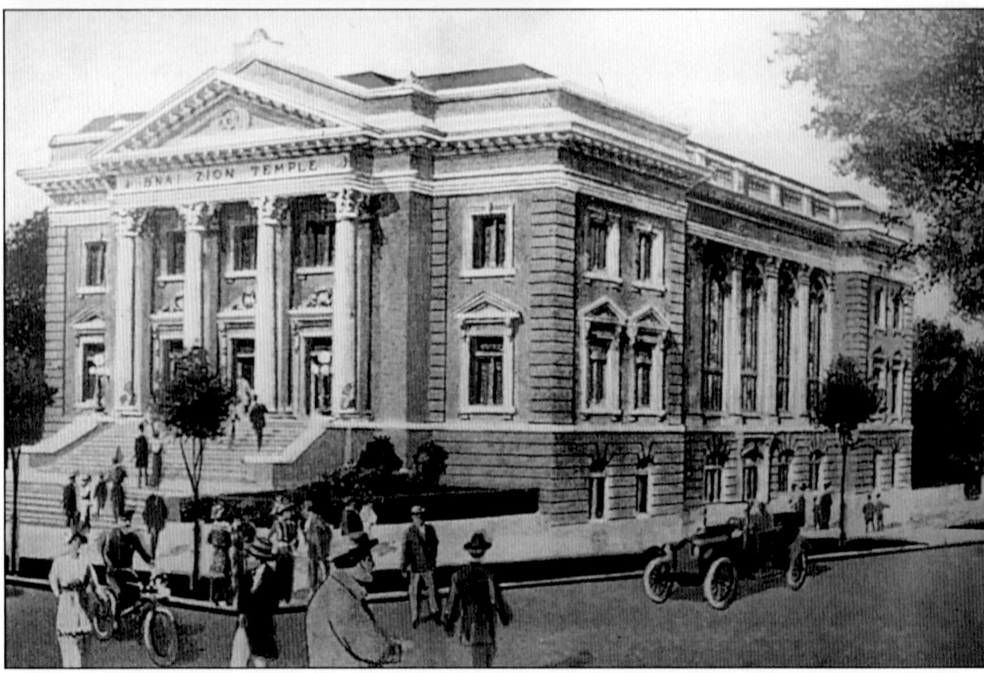

As early as 1906, there had been discussion of building a larger synagogue for B'nai Zion but it wasn't until 1913 that the Temple Guild raised and donated $10,600 to purchase two lots at the northwest corner of Cotton and Common Streets. An architect, Edward Fairfax Neild of Shreveport, was hired to design a new temple. The design approved by the building committee and congregation is the one seen here.

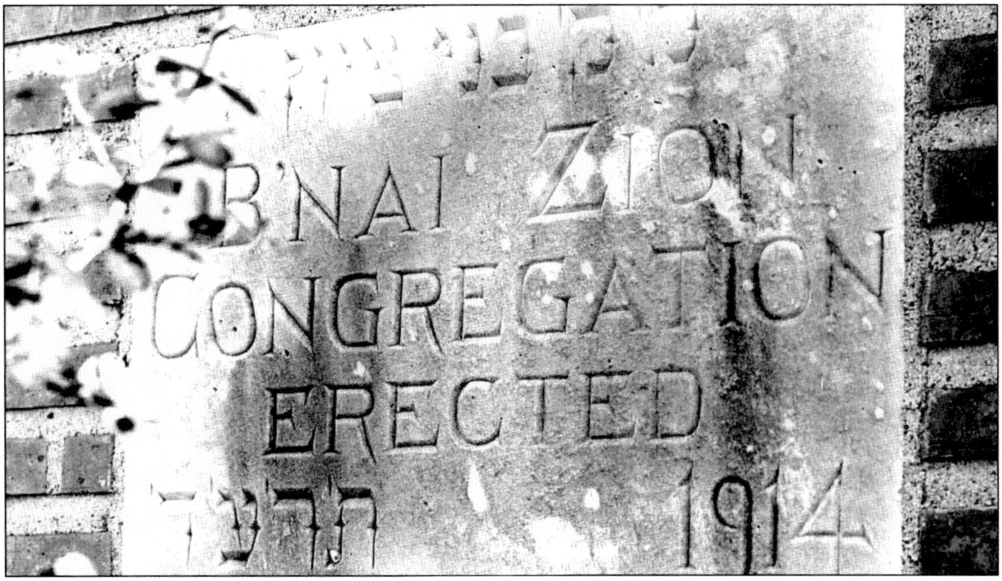

The cornerstone of the new temple was laid on April 26, 1914. At the same time, the cornerstone of the 1869 temple was opened and removed, to be placed in the wall of the new synagogue. Ten members of the congregation who had been present at the laying of the 1869 cornerstone were also present at the laying of the 1914 cornerstone. As the new temple arose, the old one went on the market. It was sold to the First Christian Science Church and would be used by that congregation through the 1920s. It was demolished in 1929.

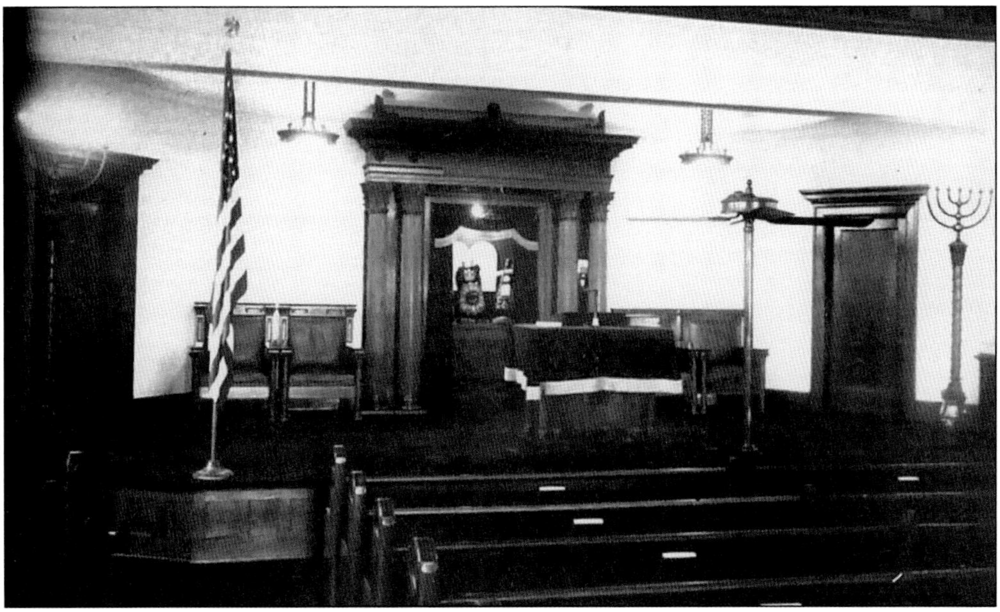

The interior of the new temple featured a Robert Morris pipe organ, a neo-classical ark donated by the Bernstein family, 10 magnificent stained glass windows believed to have been made by Lafarge (the installation of these was delayed until after the end of the First World War), Bohemian pressed glad light fixtures, and free-standing fans to keep the prayer hall cool in the sweltering Louisiana summers. Interior design was by Paul Heerwagen working together with architect Neild.

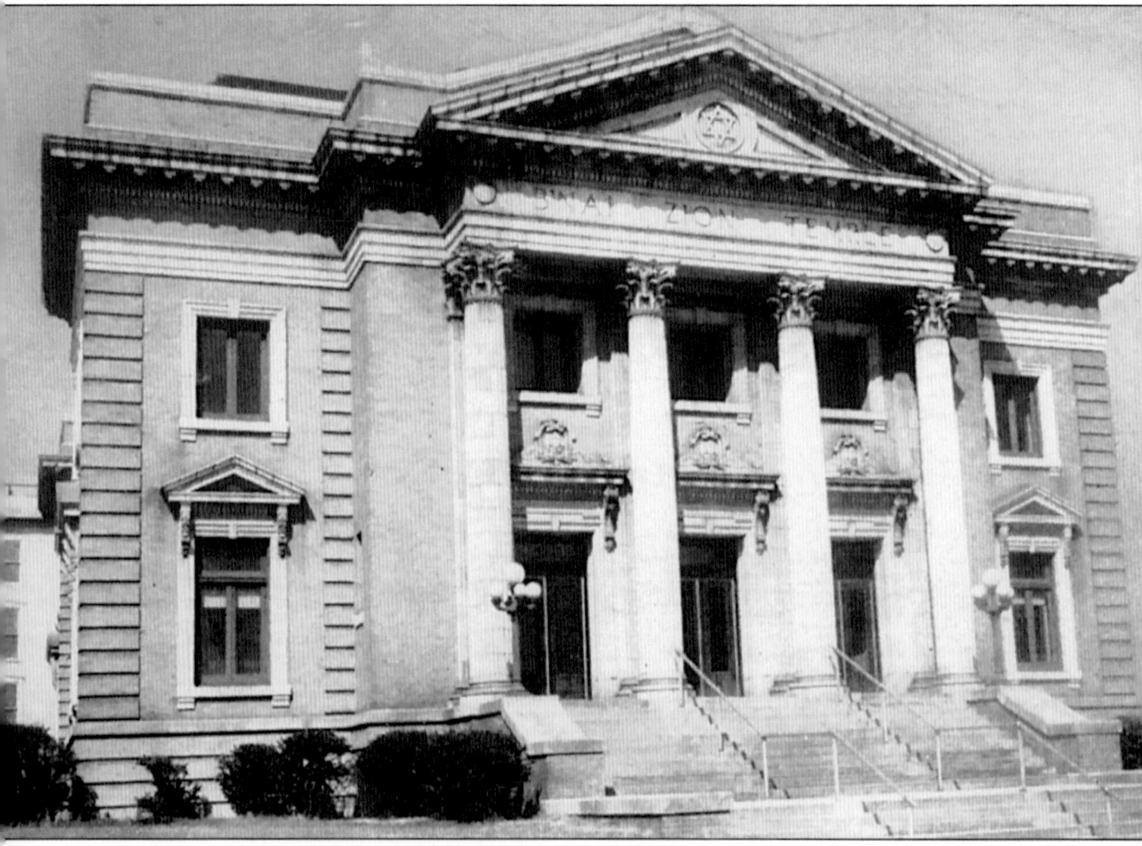

The new temple, completed at a total cost of $86,000, was dedicated on October 22 and 23, 1915. Rabbis Jacobson and Saenger of Shreveport, Rabbis Maximillian Heller and Emanuel Sternheim of New Orleans, and Rabbi David Philipson of Cincinnati, Ohio all participated in the dedication services. Rabbi Max Samfield, who had presided over the dedication of the 1869 temple was also scheduled to participate but died just days earlier. Temple president Herman Herold, together with Emanuel Phelps and Michel Bernstein, carried the Torah scrolls from the old temple to the new. Building committee chairman Ernest Bernstein kindled the *ner tamid*—the eternal light—above the ark. From that day forth, the congregation was never again called by any name other than B'nai Zion.

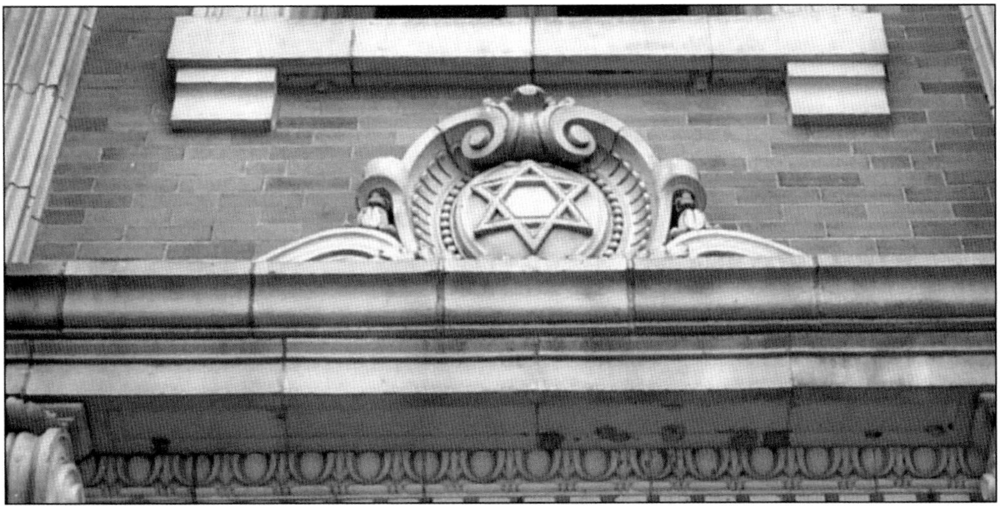

The Cotton Street synagogue of B'nai Zion Temple is rich in detail. The brick and terra cotta used in the building were all manufactured locally and have withstood the ravages of time admirably. The building is Greek Revival in basic design but its overall character is in the high style of the Beaux Arts movement. Throughout the building's ornamentation may be found examples of the *magen David*, the star of David, which symbolizes the Jewish faith. For its architectural as well as its historical importance, the Cotton Street temple was placed on the National Register of Historic Places on January 21, 1994.

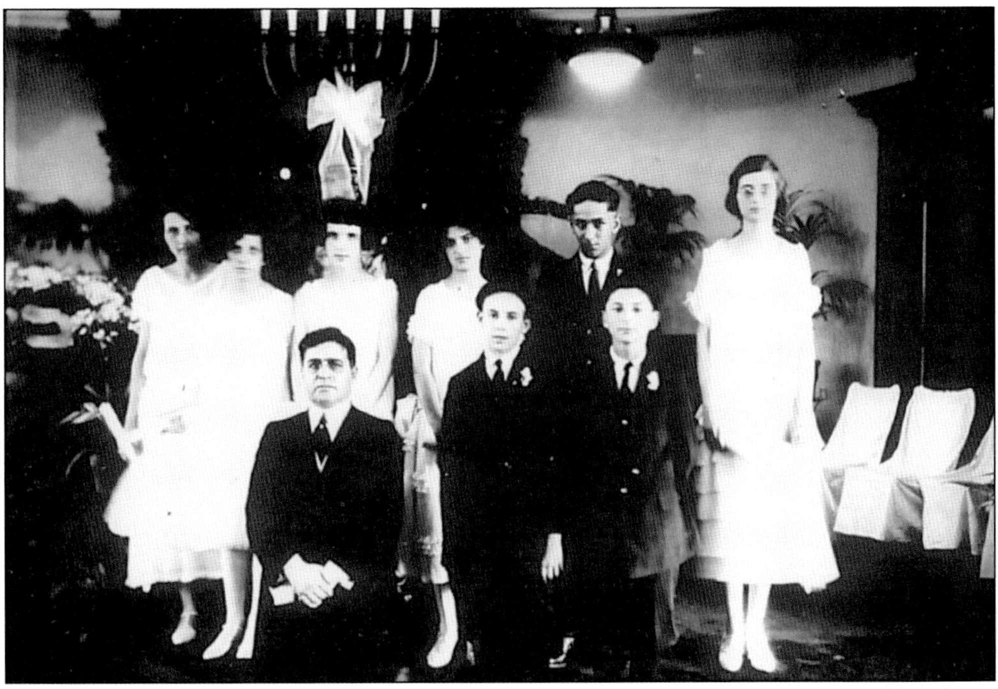

In 1919, Rabbi Jacobson departed and a search was made to fill his place. In 1920, Rabbi Abram Brill came to B'nai Zion Temple from Meridian, Mississippi. He is seen here with the 1924 confirmation class on the *bimah* of the Cotton Street temple. Behind him, from left to right, are Lois Phelps, Therese Simon, Babette Wiener, Rachel Groner, Joe Murov, an unidentified person, Sidney Weiss, and Isabel Wiener.

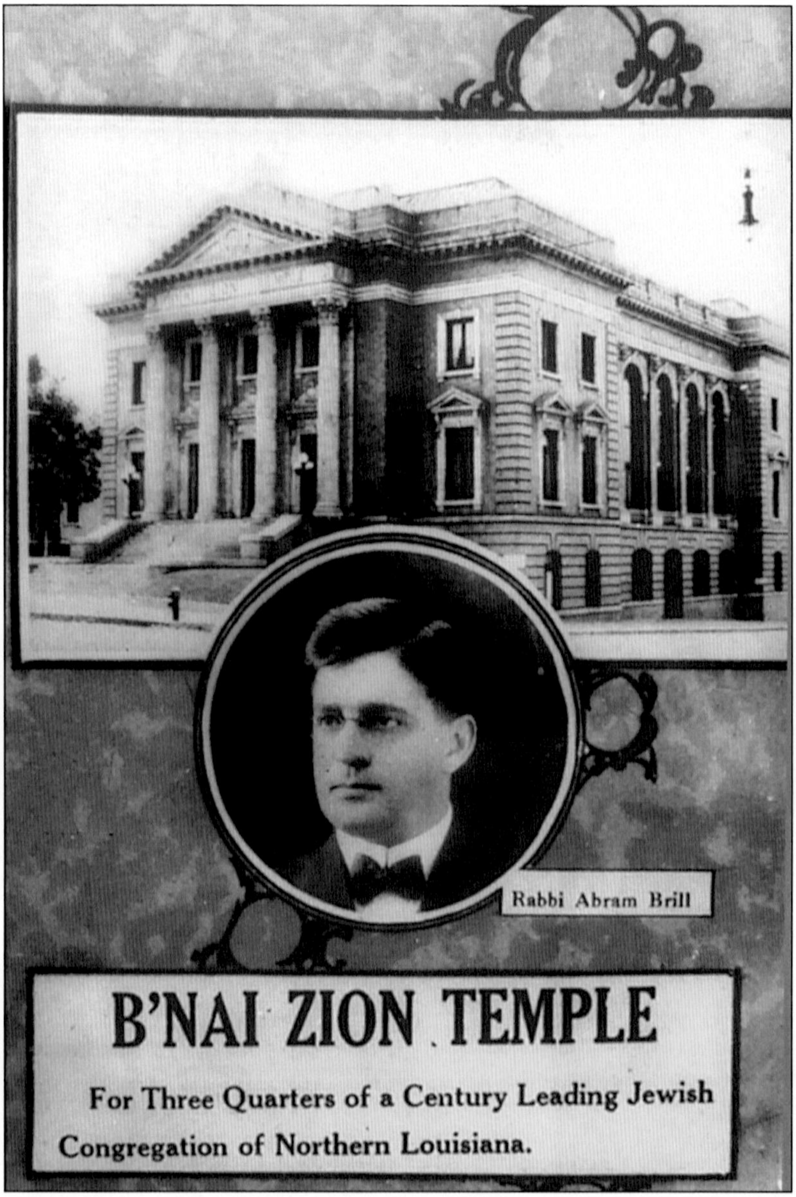

Rabbi Abram Brill was born in Ogdensberg, New York in 1876 and grew up in Rochester, New York. He was ordained at Hebrew Union College in Cincinnati, Ohio and served congregations in Helena, Arkansas; Wheeling, West Virginia; Greenville, Mississippi; Bellaire, Ohio; Demopolis, Alabama; and Meridian, Mississippi before coming to Shreveport. Rabbi Brill was a strong proponent of Classical Reform Judaism and of ecumenism. When, in 1920, nearby St. Mark's Episcopal Church was damaged by fire, Rabbi Brill opened the temple to the church to hold services. Similarly, when First Baptist Church was remodeling in 1920, and First Methodist in 1938, both made use of the temple's facilities for their Sunday schools. A popular rabbi and outspoken civic leader, Brill was popular both within and outside of the Jewish community. He remained rabbi until ill health forced his retirement in 1940. In 1942, he moved to Montclair, New Jersey to live with his daughter and there died in 1943, much mourned by the temple he so loved.

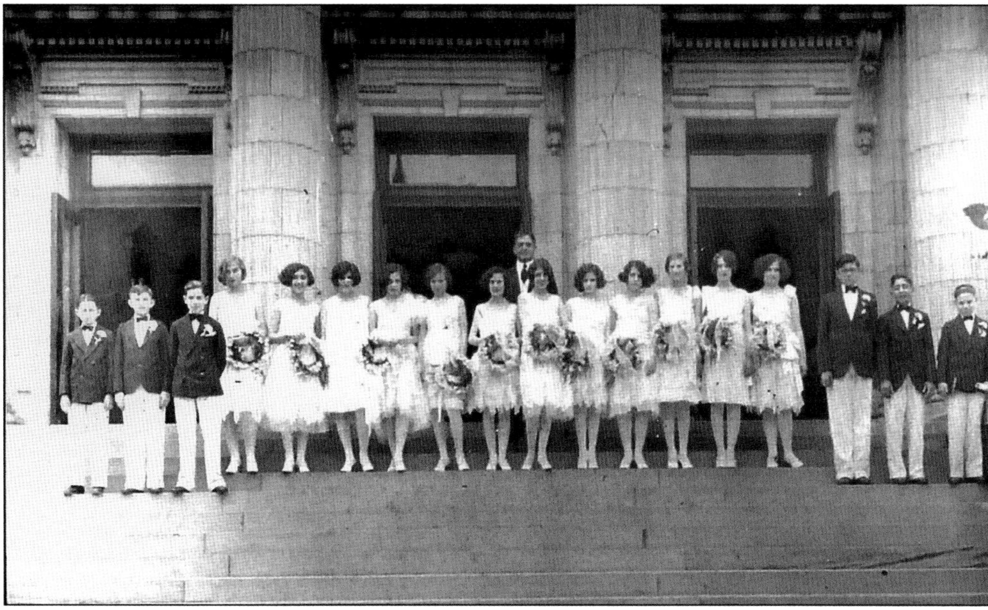

Shown here are two confirmation classes from the Brill era at B'nai Zion. At top is the 1928 class showing, from left to right, Julian Weinstein, Abe Murov, Ernest Bernstein Jr., Lottie Benson, Doris Muslow, Helen Goetschel, Ruth Rabe, Bertha Meyer, an unidentified person, Rosabel Lieber, an unidentified person, Reva Siegel, Leah Willer, Kathryn Kaufman, Minnie Florsheim, Herman Herold, Hyman Manhein, and Alfred Zeve. Rabbi Brill stands behind the group near the center. Below is the 1936 class. The order is unknown but the members of the class were Gloria Bodenheimer, Bertha Bodenheimer, Flora Mae Blumberg, Marion Cahn Jr., Seymour Florsheim Jr., Harvey Groner, Milton Holland Jr., Roy Kern, Gwendolyn Jane Levi, Ben Levy Jr., Saul Levinson, Carolyn Loeb, Muriel Selber, Carolyn Phillips, Carolyn Picard, Jacob Solomon, David Stern, Henri Wolbrette II, and Louis Zeve Jr. Rabbi Brill stands at center, to the right of the fan.

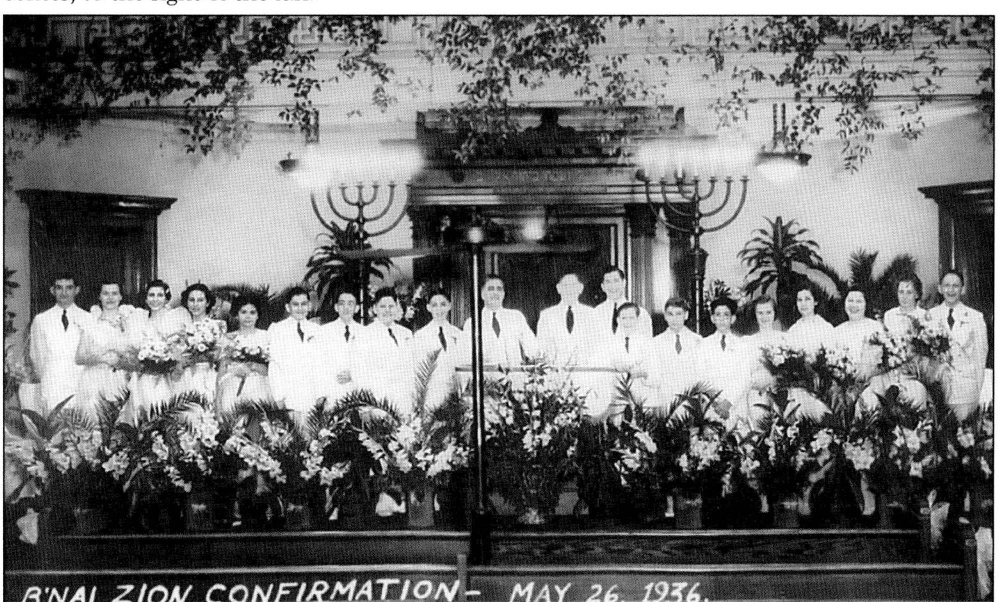

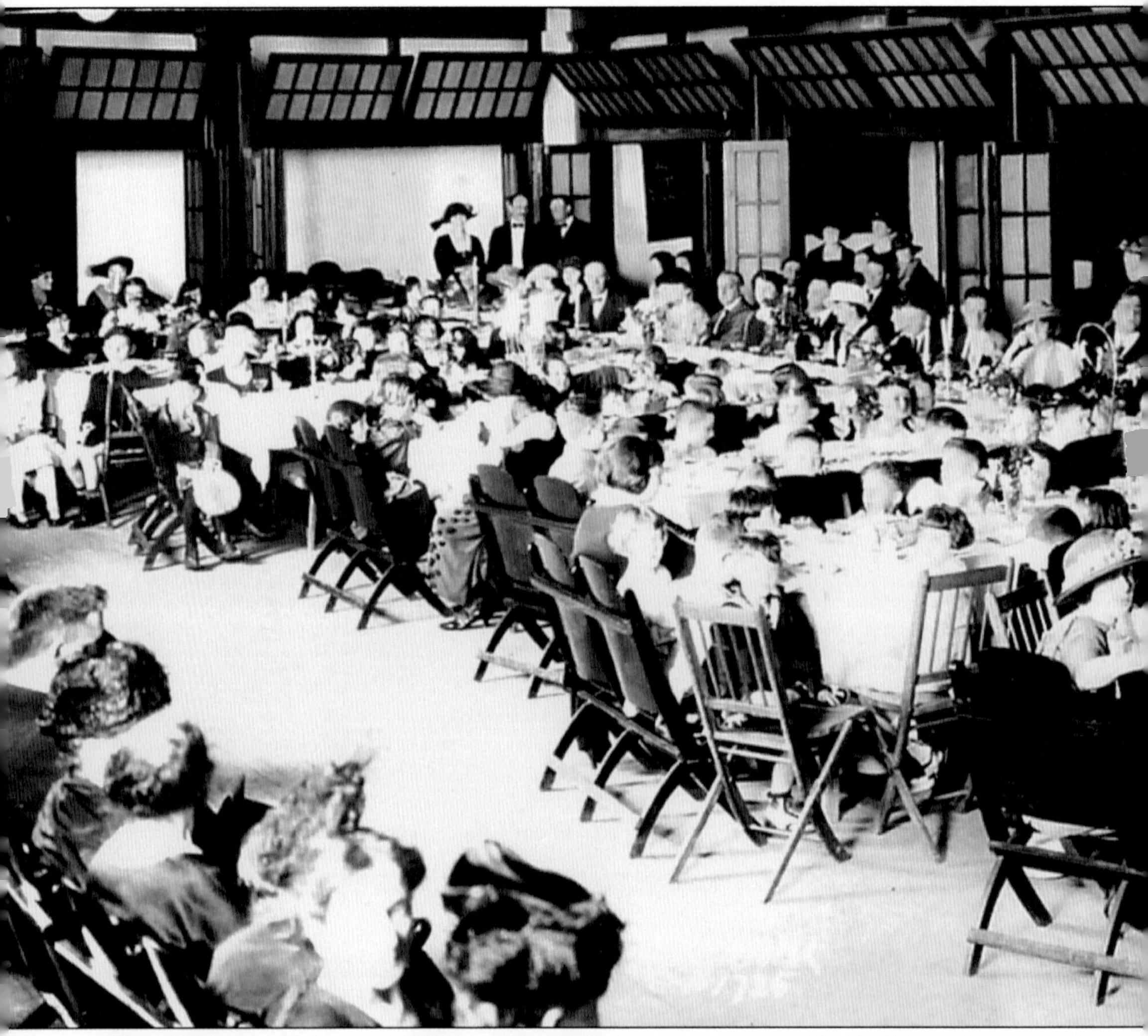

This is Passover Seder in 1925. The scene is in the basement social hall of B'nai Zion Temple on Cotton Street. In the middle of the third bay from the right, Rabbi Brill can be seen leaning back to see the camera. Mrs. Brill, the former Edna Goldstein of Greenville, Mississippi, whom the rabbi married in 1902, is next to him (with hat, leaning on table). Seated in the middle of

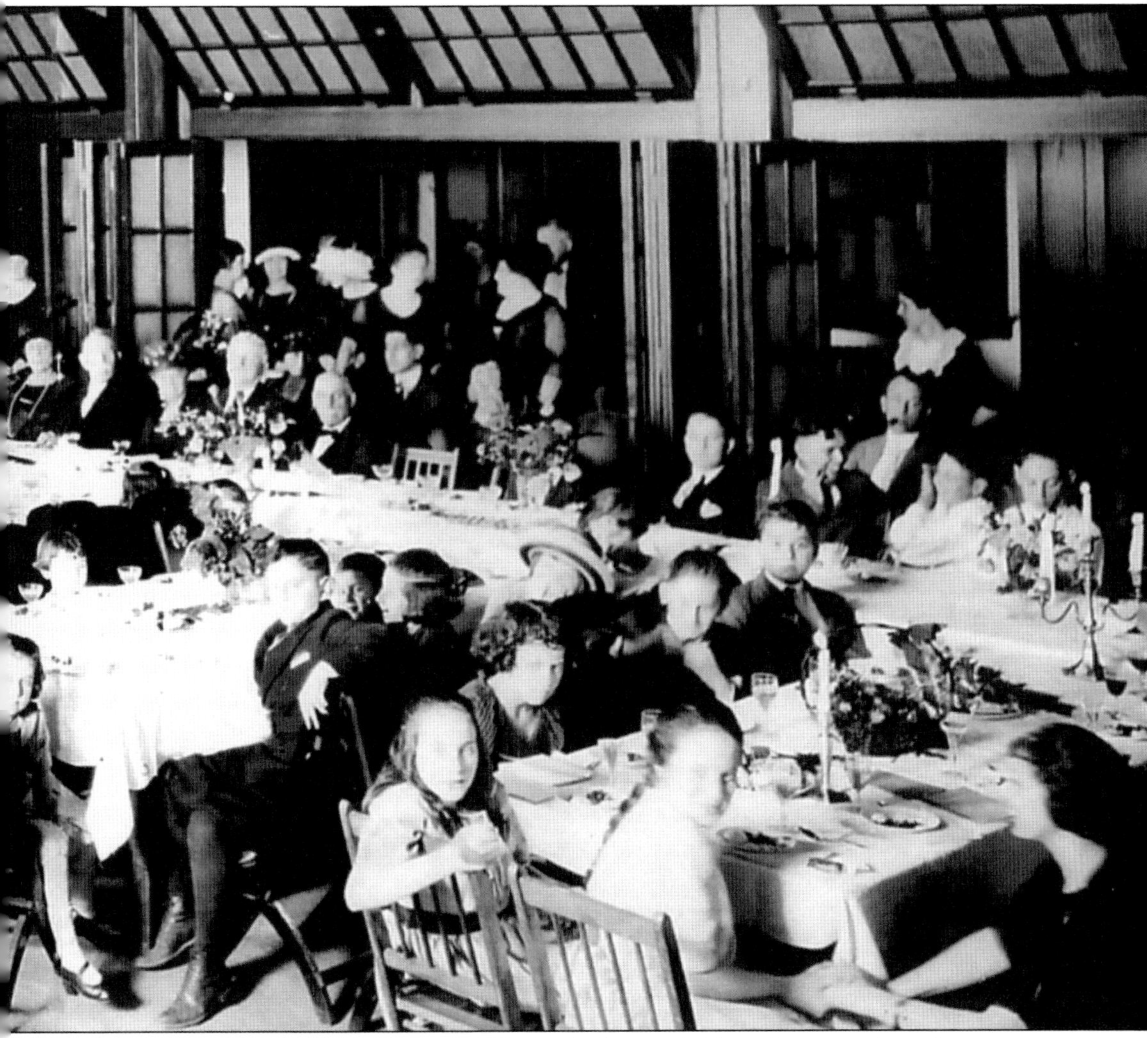

the second bay from the right is Emanuel Phelps (in bow tie). Note that several gentlemen wear tuxedos. Community seders held at the temple have always been an important part of B'nai Zion's Passover observance.

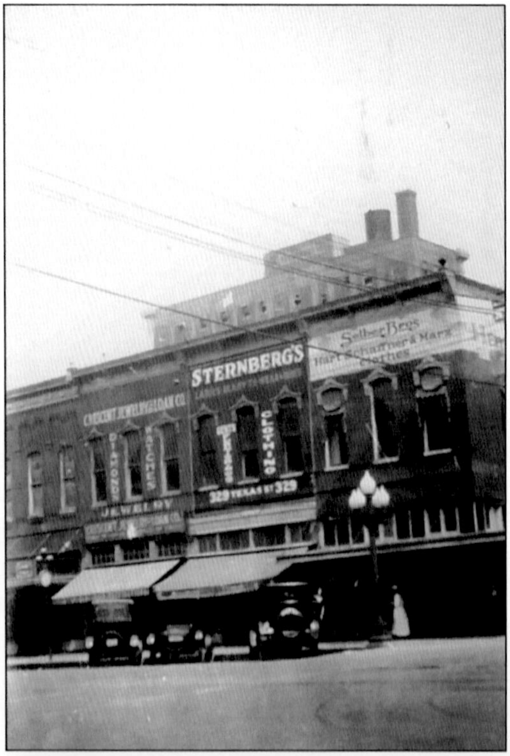

Shown here is the south side of the 300 block of Texas Street in 1920. The Crescent Jewelry and Loan Company, owned by Joseph and Samuel Rubenstein, Sternberg's Clothing Store, and Selber Brothers Clothing are prominent. Across the street were M. Levy's Sons department store and the Young Men's Hebrew Association. Nearby on Texas were Nathan's clothing store, Stein's, Silver's, Silverberg Jewelers, A. Goetschel Jewelry Company, and others.

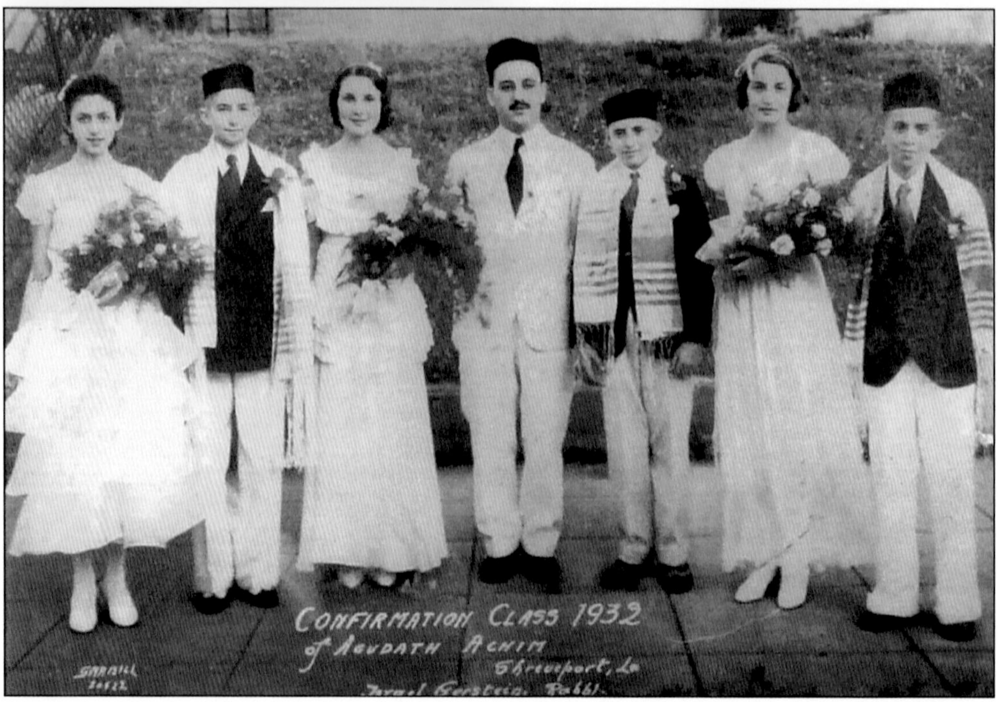

Agudath Achim's 1932 confirmation class is shown here. From left to right are Lottie Roseman, Louis Cullick, Josephine Hoffman, Rabbi Israel Gerstein, Abe Roseman, Bella Brandt, and Morris Yellen.

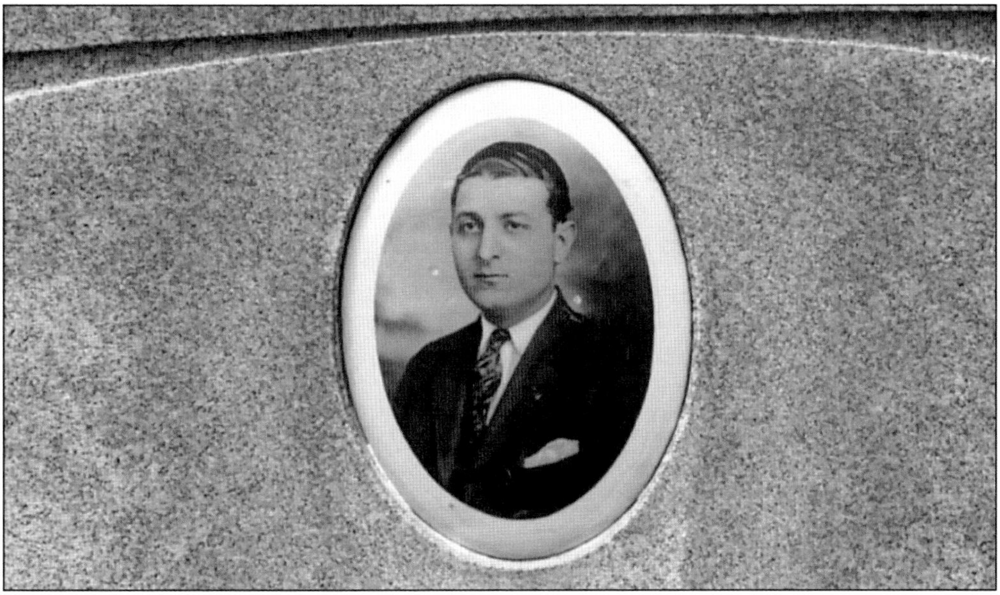

Unlike B'nai Zion, much of Congregation Agudath Achim's early 20th-century membership was made of recent immigrants, many of whom were born in Eastern Europe. One such new American was Morris Gurian (1895–1928), whose photograph appears on his gravestone at Agudath Achim Cemetery. Gurian was born in Wolma, a *shtetl* near Minsk, Russia, and came to the United States around 1920. He was naturalized a citizen in April of 1928 but was killed in a car wreck near El Dorado, Arkansas just six months later.

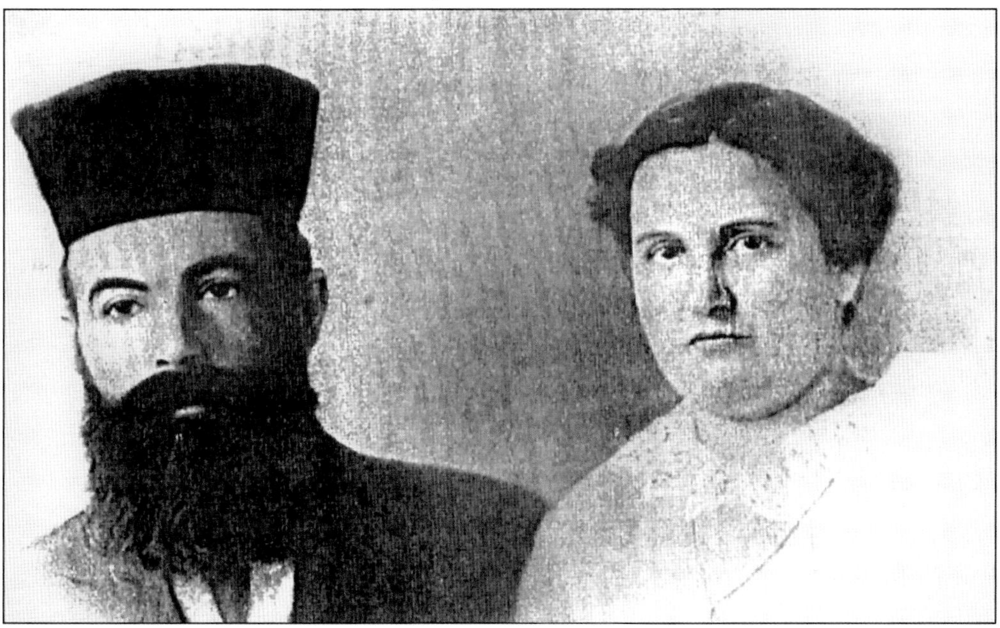

Rabbi Simon Smolensky (1883–1964) is shown with his wife Jennie (1883–1957). Smolensky was fifth rabbi of Congregation Agudath Achim. A native of Russia, where he was educated and ordained, Smolensky served congregations in Tyler, Texas and Mobile, Alabama before coming to Shreveport in 1915, serving as *shochet*, teacher, and rabbi. In 1917, he went to Calgary, Alberta, Canada, where he remained the rest of his life.

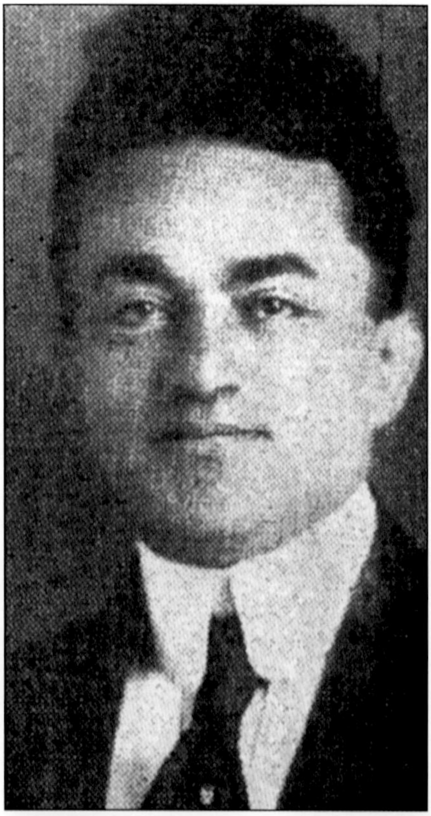

In 1922, David Stern (left) became the ninth rabbi of Agudath Achim. An accomplished writer and poet, Rabbi Stern also served congregations in Houston, Texas and Saratoga Springs, New York. Pictured below, Agudath Achim's Young Judea youth group was organized in 1926, becoming the United Synagogue Youth in 1966 but returning to the Young Judean (YJ) name in 1993. The first YJ group is seen here. From left to right are (front row) Tillie Epstein, Rose Velinsky Sachs, Minnie Frumer, Susie Gold, Bessie Abramson, Rose Gardsbane, and Esther Gardsbane; (back row) Leon Abramson, Abie Abramson, David Kaminsky, Charlie Yellen, and Sam Rubenstein.

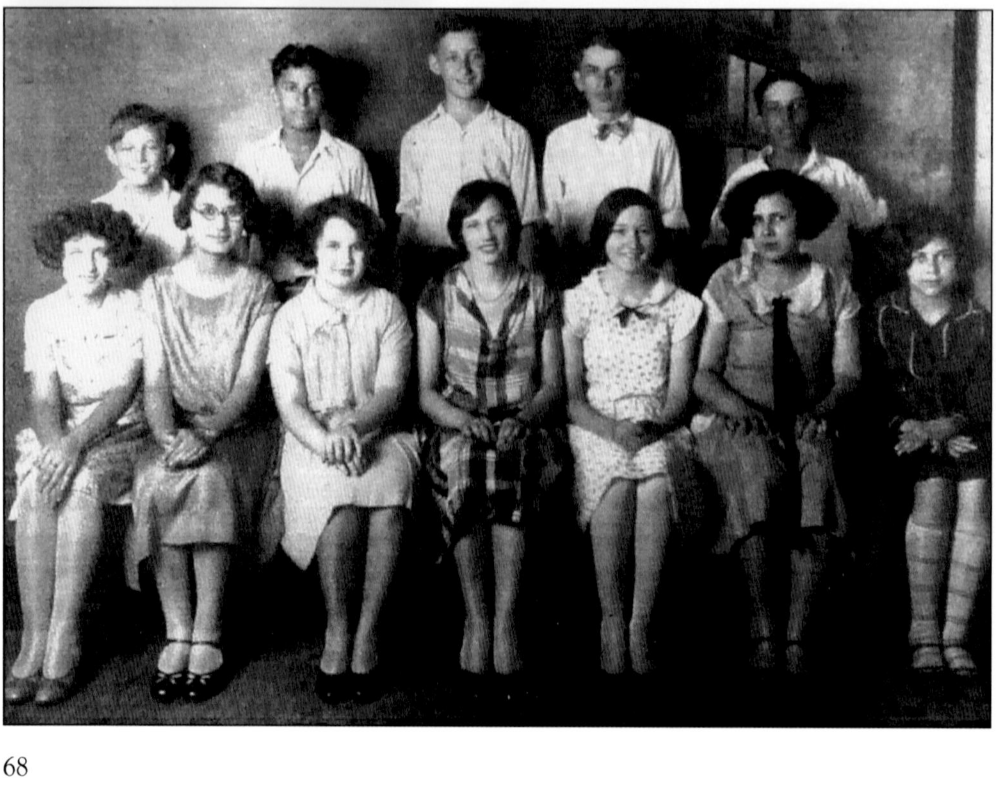

Rabbi Israel Gerstein (left), a native of Lodz, Poland, came to Agudath Achim in 1930 when he was 26 years of age. Previously he had been rabbi of Congregation Ohev Zedek in Denver, Colorado. In Shreveport, Gerstein served as president of the local B'nai B'rith lodge and was chairman of the Texas-Louisiana Zionist Federation. In late 1935, he became rabbi of congregation B'nai Zion in Chattanooga, Tennessee, but later immigrated to Israel, where he was killed in a car wreck shortly after that nation was born. Shown below, a predecessor of Rabbi Gerstein was Rabbi Charles Blumenthal, a native of Russia and a former rabbi in Toledo, Ohio and Buffalo, New York. He served Agudath Achim from 1923 to 1926. Rabbi Blumenthal is third from left on the back row. The confirmands with him are unidentified.

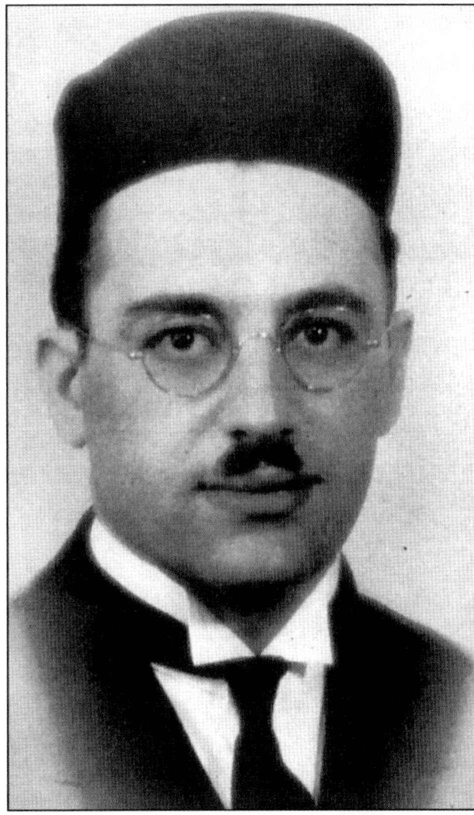

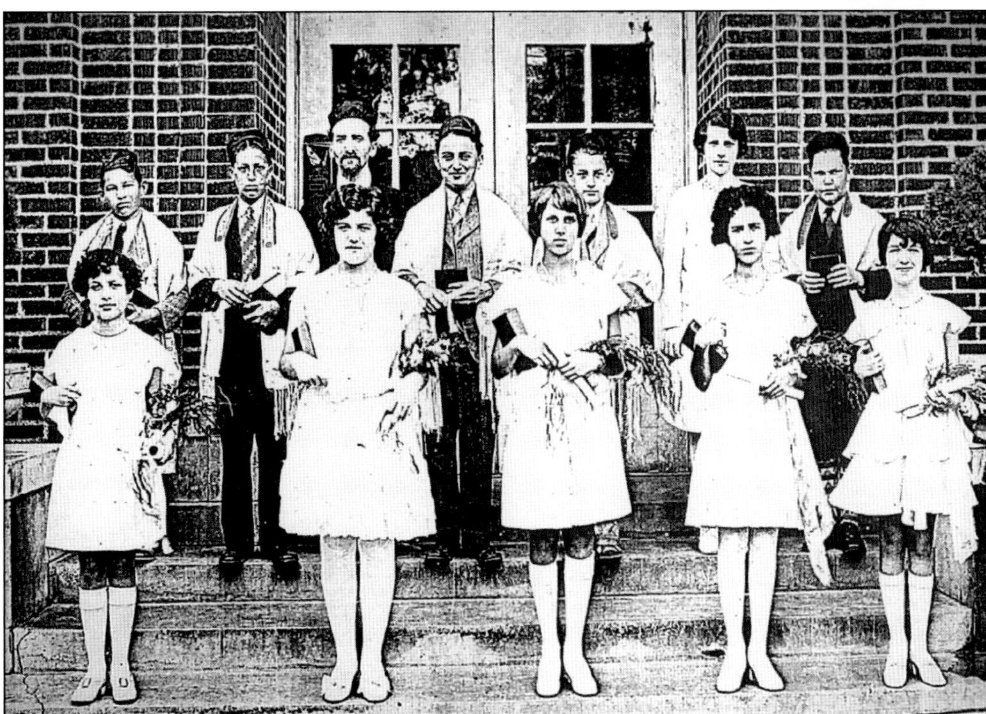

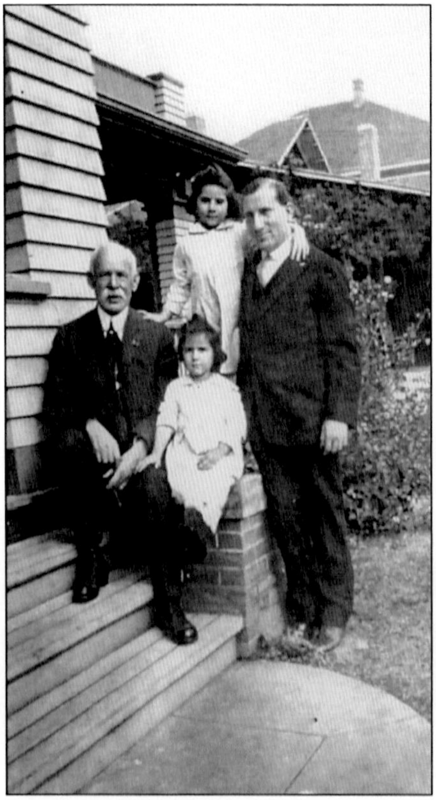

One of Shreveport's most influential figures of the early 20th century was Philip Lieber (1888–1977). In 1905, Lieber joined the Shreveport Mutual Building Association as assistant secretary and by 1921 he was president, a post he held until 1958. In 1934, it became First Federal Savings and Loan Association. Even after retirement, Lieber was influential in the firm, helping to design its round headquarters building on Line Avenue in 1961. He is seen here in 1920 with daughters Rosabel (Shavin), standing, Elizabeth (Fox), and neighbor ex-mayor Ben Holzman at their Egan Street home.

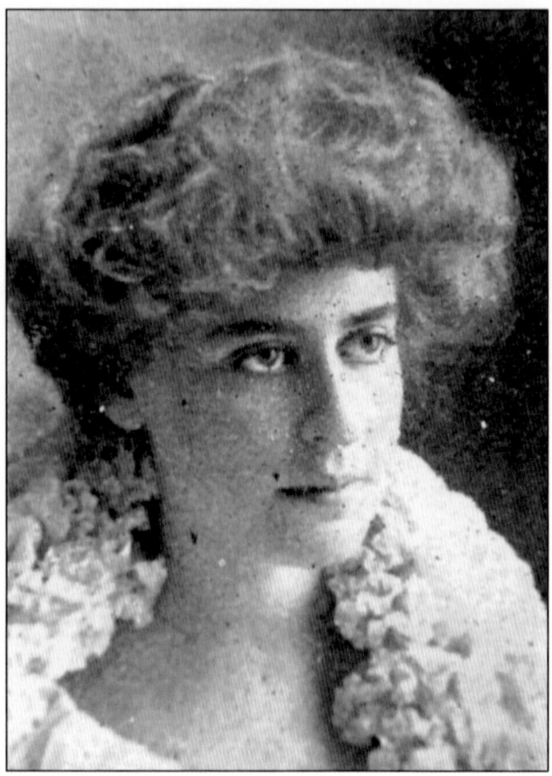

Rai Zodiag, daughter of merchant Herman Zodiag and his wife Rosa Sour Zodiag, is thought to have been the first Jewish debutante in Shreveport's general society, making her debut in 1902. She later married Edgar Friedenberg, manager of her father's store. Their children were Elizabeth Friedenberg, a painter of some note, and Dr. Edgar Z. Friedenberg, an internationally recognized psychologist and author.

Elias Goldstein (1883–1962), son of Prof. Samuel Goldstein (see page 49), was a partner in the firm of Blanchard, Walker, Goldstein, and O'Quinn, which grew to be the city's largest law firm. He was also a partner with developer A.C. Steere in creating the South Highlands and Broadmoor neighborhoods of Shreveport. From 1942 to 1943, he was president of B'nai Zion Temple. Goldstein's 818 Unadilla mansion is still a South Highlands landmark. He served on the Caddo Parish School Board in the 1920s and was instrumental in initiating the free distribution of milk to all public school children, a program he initially funded from his own pocket.

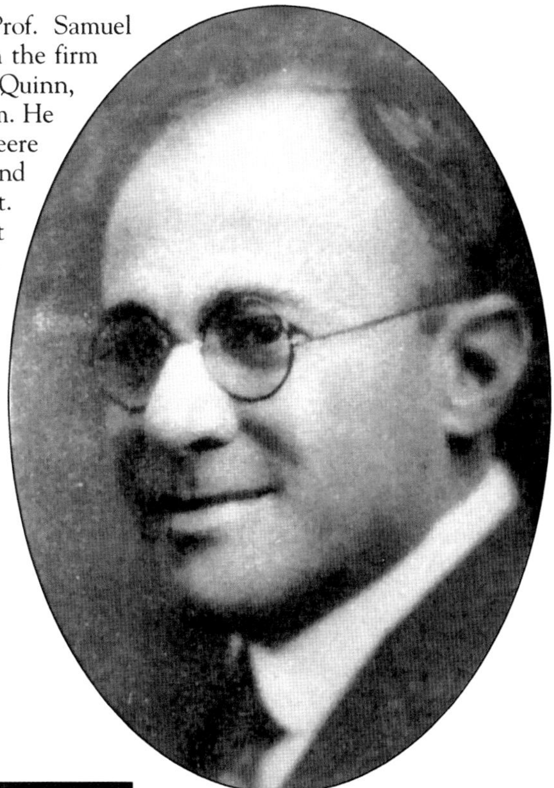

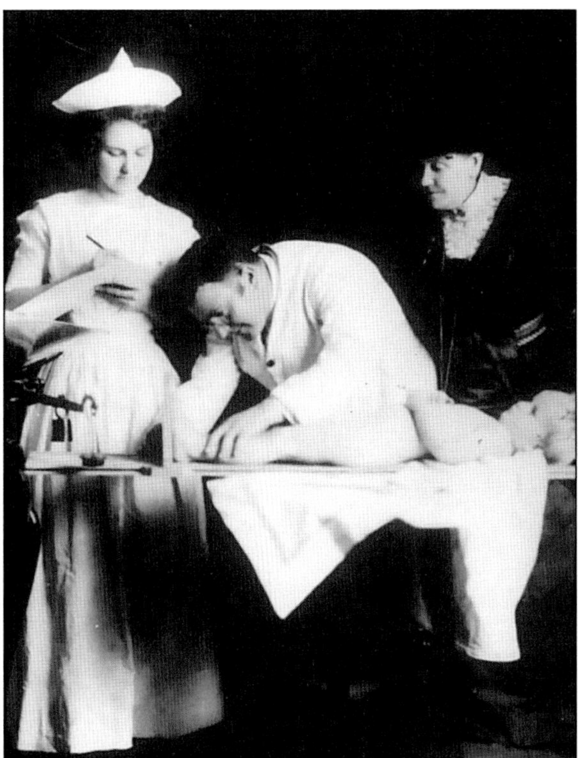

Dr. Jacob Mahne Bodenheimer (1883–1965), a grandson of the first Jewish settler in northwest Louisiana, Jacob Bodenheimer (see pages 10 and 15), was a prominent Shreveport physician and president of the Shreveport Medical Society in 1920 and later for many years, its historian. An early proponent of vaccinations, Bodenheimer was noted for bringing free medical attention to rural and underprivileged children each year at the Louisiana State Fair. He is seen here around 1910 examining a small patient.

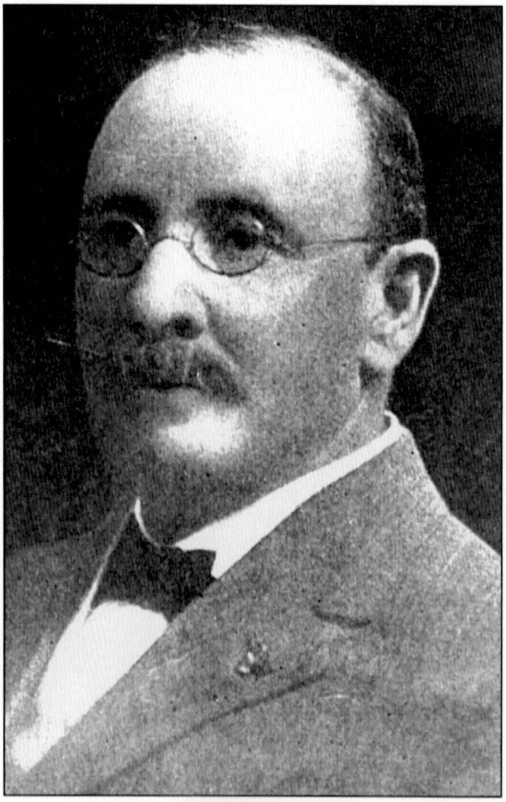

Emanuel Mahne Bodenheimer (1860–1939), son of pioneer settler Jacob Bodenheimer, was the only mayor of the village of South Highlands, a suburb of Shreveport created by Elias Goldstein and A.C. Steere in 1911 and annexed to Shreveport in 1927. During his time in office, Bodenheimer conducted his duties from the village hall (below), which still stands just off Thornhill Avenue near Ontario Street. At the time, it was purported to be the smallest town hall in the United States and possibly the second or third smallest in the world.

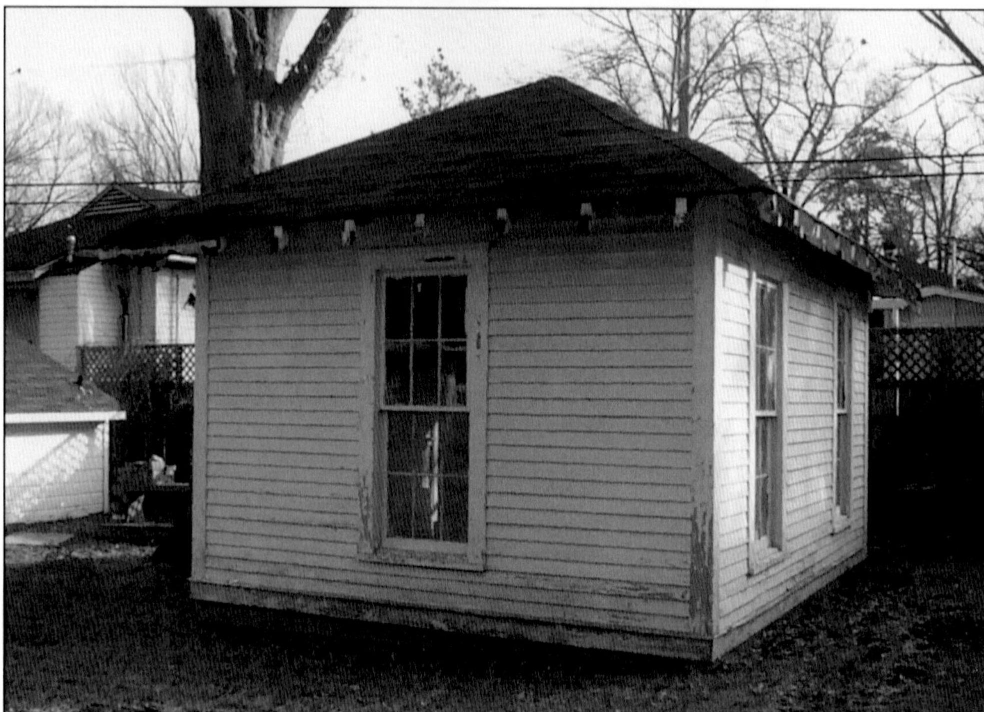

In 1916, David B. Samuel (1874–1937) became the first Jew to serve as a judge in northwest Louisiana. A former state representative from 1912 to 1916, Judge Samuel presided over Shreveport City Court until his death. From 1923 to 1926, he served as president of B'nai Zion Temple.

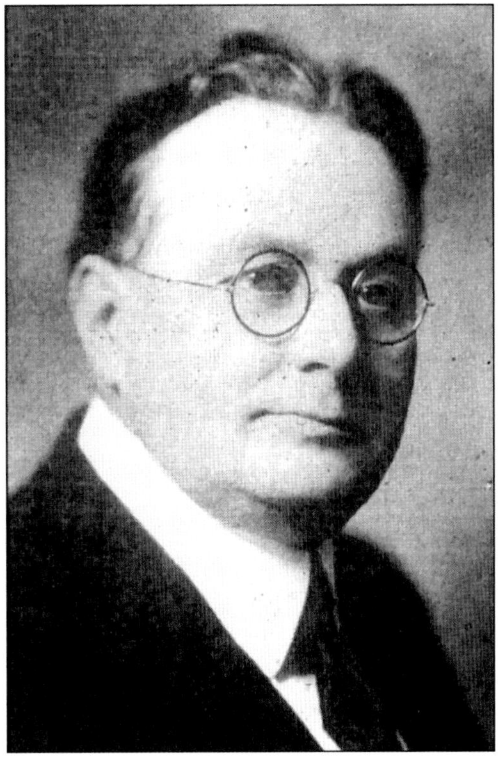

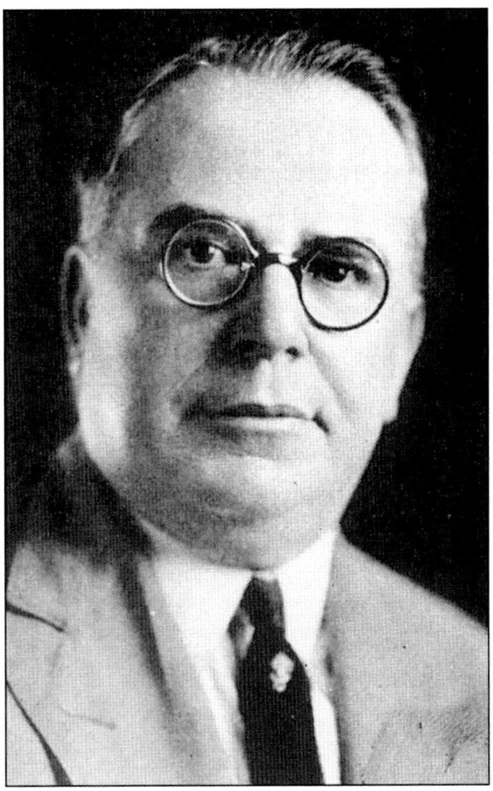

William Rex "Billy" Hirsch (1880–1954) received his middle name because a Mardi Gras parade was passing his home at the time of his birth. He was known, however, as Billy. Starting out as a messenger boy, he soon opened a cigar stand in the Phoenix Hotel (then the city's best) and in 1907 partnered with Eugene Leman to establish the Hirsch and Leman Company, a long-lived bookstore and stationary firm. From 1912 until his death, he was on the board of the State Fair and was for many years its president. The Hirsch Memorial Coliseum at the fairgrounds is a memorial to him.

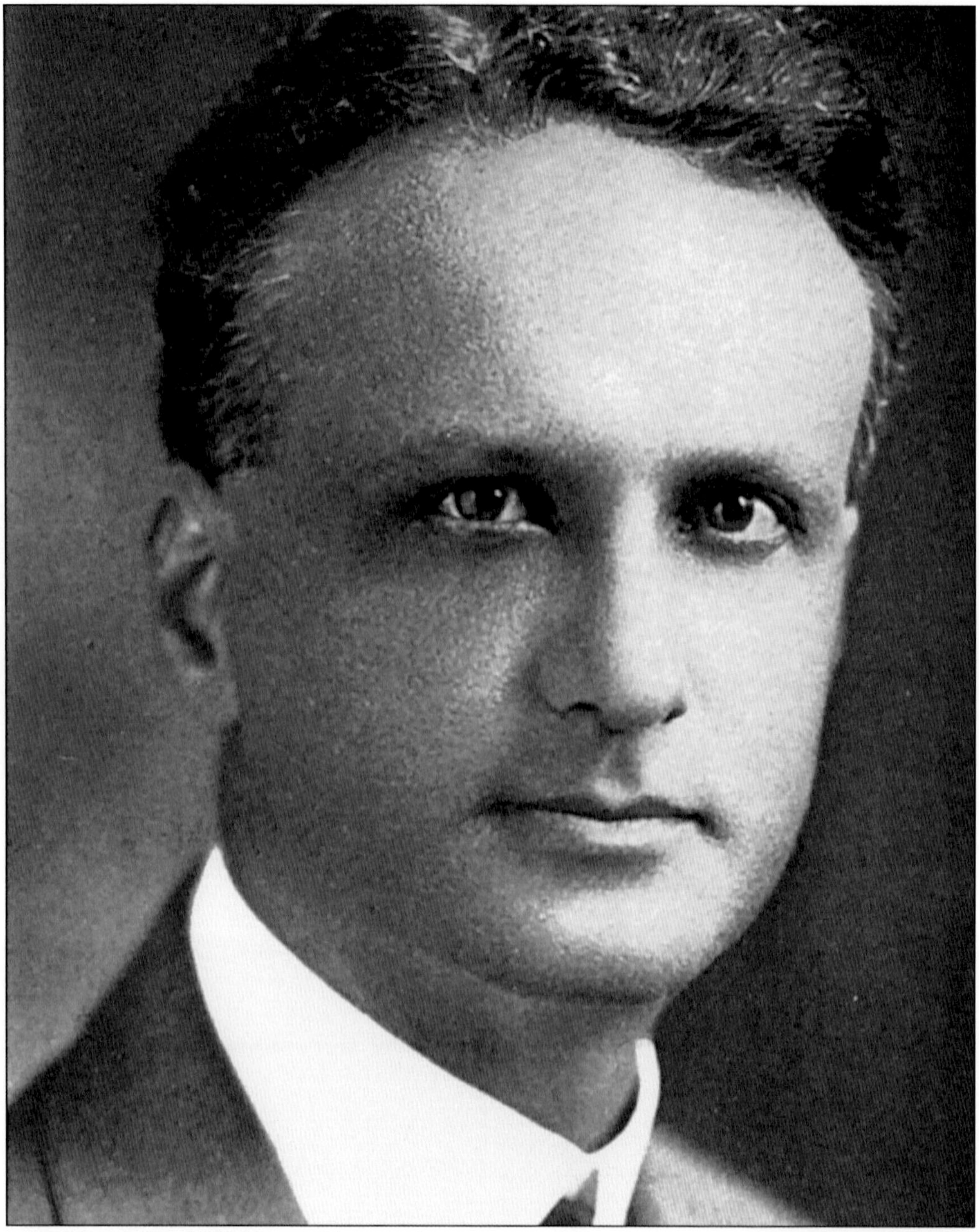

Sidney Levy Herold (1880–1950), son of pioneer merchant Simon Herold (see page 19), began his law practice in Shreveport in 1901, becoming the first attorney in the area to specialize in oil and gas law, soon to be a significant field during Shreveport's oil boom years, which lay just ahead. The arguments used in Herold's successful 1913 challenge to the parish public schools' practice of daily Bible reading was influential in the 1963 United States Supreme Court's ruling that public school prayer was unconstitutional. In 1921, Herold was a member of the State Constitutional Convention. An ardent Zionist and supporter of Zionist causes and organizations from the 1910s forward, Herold visited Palestine and, just before his death, the new State of Israel, where he was honored by that nation's government for his work in the cause of Zionist support.

Miss Hattie Schuster, a native of St. Louis, was one of Shreveport's prominent early 20th century educators. In 1901, she established the city's first kindergarten and later introduced the concept of kindergarten and pre-school education into the Caddo public school system. With Rachel Goldenberg and Elias Goldstein, she worked to establish the first school lunch program for public school students, the pilot of which was the Travis Street School cafeteria, originally run by the Council of Jewish Women.

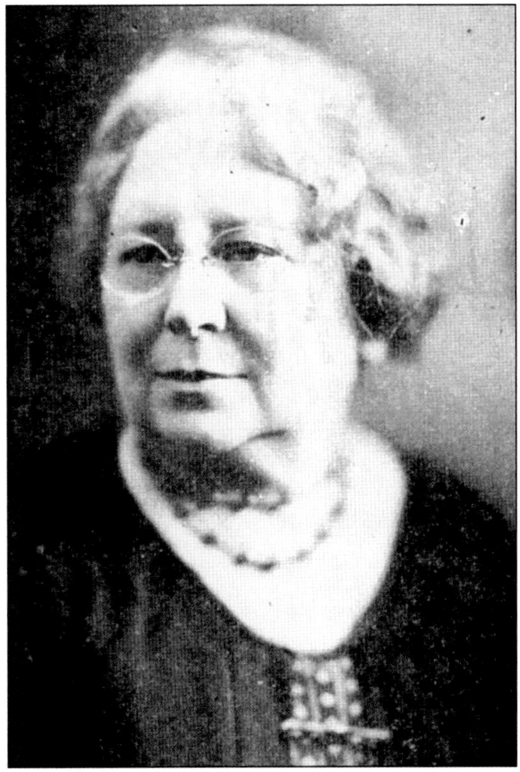

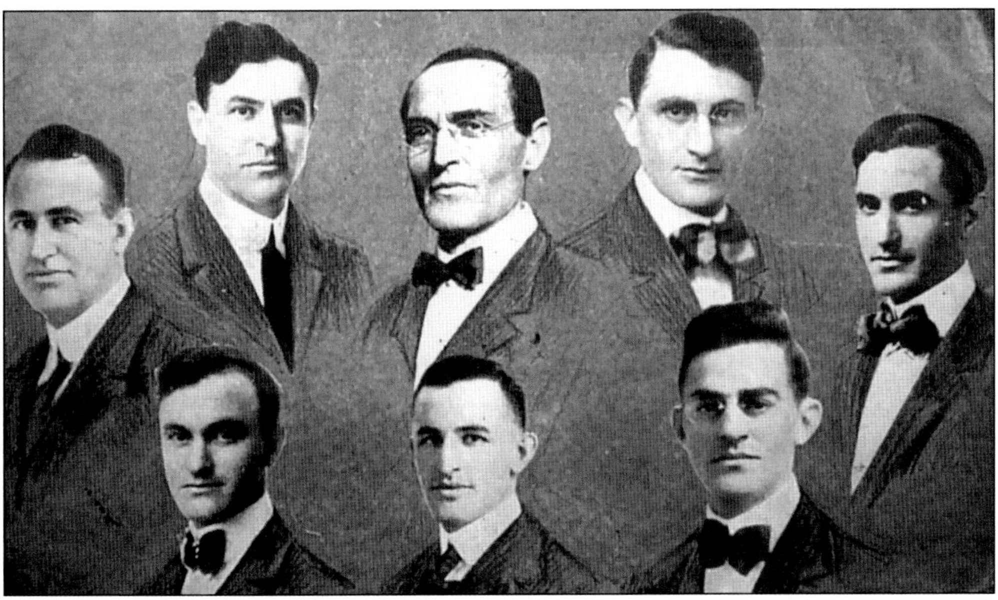

Among the many clothing stores of Shreveport that were owned by members of the Jewish community early in the 20th century, one of the best known was Benson's, founded by Joseph Benson (1858–1932), originally of Pine Bluff, Arkansas. Shown here on a c. 1915 advertising envelope is Joseph, at center, surrounded by his sons (and employees), Charles, Frank, Hamilton, Louis, Meyer, Morris, and Sayle. Benson was also builder of the Medical Arts Building downtown, now known as Travis Place Tower.

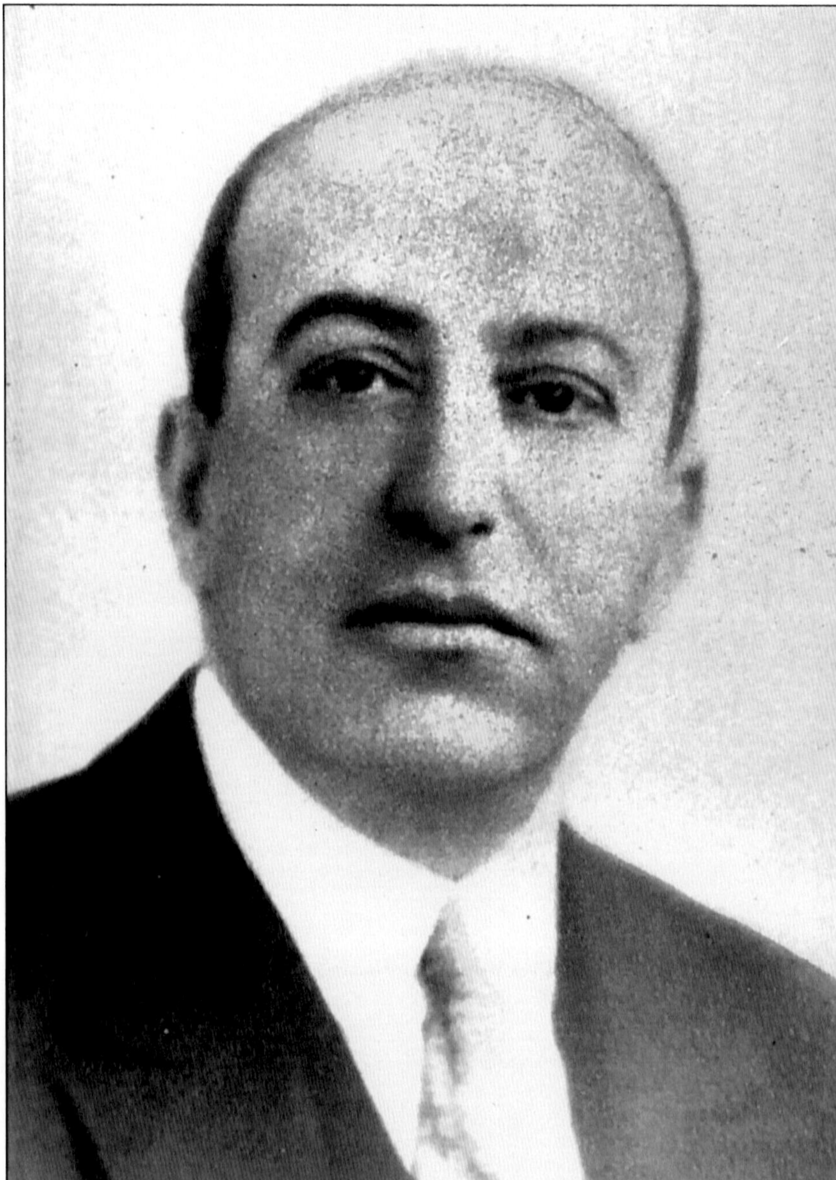

Julian Henri Saenger (1873–1932), son of Rabbi Israel Saenger (see pages 56–57), together with his brother Abraham, founded the first all-night drug store in the city, ran a patent medicine business, and finally found their niche in the theatrical line. In 1911, Julian, who with his brother had already run a nickelodeon, organized the Saenger Amusement Company, booking vaudeville shows and featuring motion pictures, then a new and curious attraction. Later, in partnership with Harry Ehrlich, Saenger-Ehrlich Enterprises built theaters throughout the South as well as in Central America. The company's headquarters after 1925 was the sumptuous Strand Theatre of Shreveport, but New Orleans's Saenger, Texarkana's Perot, and many now-vanished vaudeville palaces throughout the southern United States were also built by the partnership. In 1929, the Saenger Company sold its huge holdings to Paramount in the largest theatrical purchase in United States history up to that date. Three years later, Saenger died suddenly in his French Quarter home in New Orleans.

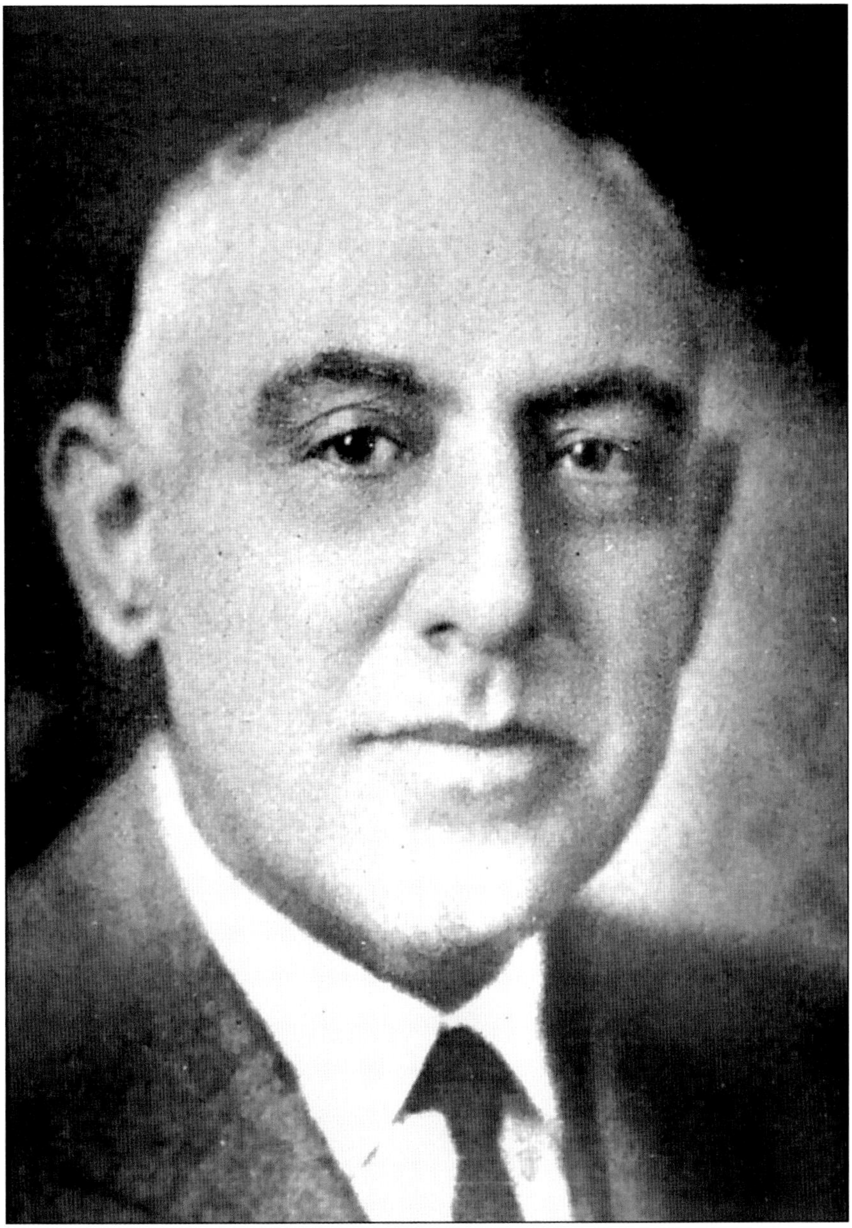

Harry Ehrlich (1875–1933), grew up in Texarkana, Texas, but came to Shreveport at the age of 22, working as a bill-poster for the Grand Opera House. Working his way up to manager of the Opera House in only three years, he and his brothers Simon and Joseph went into partnership, opening theaters throughout Louisiana, Mississippi, eastern Texas, and southern Arkansas. Later merging his holdings with those of Shreveport theatrical pioneer Julian Saenger, he helped to form Saenger-Ehrlich Enterprises. After the dissolution of the business and sale to Paramount, Ehrlich was co-organizer of the Castle-Ehrlich-Hirsch Shows, a traveling carnival and circus. Above all else, Ehrlich was noted as a philanthropist, furnishing thousands of pairs of shoes to needy children and giving free tickets to his shows for those who could not afford them. He was also a major benefactor of many local charitable organizations, orphanages, and organizations for the poor and elderly.

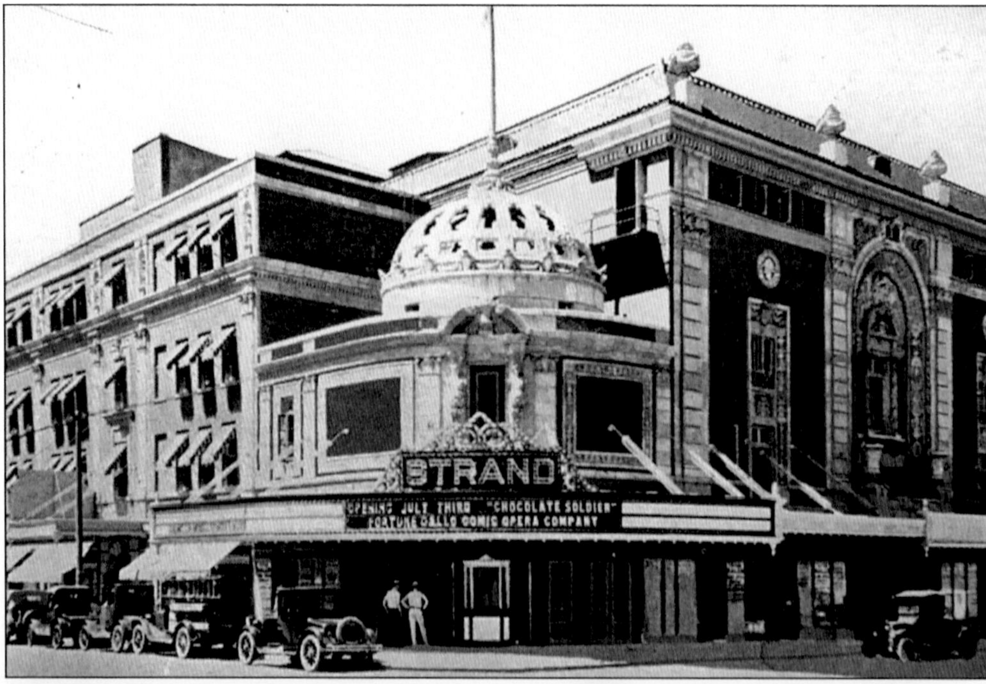

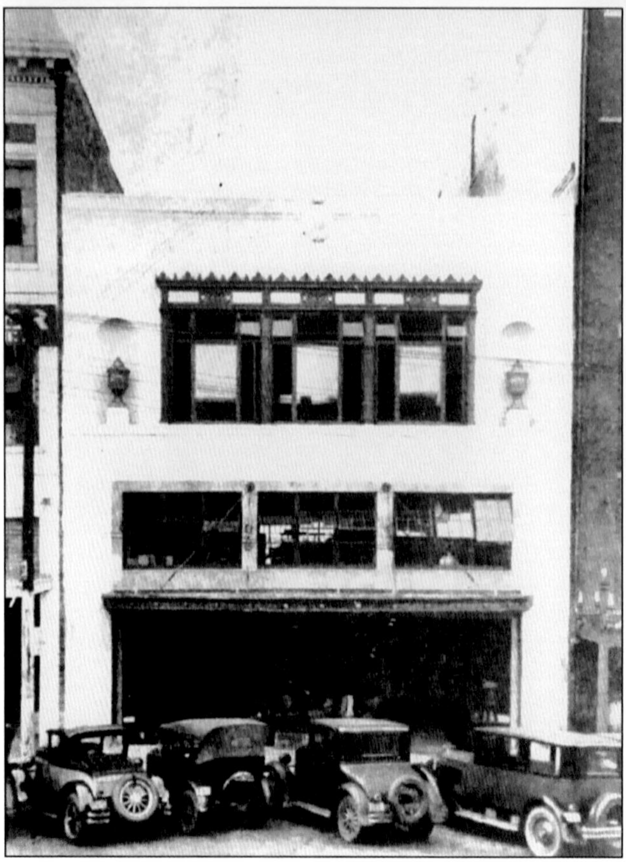

Shreveport's Strand Theatre, built by Saenger-Ehrlich Enterprises in 1924–1925, remains to this day the city's most important entertainment venue. Headquarters of the Saenger theatrical empire, the theater was designed by architect Emile Weil of New Orleans, and its rich interior ornamentation was designed and executed by Paul Heerwagen, who also did the interior design work on the Cotton Street synagogue of B'nai Zion Temple.

Zodiag's, on the 600 block of Texas Street, was the city's premiere ladies clothing and millinery store of the 1920s. Begun as a dry goods store by Herman Zodiag, a native of Austria, the business grew to become a top-shelf specialty shop and was the first store in Shreveport to employ a resident buyer in New York.

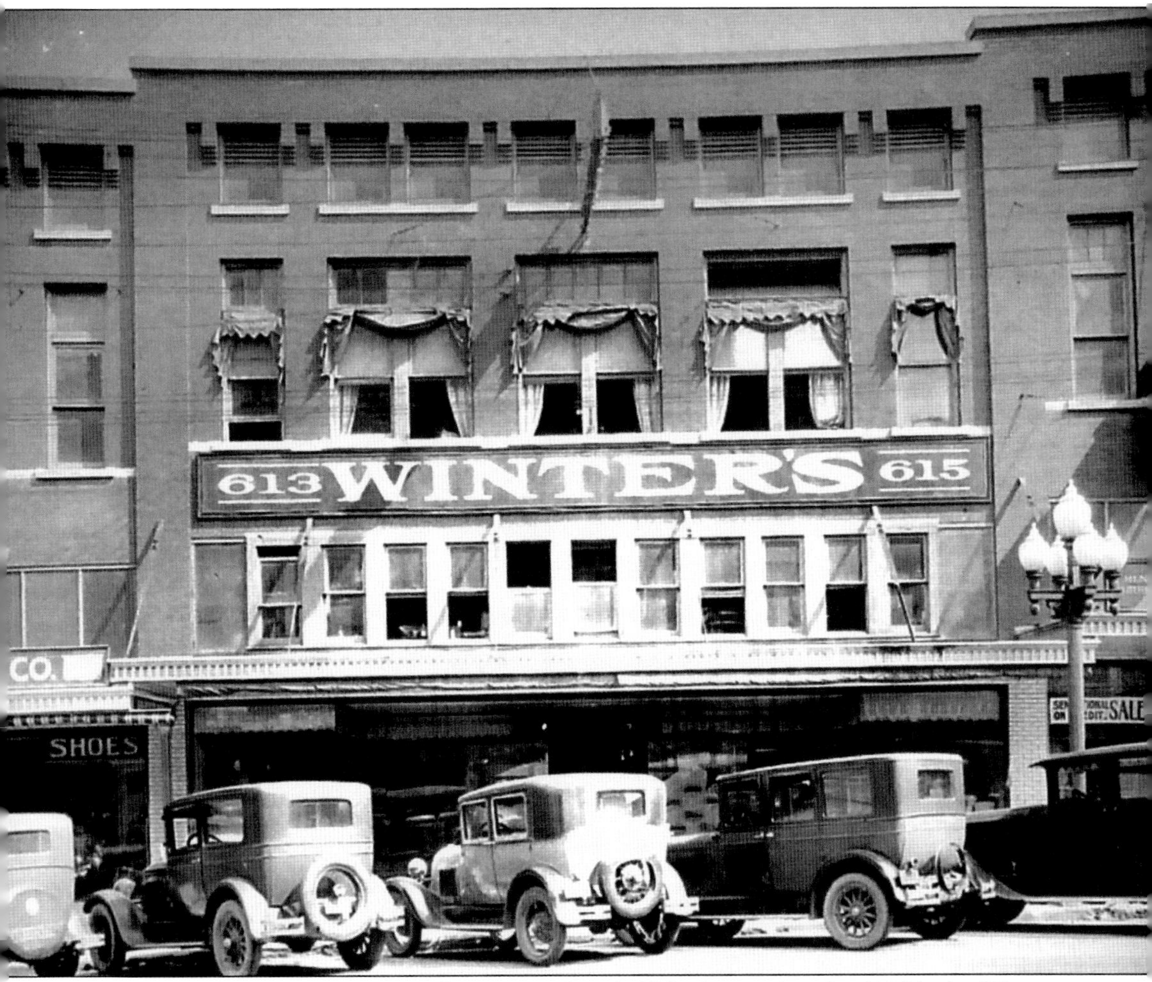

By the 1920s, the Winter Company (see pages 10 and 12) had moved to the 600 block of Texas Street and was well-established as the city's oldest operating retail store. Famous for its display windows and slogan "Watch Winter's Windows," the department store was left under the management of Sidney S. Weisman when his brother-in-law, Henry A. Winter, left Shreveport for Denver, Colorado. Weisman tried valiantly to pull the store through the Depression but economic woes finally took their toll, and in 1935, the store closed its doors forever. Weisman, however, opened Weisman's toy store, successor to the Winter Company's toy department, which had begun in 1919. Weisman's remained in operation until 1966 when it was sold to the Baskind family, becoming Toy Fair, which remains in business still.

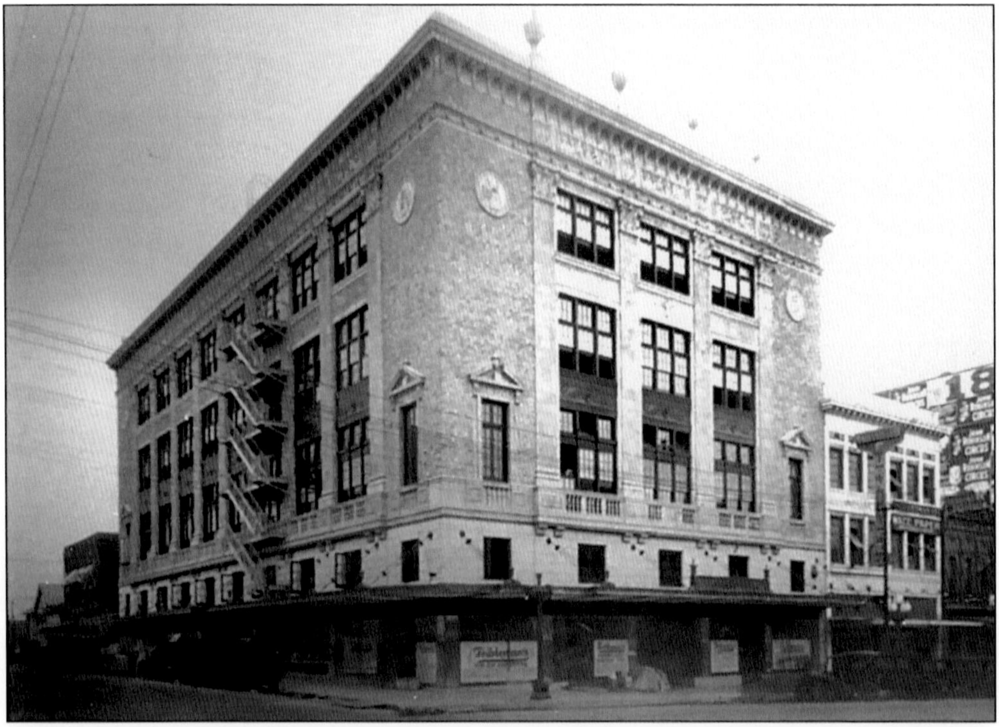

Here are exterior and interior views of Feibelman's department store, opened in 1925 at the northeast corner of Texas and Louisiana Streets. The first department store with escalators and the first to issue its own credit cards, Feibelman's was a precursor of today's discount stores. At the time of its opening, it was among the largest retail stores in the city of Shreveport. Later sold to Sears Roebuck and Company, the store was known locally as Feibelman-Sears until 1960.

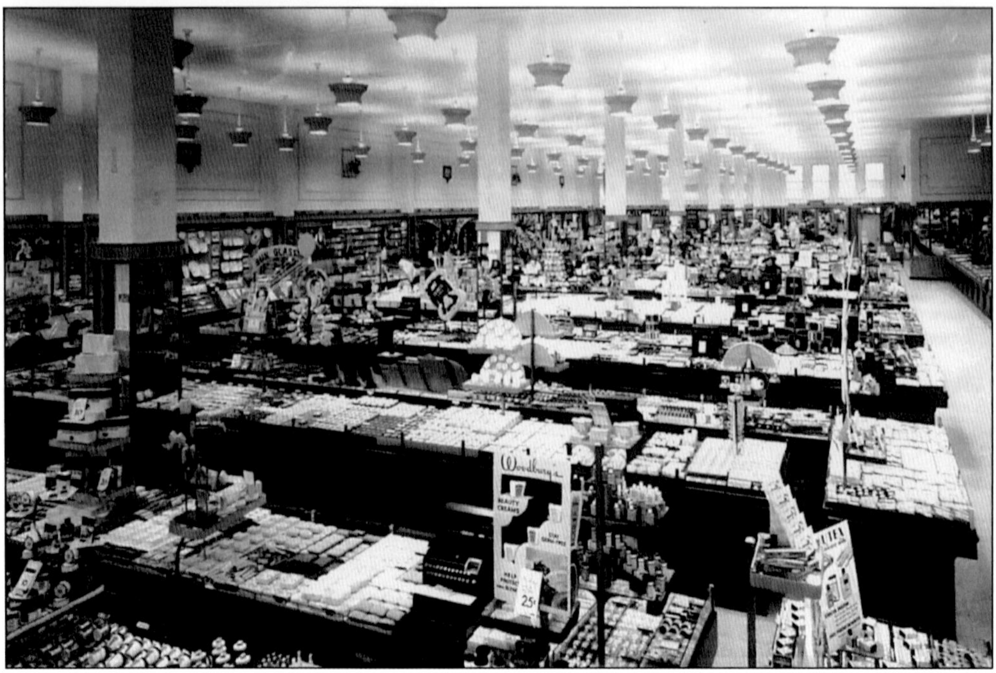

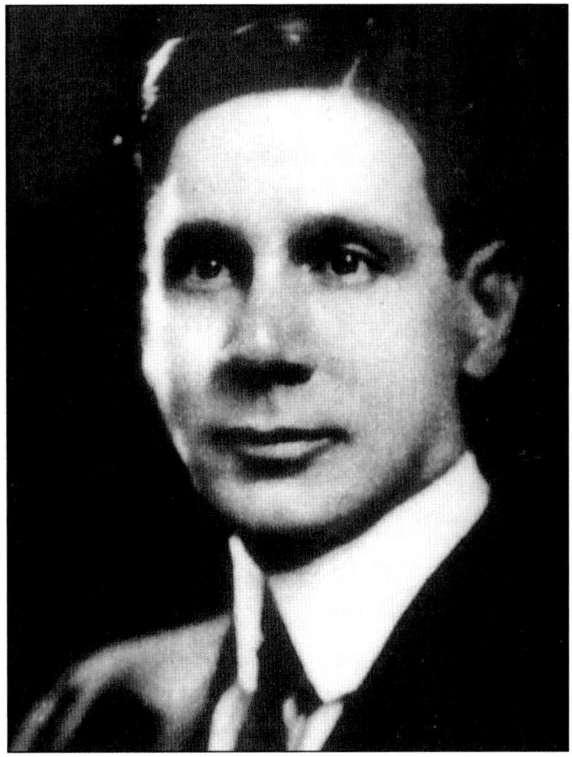

Michaelis Lewis Bath (1881–1945), a native of St. Louis, Missouri, grew up in Shreveport and worked during his school years for a St. Louis-based stationery company. In 1905, he founded his own stationery, engraving, binding, and office supply house—the M.L. Bath Company (bottom), which is still in business. The son-in-law of William Winter (see page 47), Bath was a leader in local business and civil affairs. He served as president of the chamber of commerce, the rotary club, the local red cross, the local blood bank, and the Red River Valley Improvement Association. He and his wife Leona (d. 1967) were also influential in the establishment of the Community Chest, now the Community Foundation of Shreveport-Bossier.

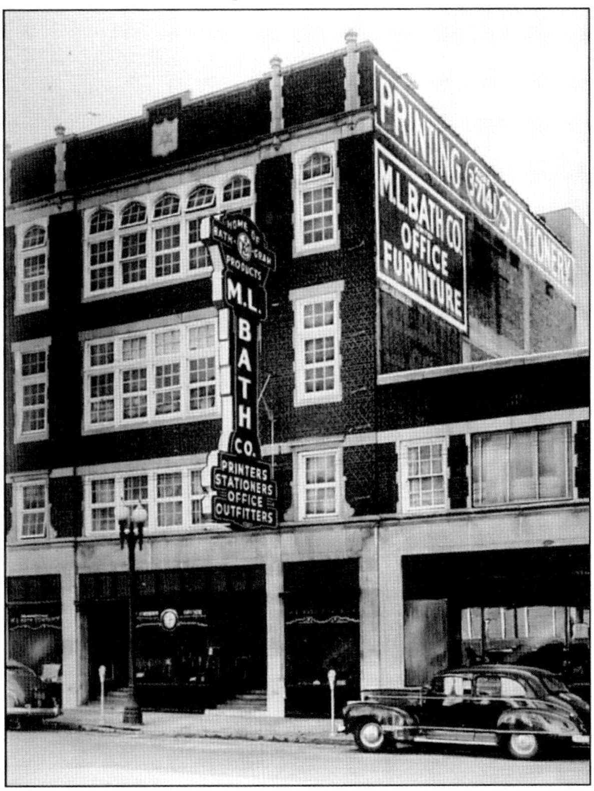

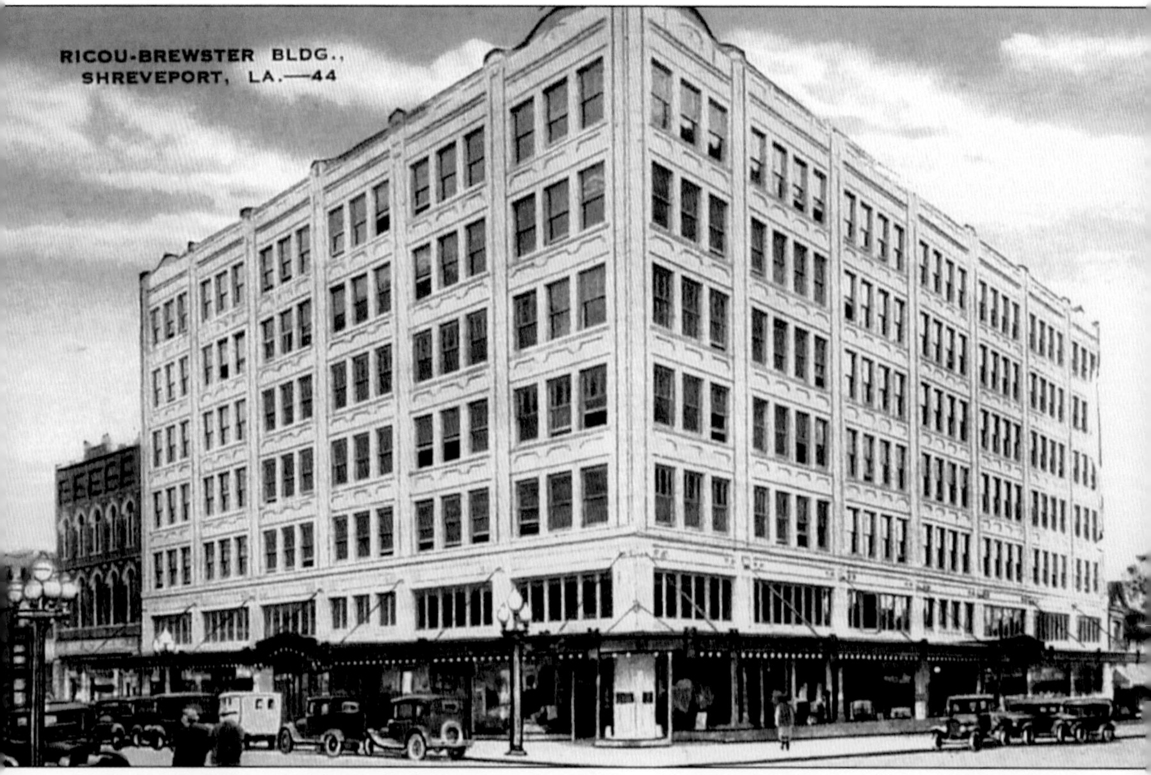

In 1925, Selber Brothers clothing store moved from 331 Texas Street (see page 66) where it had been located since 1907. Founded in Baton Rouge in 1896, Selber's moved to Shreveport 11 years later. By 1925, the store had grown from a small, men's ready-to-wear shop into one of the city's foremost department stores, occupying a substantial portion of the new Ricou-Brewster Building. When Selber's constructed a new store two blocks away in 1956, the Ricou-Brewster Building became home to M. Levy's Sons, which would operate there until its closure in 1980. The building was demolished in 1996.

E. Bernard Weiss (1898–1954), originally of Abbeville, Louisiana, came to Shreveport in 1920 to manage the local store of the Goldring Company, a clothing store founded by his uncle, Dave Goldring of Alexandria, Louisiana.

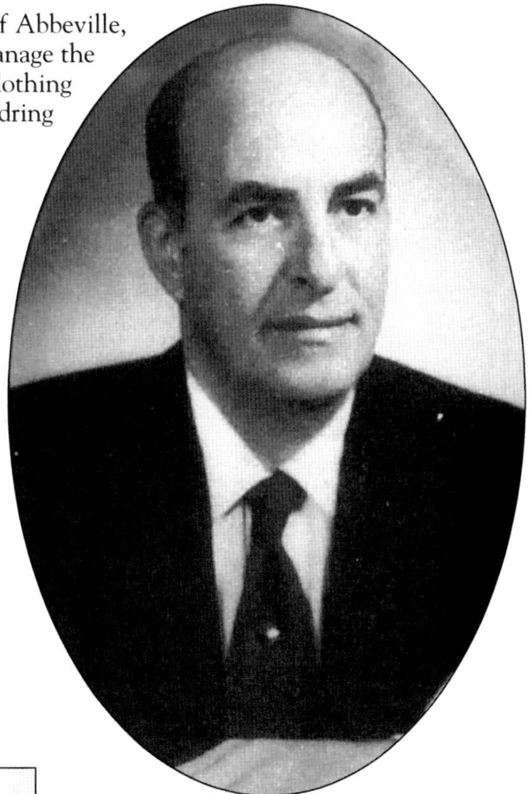

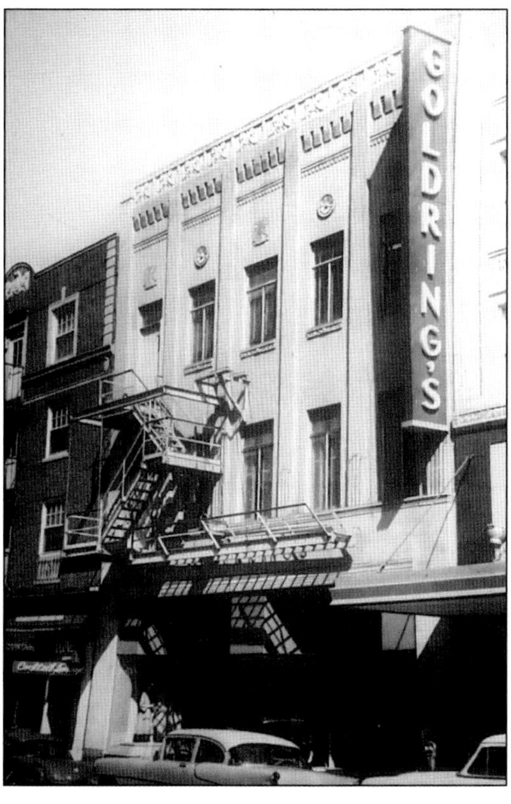

The Shreveport store, in the 400 block of Milam Street, remained in operation until the 1980s, though the firm still exists in Shreveport as Goldring's (albeit a mere shadow of its former self) and in Alexandria as Weiss-Goldring and Company. In January 1954, Bernard Weiss and his brother Milton, of Dallas, were among a dozen victims of a plane crash over Shreveport's Wallace Lake, which also took the lives of Thomas Braniff of Braniff Airlines and a number of prominent Shreveport businessmen. Seymour Weiss, a third brother, had been a leading figure in the administration of Gov. Huey P. Long.

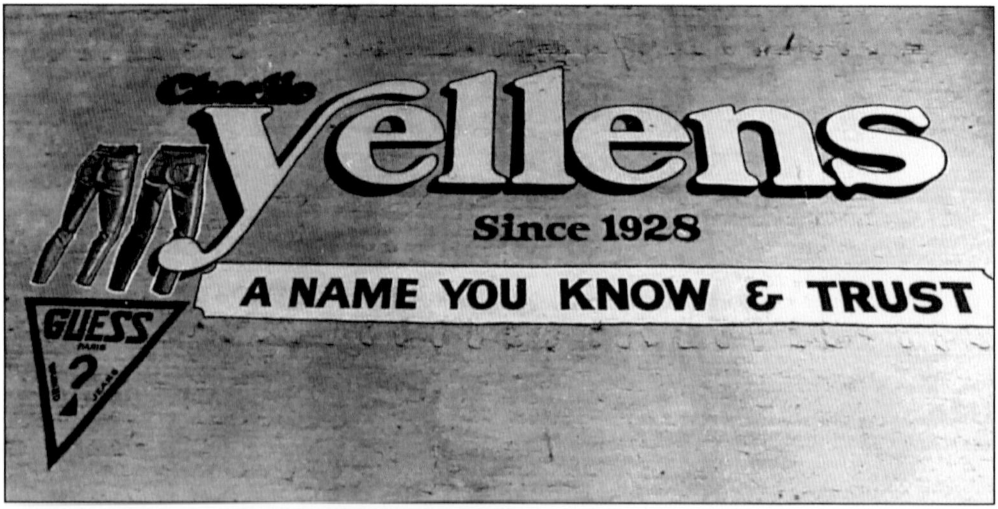

Yellen's Clothing Company was founded by Nathan Yellen (1882–1968) in 1928. Yellen had been a confectioner and had worked for Florsheim Dry Goods. His new store prospered, and was later run by his sons, Harry and Charlie. After Harry's death in 1967, Charlie ran the company solo. It continued to operate until 1996, eight years after Charlie's death. Yellen's was Shreveport's last small, men's ready-to-wear and tailor shop.

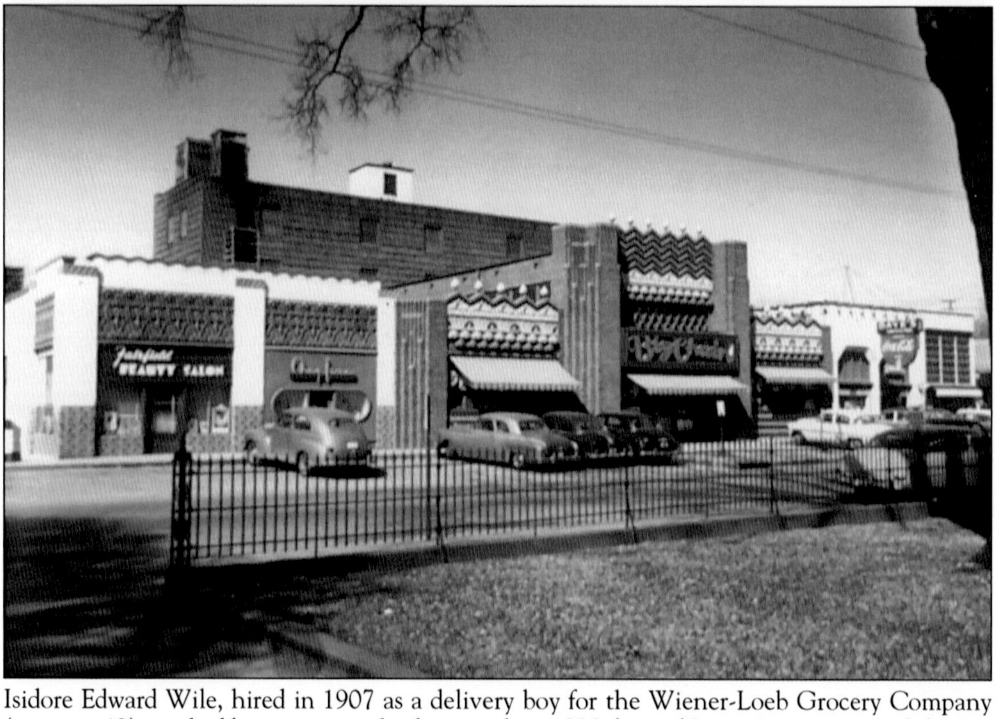

Isidore Edward Wile, hired in 1907 as a delivery boy for the Wiener-Loeb Grocery Company (see page 40), worked his way up in the firm until, in 1922, he and Louie Levy organized the Big Chain Grocery Company, initially a subsidiary of Wiener-Loeb, which they then purchased, merging the two. The first store was located in the Levy Building (see page 46) but in 1924, the landmark Art Deco supermarket shown here was constructed on Fairfield Avenue to house the firm. Designed by Samuel G. Wiener, it was the first of many Big Chain supermarkets that would dot the city and serve as models for supermarket development nationally.

Abe Meyer (1852–1930) was an investor in real estate, owner of a plantation, vice-president of City Savings Bank and Trust, and a member of the building committee of B'nai Zion Temple's Cotton Street synagogue. In 1924, he built the Alvin Building (below), named for his son, Alvin Felix Meyer (1894–1923), who had succumbed to injuries sustained in the First World War. Designed in the Tudor Revival style beloved of Beulah Meyer Stagg, Abe's daughter and Alvin's sister, the Alvin Building long housed the Harmony Club, a Jewish social and service club established in 1881 as successor to the Concordia Club, founded in 1869.

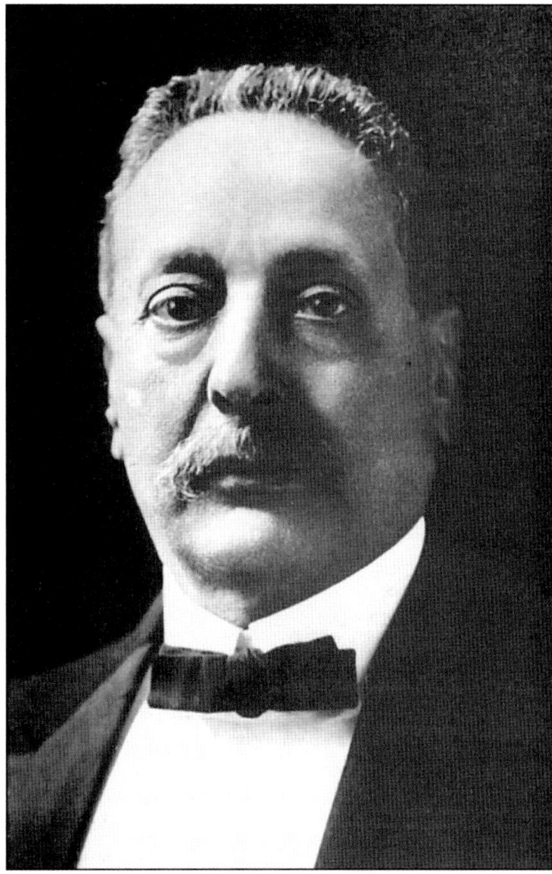

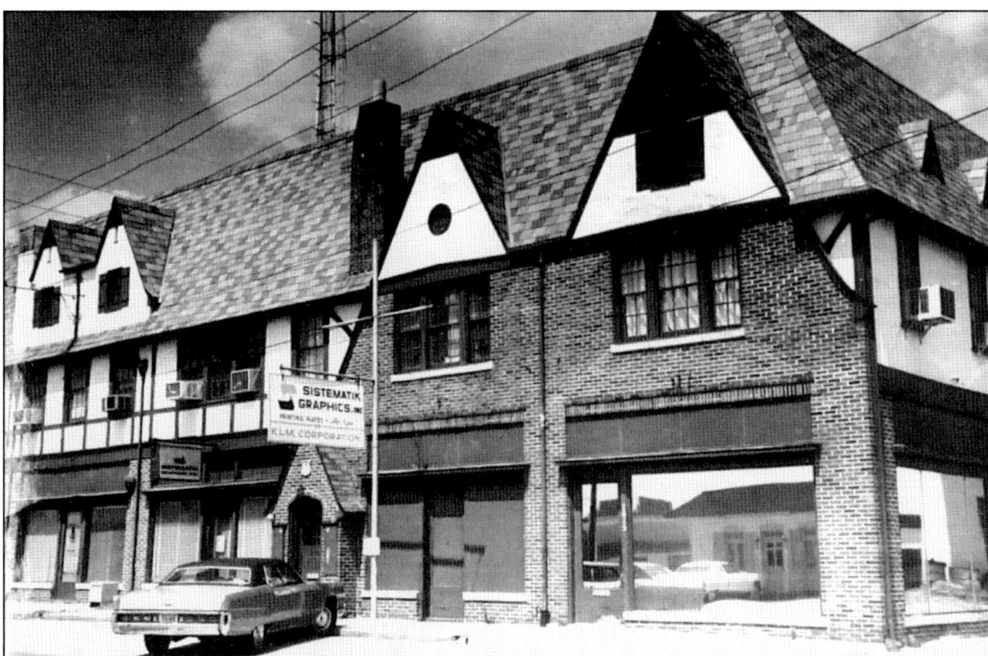

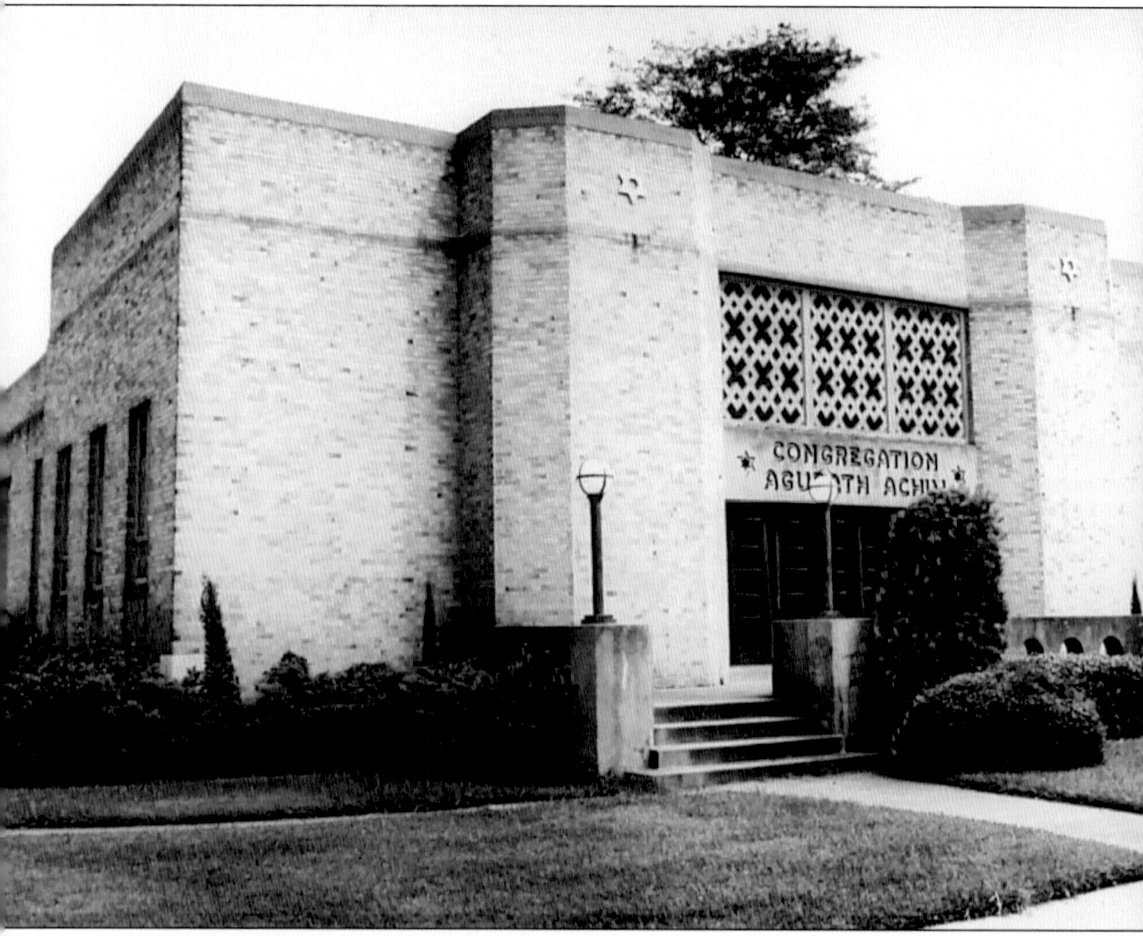

In 1926 Agudath Achim Congregation purchased property on Line Avenue at the head of Margaret Place with plans to construct a Hebrew school there. The congregation was outgrowing its synagogue at Fannin and McNeill Streets, however, and in 1927 it was determined that the best use for the property would be as the site for a new synagogue. The new synagogue was not built until 1938. Seymour Van Os, a member of B'nai Zion Temple, was chosen as the architect. Although an orthodox *shul*, the *bimah* was placed upon a stage at the rear of the sanctuary, in front of the ark. This was a radical departure from the traditional arrangement familiar to the congregation's mostly Eastern European membership. The downtown *shul*, as with synagogues in Europe, had had the *bimah* at the center of the sanctuary. Men and women still were seated separately, however. On May 14, 1939, the new synagogue was dedicated.

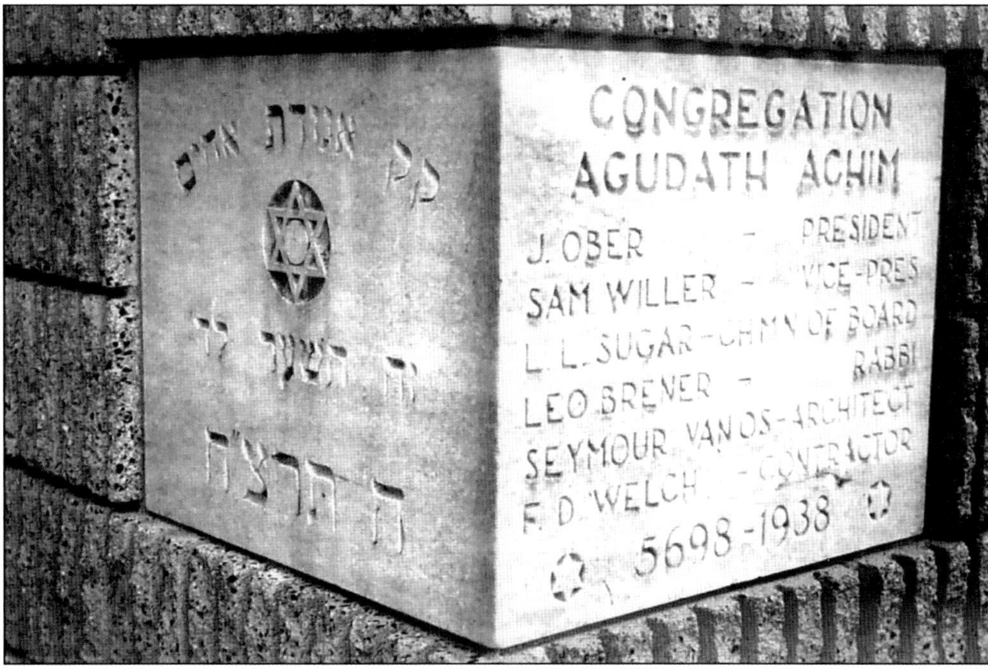

The cornerstone of the Line Avenue synagogue was laid with much fanfare on June 20, 1938. Rabbi Leo Brener led the services, which included Rabbi Abram Brill of B'nai Zion, Rev. James Owens of St. Mark's Episcopal Church, Mayor Sam Caldwell, and numerous others.

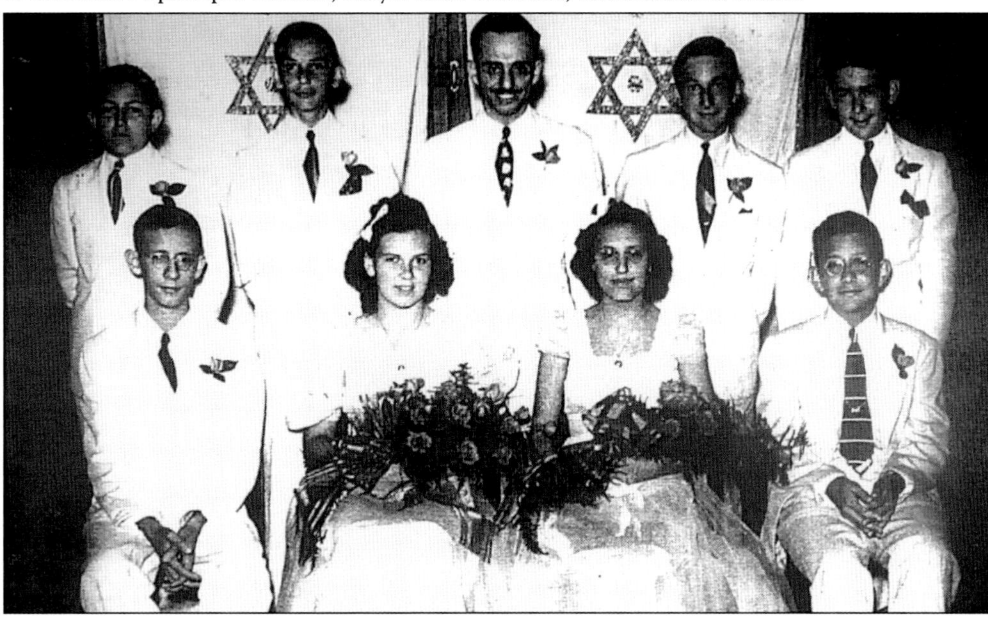

Rabbi Brener (1909–1989), a native of New Orleans, to which his parents had emigrated from Poland, came to Agudath Achim in 1934 and would remain as rabbi for the next 40 years and as rabbi emeritus thereafter (see also page 110). Shown is Rabbi Brener with the 1942 Agudath Achim confirmation class. From left to right are (front row) Raphael Atlas, Pearl Vedlitz, Dorothy Strausman, and Daniel Lincove; (back row) ? Katz, Ike Muslow, Rabbi Brener, Irwin Muslow, and Elliott Samuels.

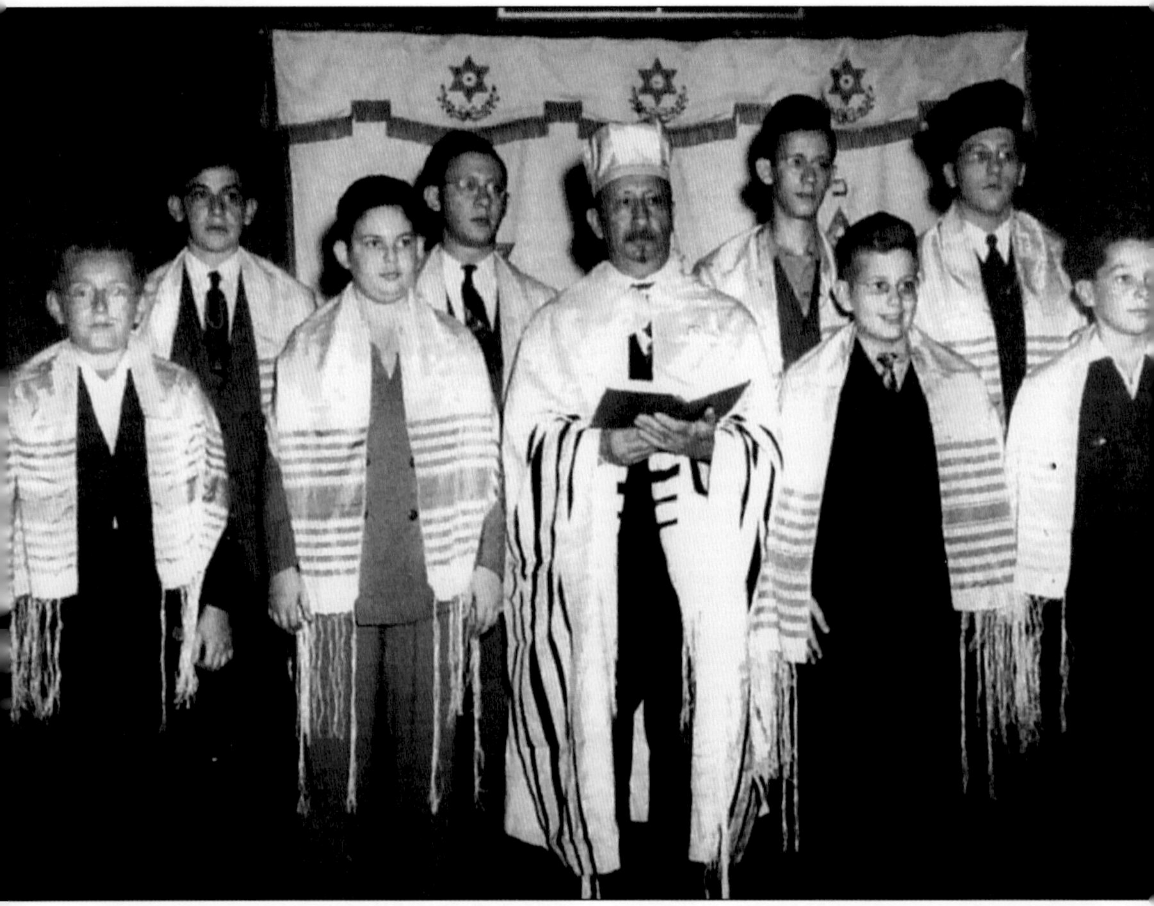

The cantor has traditionally been an important part of orthodox religious services. In the early days of Shreveport's orthodox community the cantor and *shochet* (kosher butcher) were often the same thing. In several instances, the rabbi served all three roles. Agudath Achim has employed at least 11 cantors—Jacob Cantor, Elias Atlas, Elias Renov, Arthur Rosenwasser, Paul Stone, and Monty Pomm being the longest tenured. Pomm, a native of Great Britain with a booming melodious voice, became cantor when he arrived in Shreveport in 1977 to assume the post of executive director of the Jewish Federation. In 1993–1994, he would also serve as interim rabbi, making *aliyah* to Israel in 1995. Above is the 1940 High Holiday Choir. From left to right are (front row) Norman Chapman, Harvey Schwartzberg, Cantor Elias Atlas, Sig Spitzer, and Harold Friedman; (back row) Elliott Samuels, Raphael Atlas, Harry Atlas, and Seymour Atlas.

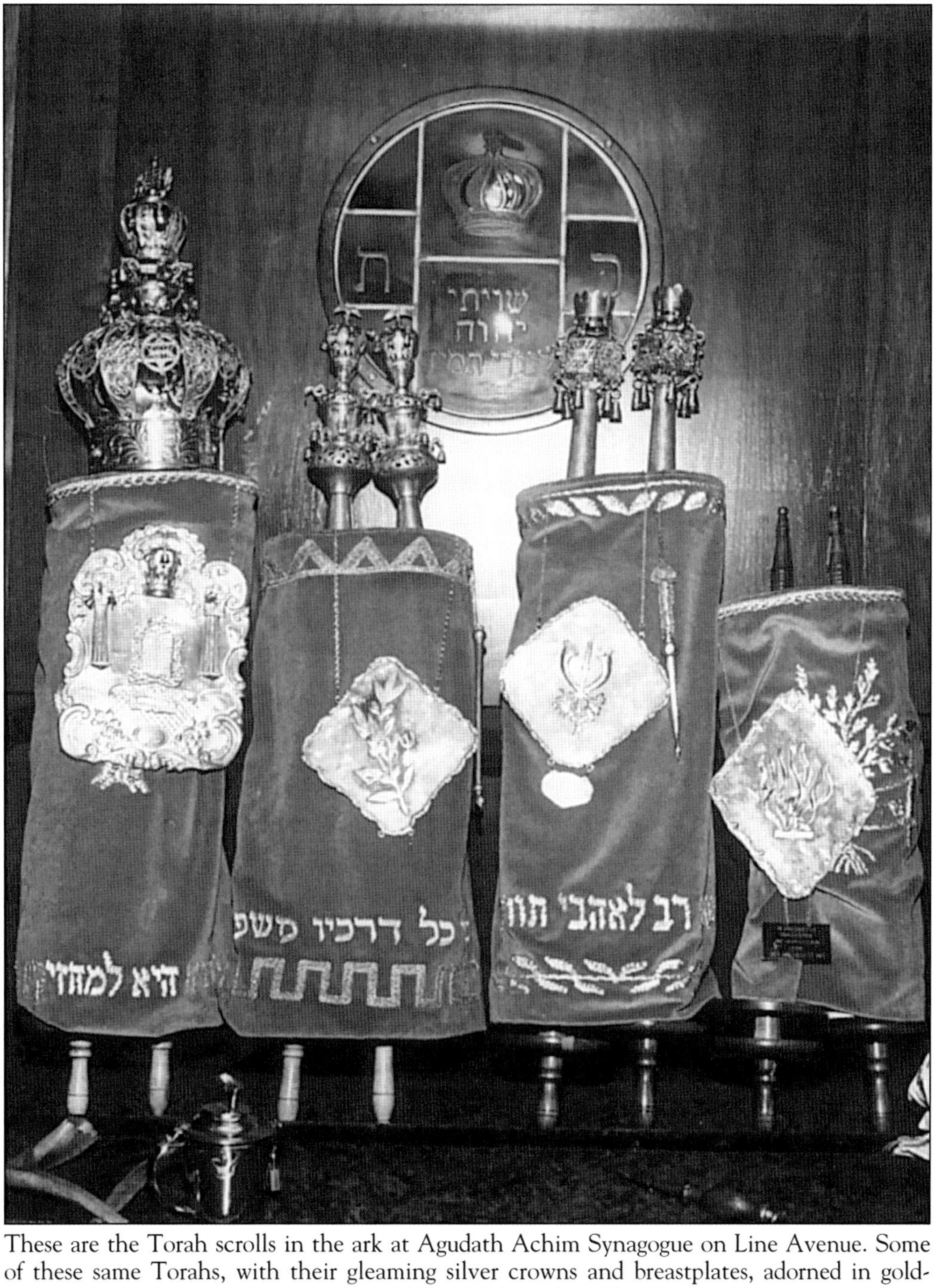

These are the Torah scrolls in the ark at Agudath Achim Synagogue on Line Avenue. Some of these same Torahs, with their gleaming silver crowns and breastplates, adorned in gold-embroidered velvet covers, were carried by hand from the old synagogue on Fannin Street to Line Avenue in 1939. In 1981, they were carried to the ark of the third and present Agudath Achim Synagogue. Thereafter, the Line Avenue *shul* became home to Rutherford House, a social service organization that has carefully maintained the old building's spectacular pink marble and polished oak ark, as well as the architectural integrity of the former synagogue's exterior.

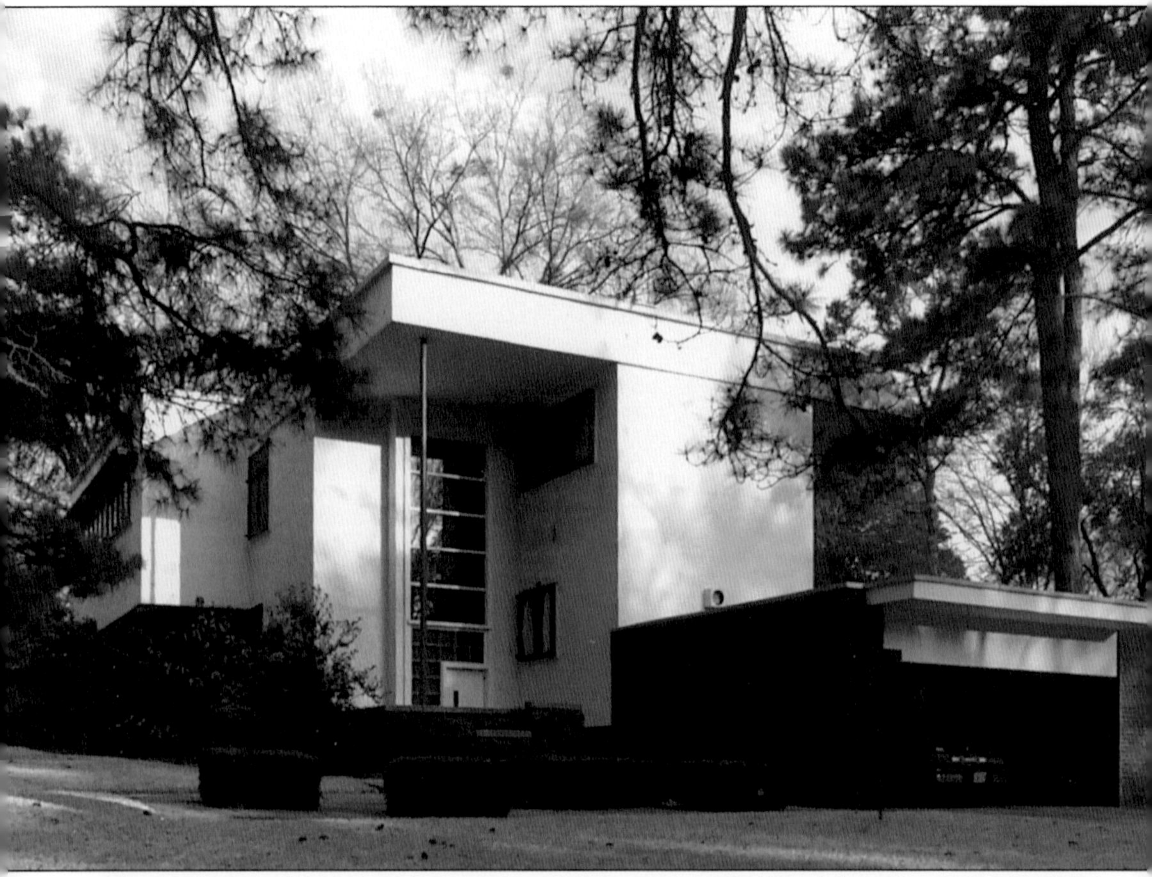

The residence of the Samuel G. Wiener family on Longleaf Road (1937) is a landmark of the International Style of architecture, a style pioneered and popularized in America by the Wiener brothers, Samuel and William. They achieved national and international acclaim for their work, which include numerous important Louisiana buildings. Indeed, owing in large measure to the Wiener brothers' residence in Shreveport, the city has one of the largest collections of significant International-Style architecture in the American South, though much of what formerly existed has, unfortunately, been destroyed or compromised. Other architects who have emerged from the Shreveport Jewish community include Bill Wiener Jr., Seymour Van Os, Ted Flaxman, Henry Schwarz, Lester Haas, and Albert Dreyfuss, who later relocated to Sacramento, California. Sam Wiener, son of architect Samuel Wiener, is today a noted artist in New York City, working under the pseudonym Evangeline Tabasco. One other architect worthy of note here is Julian Sokoloski, municipal architect for the city of Berlin, who came to Shreveport due to family connections when the Nazis came to power.

The legacy of Samuel G. Wiener (1896–1977) includes much of Shreveport's Art Deco, Moderne, and International Style architecture. The son of grocer Samuel G. Wiener, co-founder of the Wiener-Loeb Company, he grew up in a Victorian mansion (see page 40) but ultimately found his niche in the antithesis of Victorian architecture, the International Style. Heavily influenced by the German Bauhaus school, Wiener's buildings represent some of the first radical departures from traditional styles seen in the Deep South. Wiener was the first president of the North Louisiana Chapter of the American Institute of Architects.

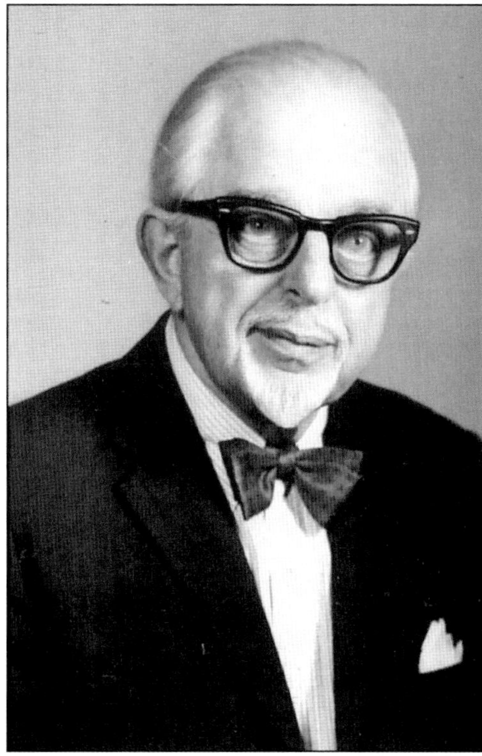

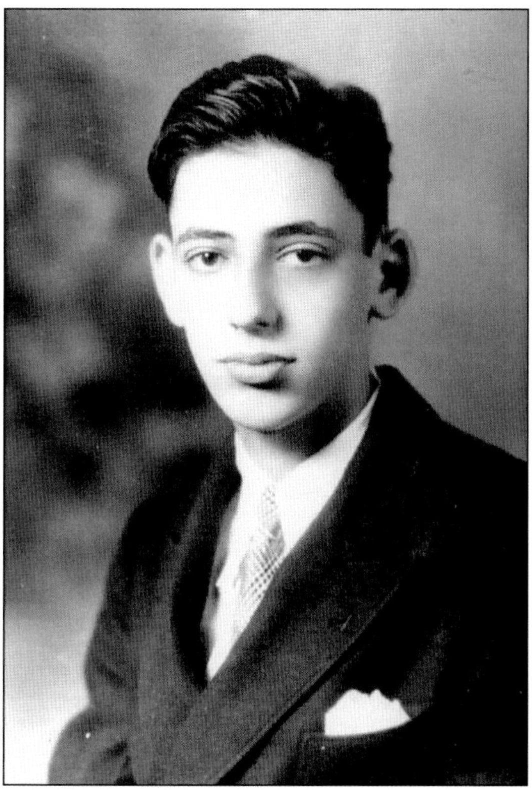

Phelps Kirsch, seen here in his youth, was the grandson of shoemaker Emanuel Phelps (see page 24). In the mid-1930s, he went to Paris where he studied under Romain de Tirtoff, better known as Erté. Like Erté, Phelps Kirsch decided to create a pseudonym of his initials, thus becoming Piqué. Eventually he changed his name to Jean-Pierre Piqué and came to be much in demand as a designer and decorator in New York. In the early 1990s, after retiring from his noteworthy career in Manhattan, Piqué returned to Shreveport where he resides today.

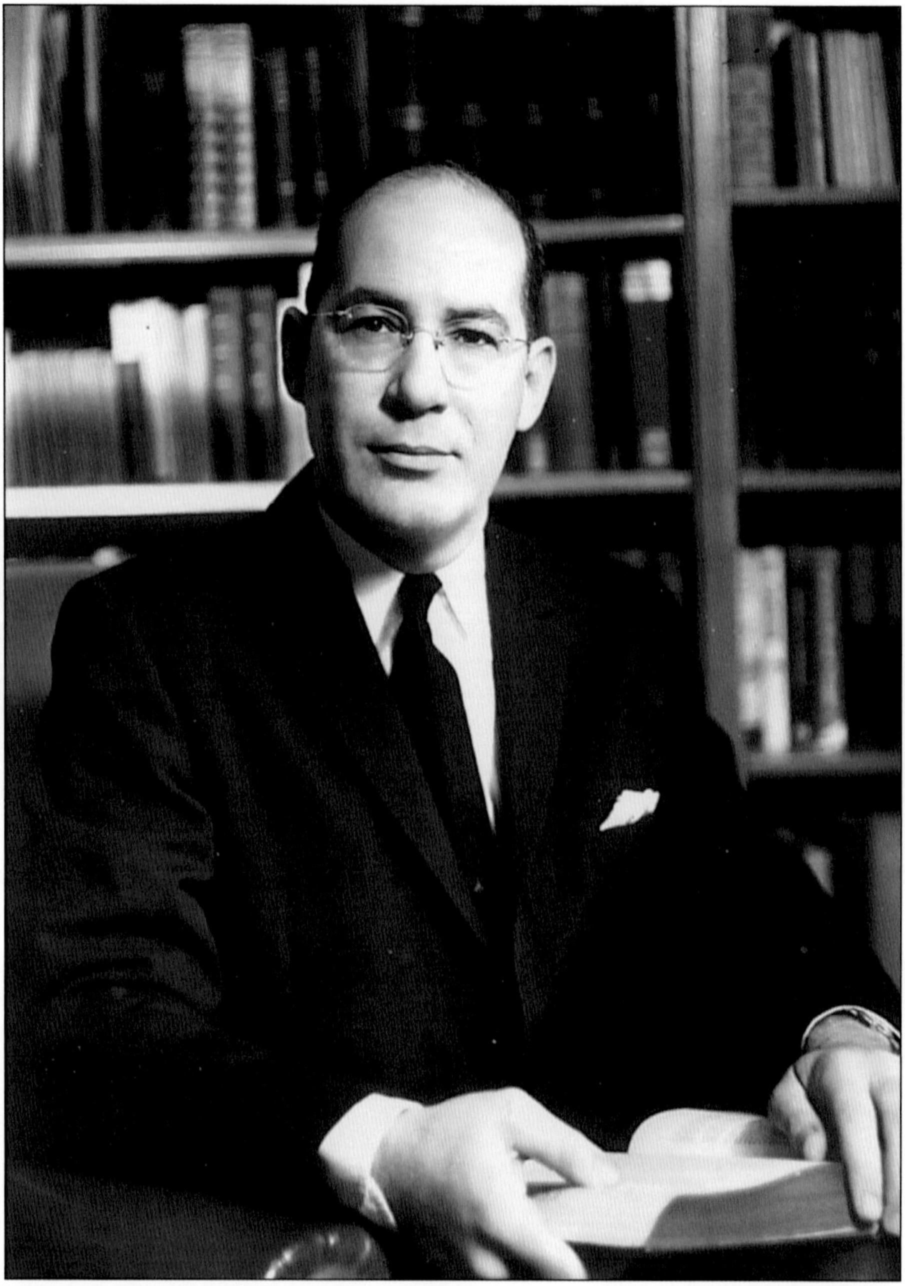

Rabbi David Lefkowitz Jr. (1911–1999), a native of Dayton, Ohio, spent much of his youth in Dallas, Texas, where his father was rabbi of Temple Emanu-El from 1920 to his death in 1955. In 1940, Rabbi Lefkowitz came to Shreveport to serve as associate rabbi of B'nai Zion Temple under Abram Brill. Rabbi Brill, however, was ill and retired within the year. Lefkowitz was then hired as the congregation's full-time rabbi. For 32 years, from 1940 until 1972, David Lefkowitz Jr. would serve as B'nai Zion's rabbi. From his retirement until his death 27 years later, he would hold the title of Rabbi Emeritus, frequently conducting or assisting his successor rabbis with services. A popular, scholarly, charismatic, and loving spiritual leader, Rabbi Lefkowitz and B'nai Zion Temple during the mid-to-late 20th century are inseparable.

During the Second World War, Rabbi Lefkowitz was called to service as a United States Army Air Corps chaplain, serving for three years in that capacity. During 1943 and part of 1944, B'nai Zion's pulpit was filled by Rabbi Max J. Merritt (1879–1963) of Berkeley, California. Rabbi Merritt is seen here standing on the *bimah* in 1944. To his left is Carolyn Marcus and to his right is Joy Goldberg, later Baskind.

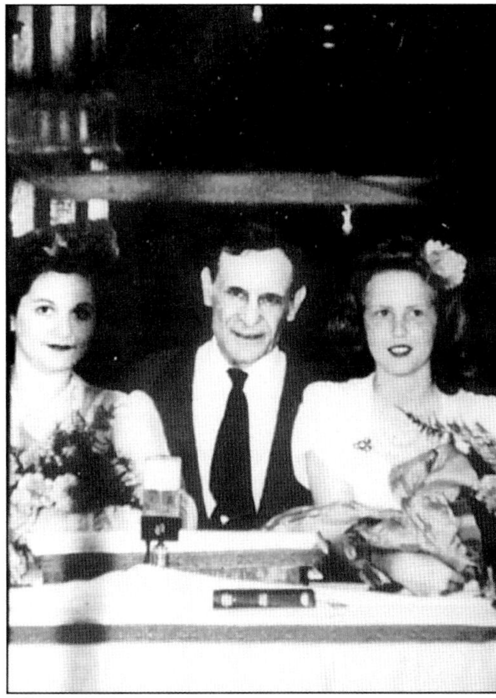

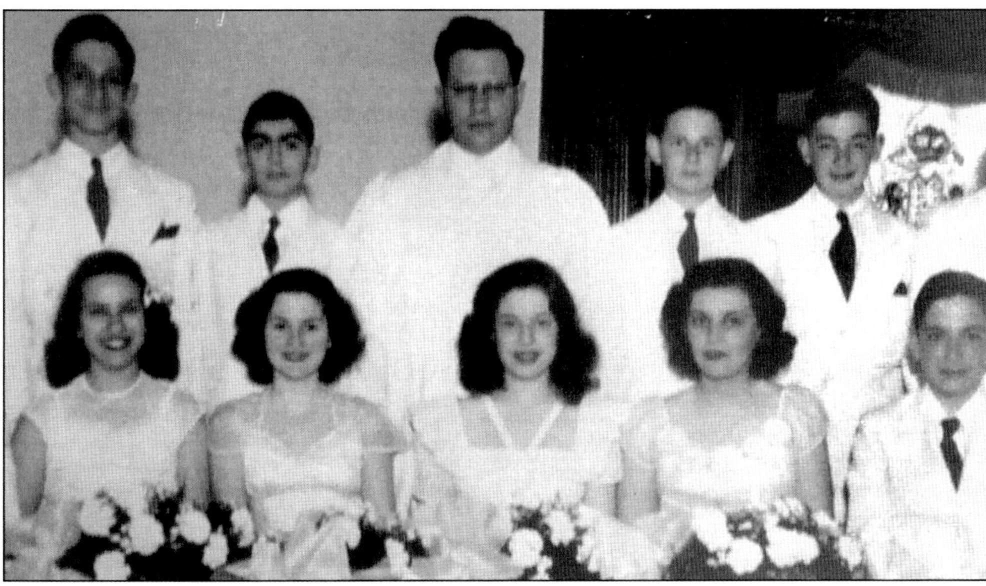

Rabbi Merritt was succeeded by Rabbi A. Stanley Dreyfuss, then a rabbinical student at Hebrew Union College. Dreyfuss later married Marianne Berlack, granddaughter of the famed Berlin Rabbi Leo Baeck. Rabbi Dreyfuss, himself a descendant of Capt. Simon Levy Jr. of Shreveport (see page 26), served as chairman of the liturgical committee of the Central Conference of American Rabbis in 1973–1975 when the *Gates of Prayer* and *Gates of Repentance* prayer books were compiled by that same committee. Rabbi Dreyfuss is seen here in 1945 with B'nai Zion confirmands. To his left are Jimmy Rosenbloom and Allen Rosner. To his right are Clifford Bayer and Fred Schrainke. On the bottom row, left to right, are Sharon Kleban, Carolyn Rudnick, Babette Braunig, Marilyn Meyer, and Charlton Meyer Jr.

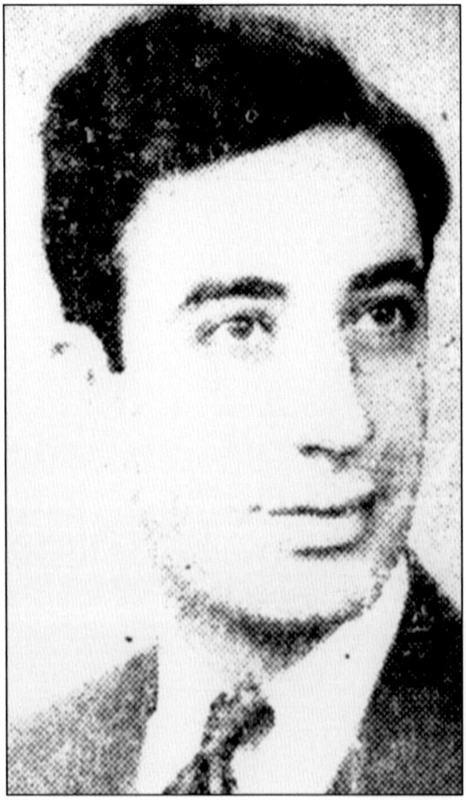

In 1945 and part of 1946, B'nai Zion was served by Rabbi Sanford Rosen, a native of Cleveland, Ohio and a student rabbi at the time of his Shreveport service. Ordained in 1947, Rabbi Rosen afterward served a congregation in Bakersfield, California and in 1951 helped to found Peninsula Temple Beth El in San Mateo, California, of which he is now Rabbi Emeritus.

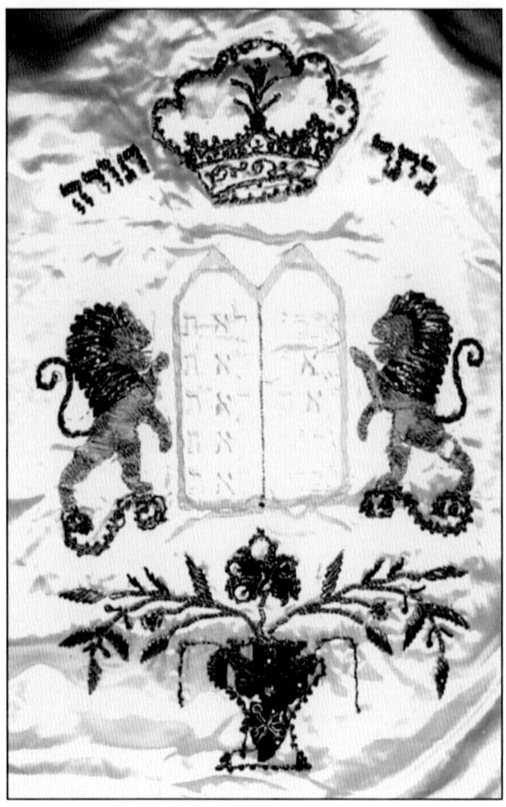

In 1945, the Selber family gave this lavishly gold-embroidered white silk Torah curtain to B'nai Zion Temple. Used continuously until the temple's move from the Cotton Street synagogue in 1956, it was then retired and now resides in the B'nai Zion archives. Two matching Torah covers of similar design were also given. These items are memorials to Isadore Selber (1887-1944), one of the original Selber brothers of Selber Brothers Department store.

In 1946, Rabbi Lefkowitz returned to Shreveport and B'nai Zion, never again to leave. Immediately after the war's end, friction between pro-Zionist and anti-Zionist congregants threatened to split B'nai Zion. The pro-Zionists were led by attorney Sidney Herold (see page 74) while Rabbi Lefkowitz stood solidly in the anti-Zionist camp, fearing a dangerous mix of religion and politics. Like many classical Reform Jews, Lefkowitz viewed Judaism solely as a religion, not a nation or a people separate from others. After the 1948 creation of Israel, however, he softened his stance and in time became a supporter of the new state, much as many others who had opposed it later did. He is seen here in his role as a leader in the local chapter of the American Legion.

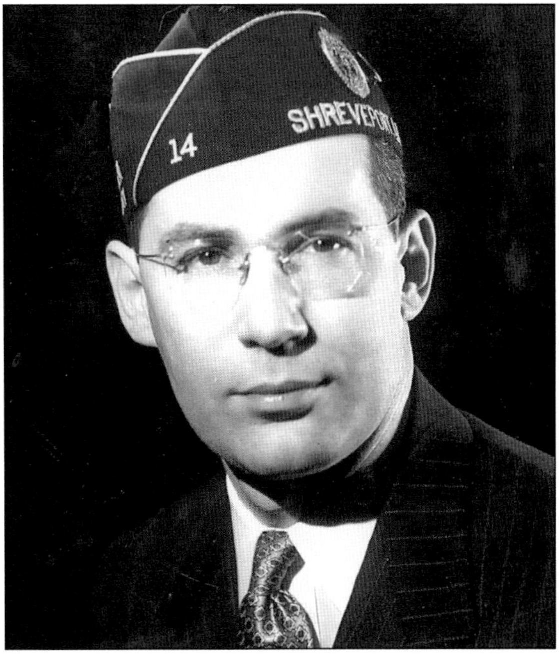

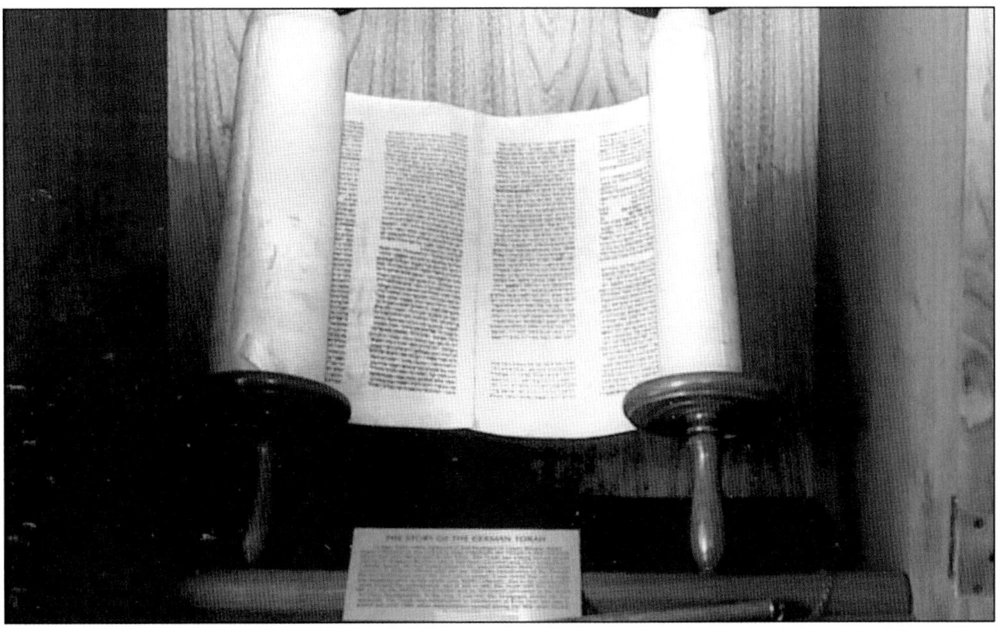

Upon his return from Europe, Rabbi Lefkowitz presented to B'nai Zion the Torah scroll of Bad Neustadt, Germany, which had been saved by a Christian farmer and buried under the floorboards of his barn. No Jews remained in Bad Neustadt at war's end and so the farmer brought this ancient and priceless Torah to Rabbi Lefkowitz, stationed in nearby Bad Kissingen. From 1946 to 1982, it saw active use at B'nai Zion but finally was retired due to wear and tear. It is now on display in the Temple foyer. While in Germany, Rabbi Lefkowitz performed the blessing of the remains of some 40,000 murdered Jews at Dachau. In 1989, Pope John Paul II awarded him the Order of Benemerenti for his humanitarianism and selfless devotion to righteous causes.

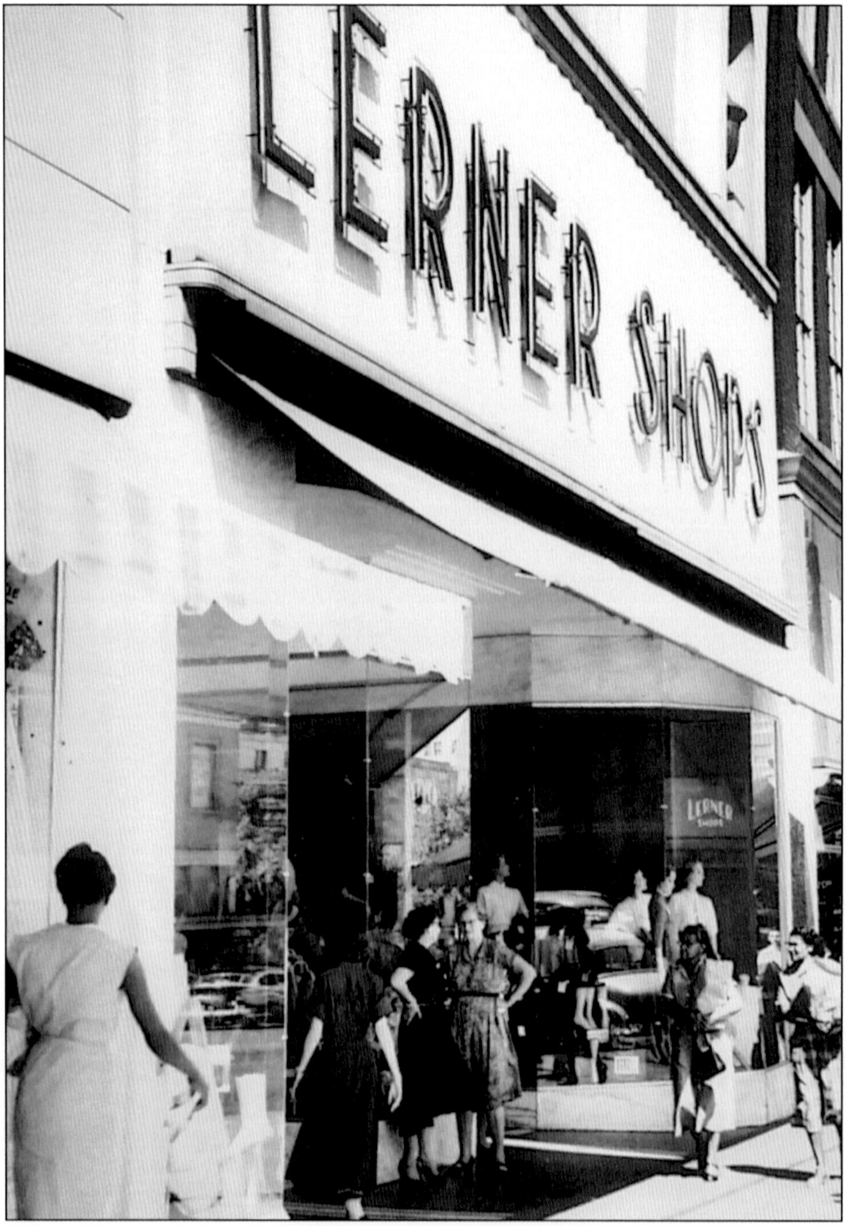

This is a photo of Lerner Shops in the 600 block of Texas Street. Successor to Zodiag's and occupying the same building, Lerner's was in operation for much of the mid-20th century. Other important 20th-century businesses owned by members of the Jewish community not previously mentioned include Cahn Electric Company, founded in 1907 by Abry S. Cahn Sr.; Brenner's Furniture Company, founded the same year by Alphonse Brenner, who took over the furniture and dry goods business of his uncle, Marks Meyer, founded some 30 years before; Louisiana Paper Company, established by John and Henry Meyer in 1903; The Fashion, a ladies' ready-to-wear store established by Isidore Rosenfield in 1920 and today perhaps the city's premier high-end ladies' clothing and couture firm, today run by Robert Rosenfield; Isidore Rosenstrauch's Globe Dry Goods Company; Schwartzberg Dry Goods, established by Joseph Schwartzberg; Bayer's Bakery; and Ritman's Dry Goods.

Four

The Modern Era
Since 1950

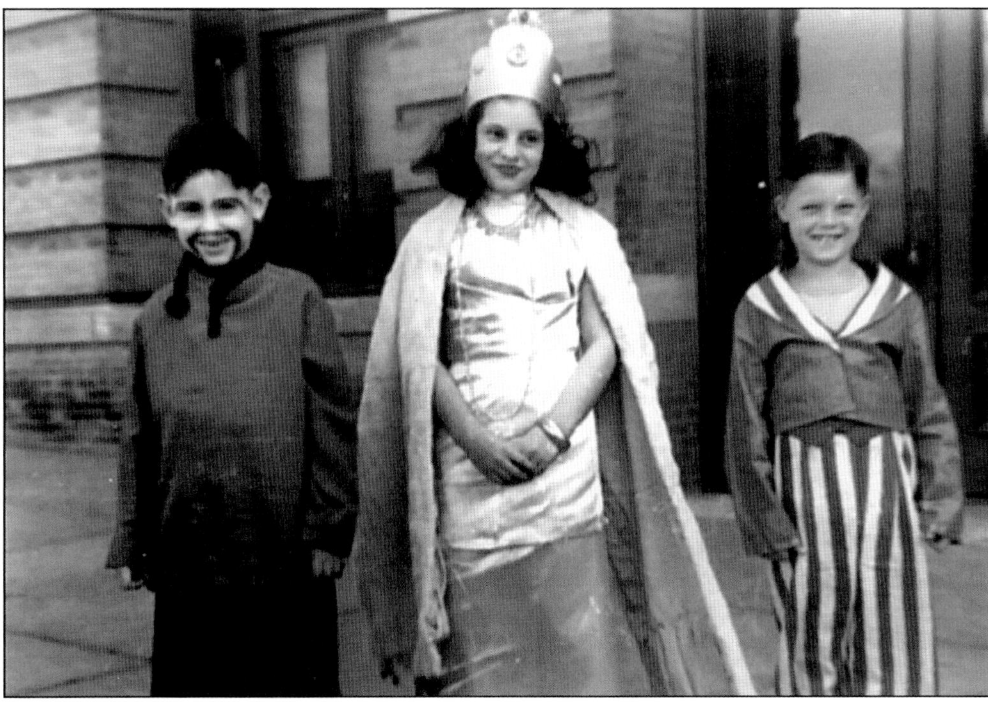

Purim carnival is shown in 1956 at B'nai Zion Temple, outside the Common Street basement-level entrance. The children are David Lefkowitz III, Helen Lefkowitz, and Henry Lefkowitz, children of Rabbi and Mrs. David Lefkowitz Jr. Today David is a physician in Charlotte, North Carolina, Helen (now Horowitz) is professor of history at Smith College, and Henry is a librarian with the Library of Congress. Purim celebrates the deliverance of the Jews of Persia from the tyrant Haman as recorded in the biblical book of Esther. The holiday is celebrated each spring with costumes, masking, and carnivals. It is especially popular with children. The year 1956 would be the last in which Purim was celebrated at B'nai Zion's Cotton Street synagogue.

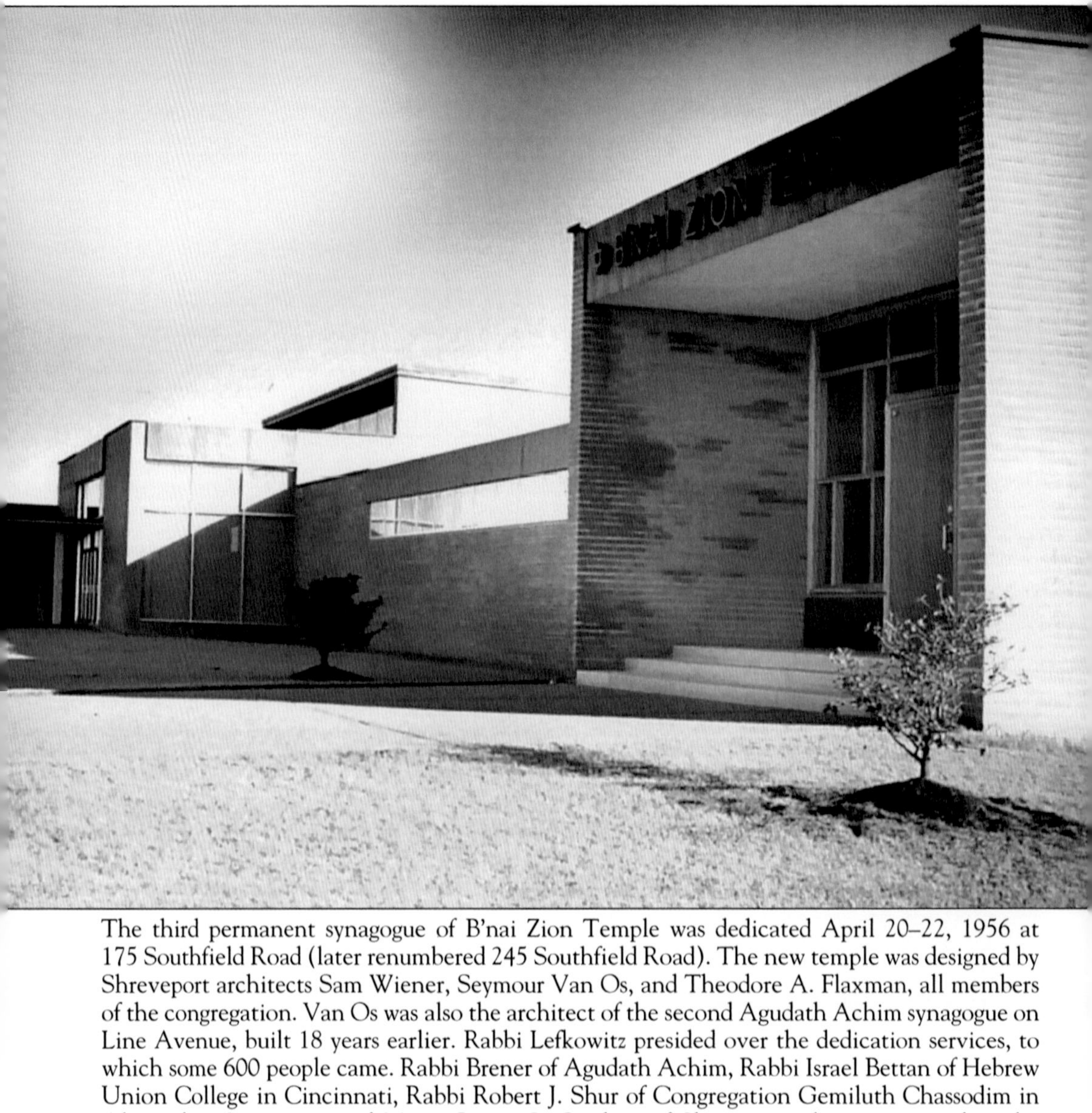

The third permanent synagogue of B'nai Zion Temple was dedicated April 20–22, 1956 at 175 Southfield Road (later renumbered 245 Southfield Road). The new temple was designed by Shreveport architects Sam Wiener, Seymour Van Os, and Theodore A. Flaxman, all members of the congregation. Van Os was also the architect of the second Agudath Achim synagogue on Line Avenue, built 18 years earlier. Rabbi Lefkowitz presided over the dedication services, to which some 600 people came. Rabbi Brener of Agudath Achim, Rabbi Israel Bettan of Hebrew Union College in Cincinnati, Rabbi Robert J. Shur of Congregation Gemiluth Chassodim in Alexandria, Louisiana, and Mayor James C. Gardner of Shreveport also participated in the ceremonies. The complex contains a sanctuary, large social hall (named in honor of David and Leona Lefkowitz in 1997), a religious school building, library, and other amenities. The facilities serve a threefold role as synagogue, Hebrew school, and community center.

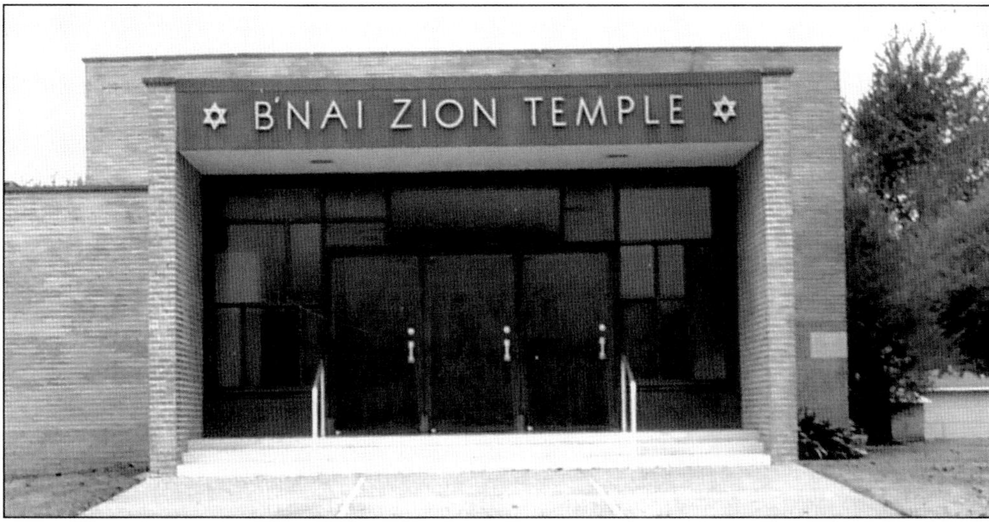

This is the main entrance to the sanctuary of B'nai Zion's Southfield Road synagogue. A larger sanctuary was part of the original plan but was never constructed. Had it been, the present one would have served as the temple's chapel. Plans for the new temple were first conceived in the 1940s when B'nai Zion was at its membership peak, with some 500 families on the rolls. Although membership declined somewhat in the post-war era, it was still substantial enough to merit a relocation to the suburbs from downtown. In 1955, when work began on the new facility, Southfield Road represented the southern city limits in the Broadmoor area of Shreveport.

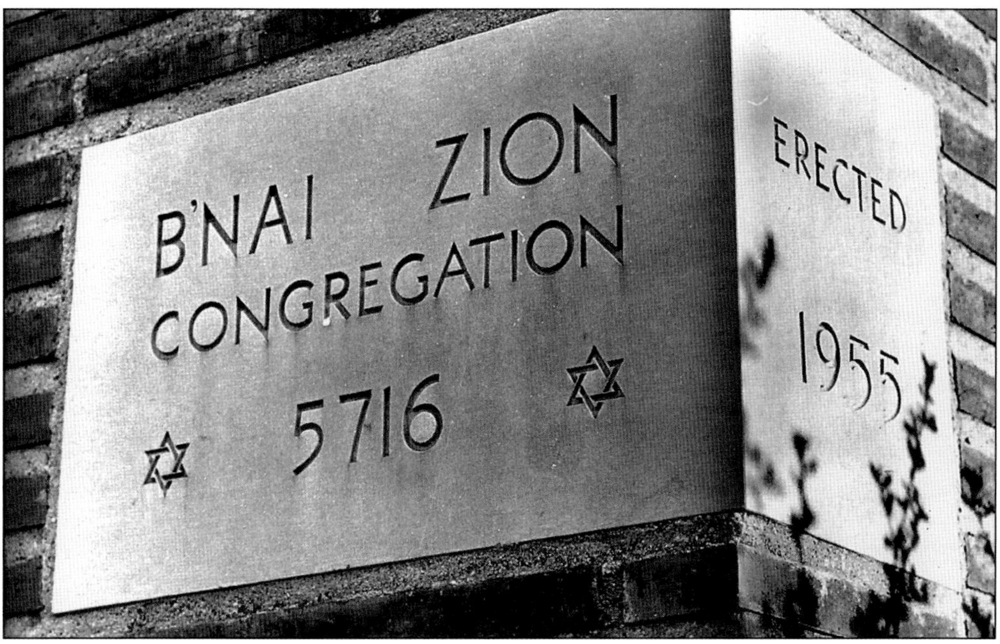

The cornerstone of B'nai Zion Temple on Southfield Road is shown here. Ground was broken for the new temple on April 29, 1955 by Rabbi Lefkowitz, temple president Henry E. Cahn, and building committee chairman Philip Lieber. The cornerstones of the two previous homes of B'nai Zion—320 Fannin Street and 810 Cotton Street—were relocated to the new temple upon its completion in 1956.

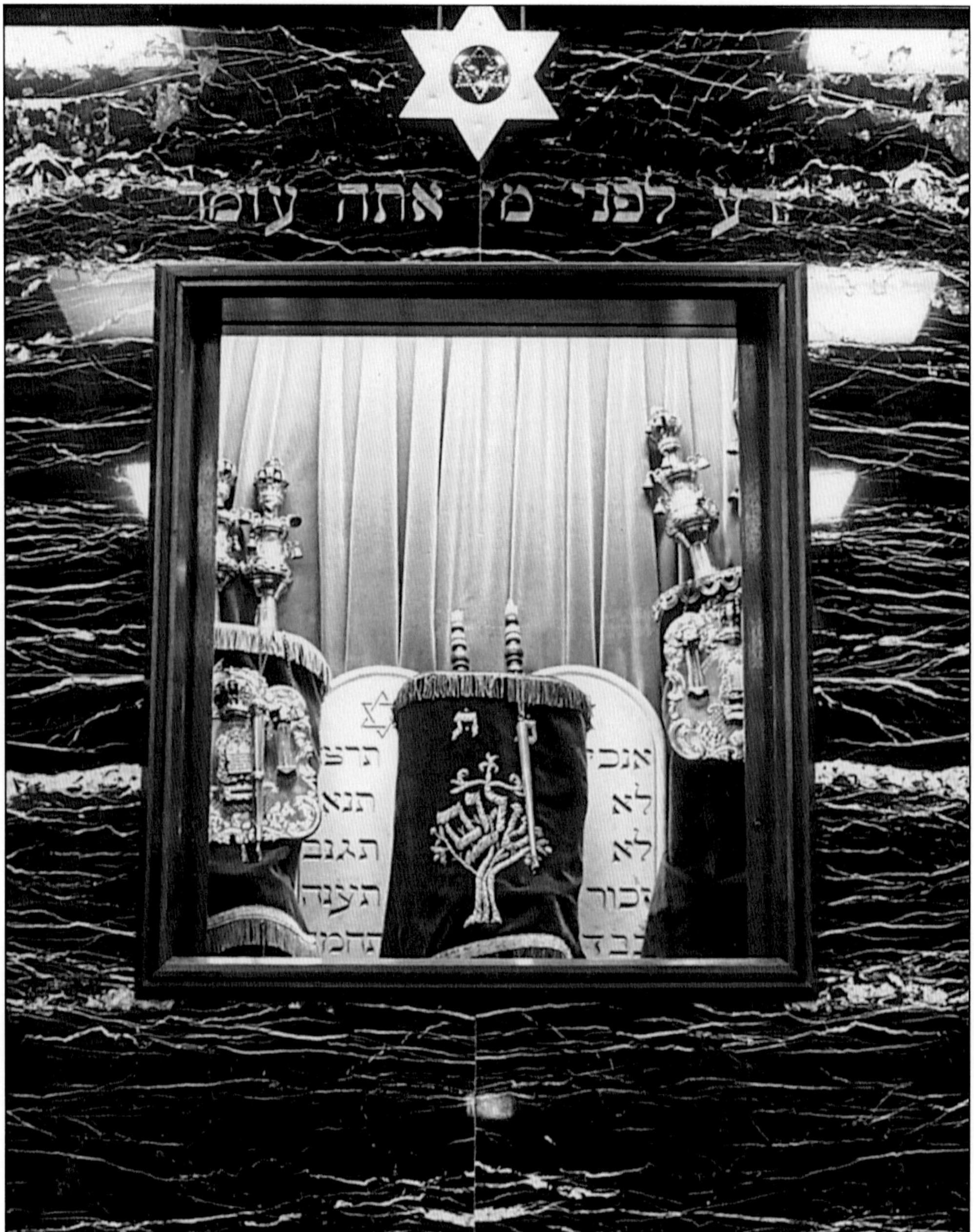

B'nai Zion's ark is the focal point of the sanctuary. Constructed of polished black stone with crystalline stratification, cut so that the grain pattern is symmetrical, the ark houses the Torah scrolls used in Shabbat and holiday worship services. Also contained within the ark are the marble tablet of the commandments, originally in the ark of the Fannin Street temple and then at Cotton Street. Incised in gilt Hebrew lettering above the doors of the ark are the words "Know before whom you stand." Above it all is the *ner tamid*, the eternal lamp, first lighted on April 20, 1956 by Seymour L. Florsheim (1878–1958), then the congregation's oldest living past president (he served from 1916 to 1917).

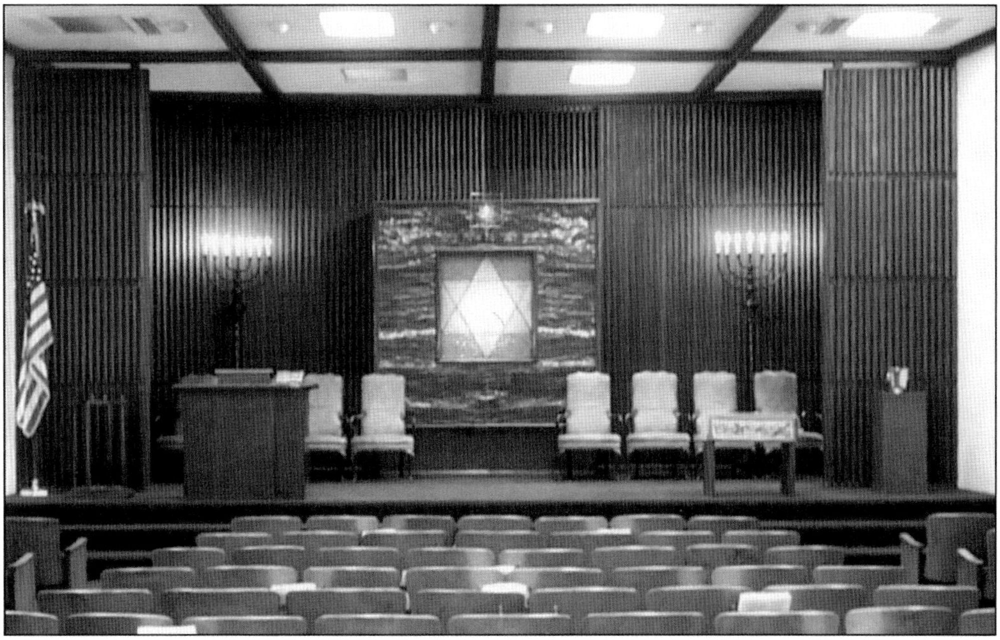

This is the sanctuary of B'nai Zion today. The ark doors are decorated by a mosaic of the *magen David* designed and created by architect Bill Wiener Jr. The bronze candelabra were brought from the Cotton Street temple. Above and behind the ark is the choir gallery and organ. The present *ner tamid* was installed in the 1970s. Additional arks are located in the parlor and Lefkowitz Social Hall. Over these hang the eternal lamps from Cotton and Fannin Streets.

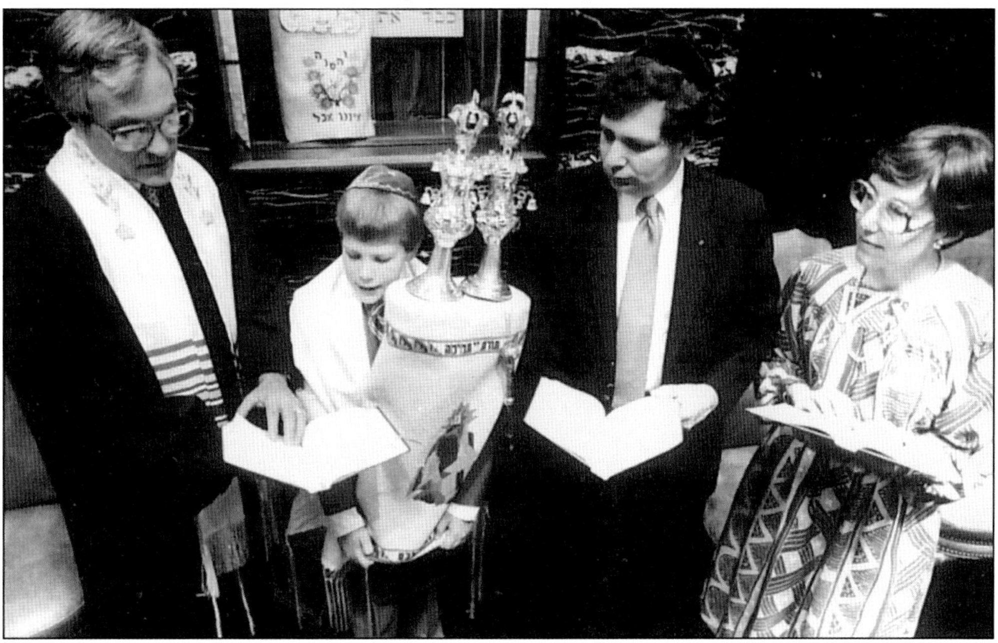

The *bar mitzvah* (or, for girls, *bat mitzvah*) ceremony is an important milestone in the life of Jewish young people, initiating them into the fold as full participants in the community. The entire family and rabbi take part in the event and its preparation, as seen here, at the *bar mitzvah* of Michael Levy. Parents Ken and Sandy Levy are at right. Rabbi Richard Zionts is at left.

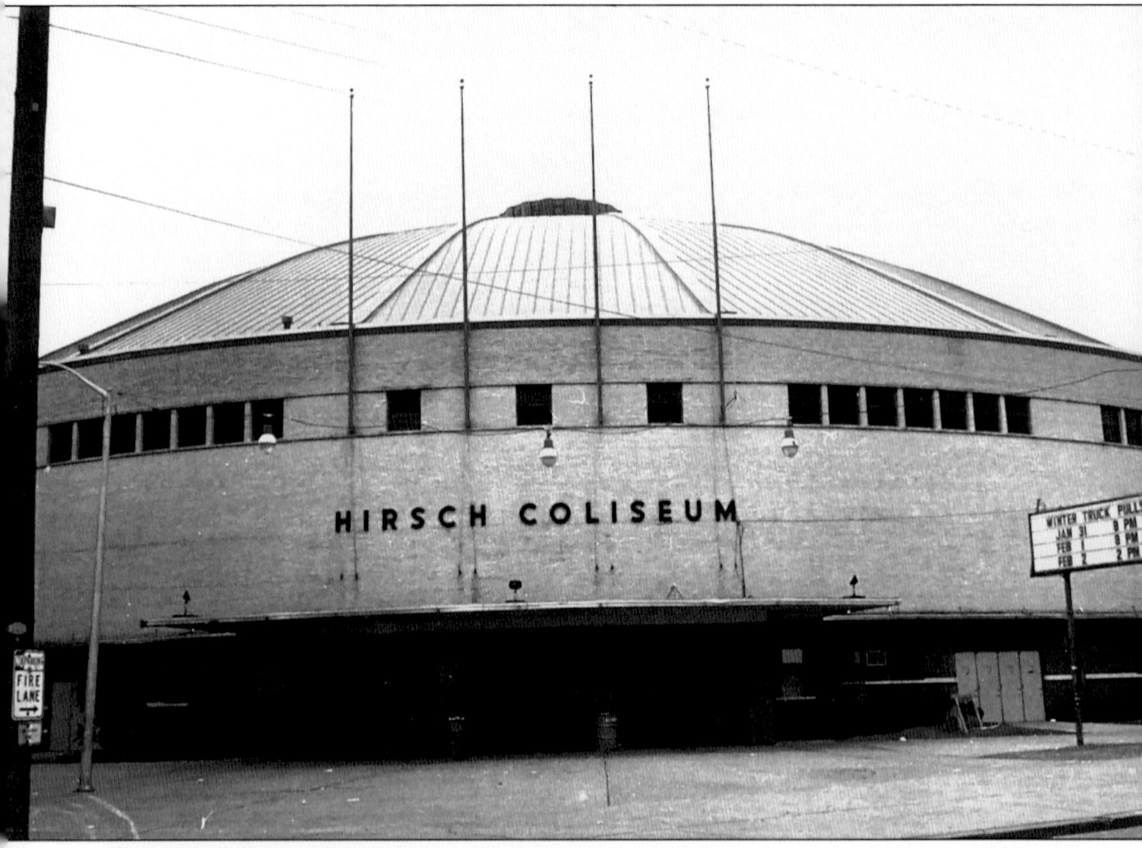

The Hirsch Memorial Coliseum at the Louisiana State Fairgrounds was built in 1954 as the Youth Building. It was shortly thereafter renamed in memory of longtime fair executive and promoter Billy Hirsch (see page 73). When completed, its dome was the largest sheet copper roof in the world. Designed by Edward Neild Jr., whose father was architect of the Cotton Street synagogue of B'nai Zion, the coliseum is almost identical to the Parker Coliseum (affectionately known as "The Cow Palace") on the Louisiana State University campus in Baton Rouge, also a Neild design. Nearby on the fairgrounds is Independence Stadium, first called Fairgrounds Stadium and designed by Samuel G. Wiener. The Hirsch Memorial Coliseum is Shreveport's largest public monument to a member of the Jewish community.

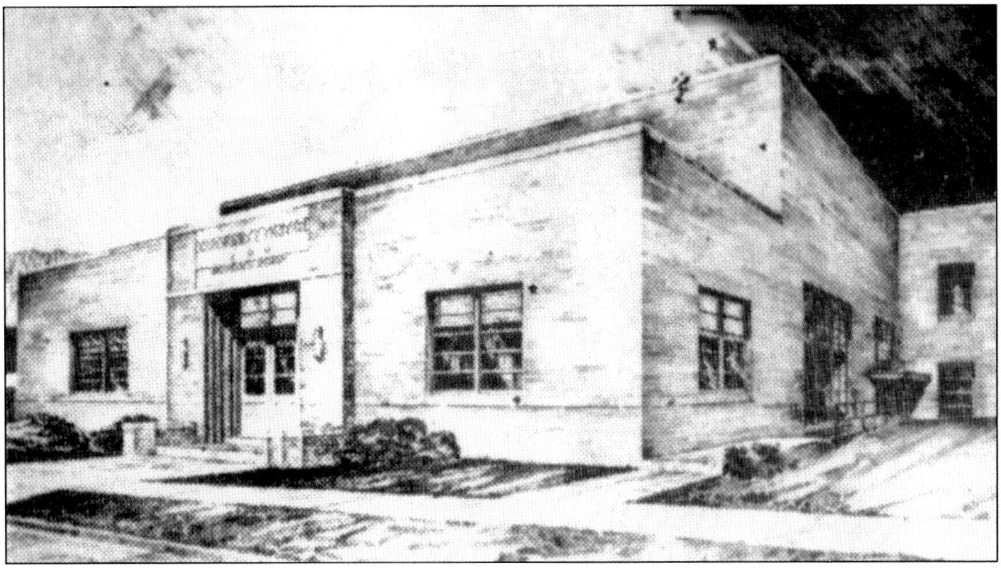

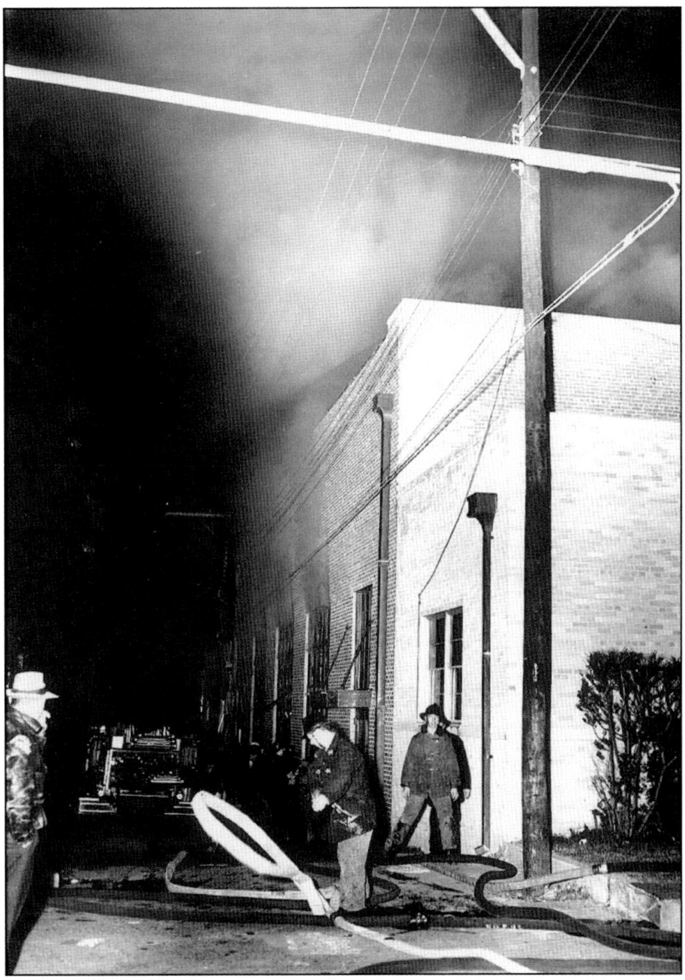

In 1950 Agudath Achim Congregation constructed a new community center (shown above) to the rear of the Line Avenue synagogue, facing Herndon Street. In 1952, the community center was renamed Muslow Hall in honor of Hyman Muslow, who was instrumental in raising the funds for its construction. It was designed by architect Henry E. Schwarz (1895–1966), a member of the congregation. The addition nearly doubled the square footage of the synagogue and included a gymnasium/social hall, classrooms, a chapel for the daily *minyan*, and a *mikveh*. In 1953, Muslow Hall was damaged by fire (shown to the right) and was extensively remodeled. It was again renovated in 1960.

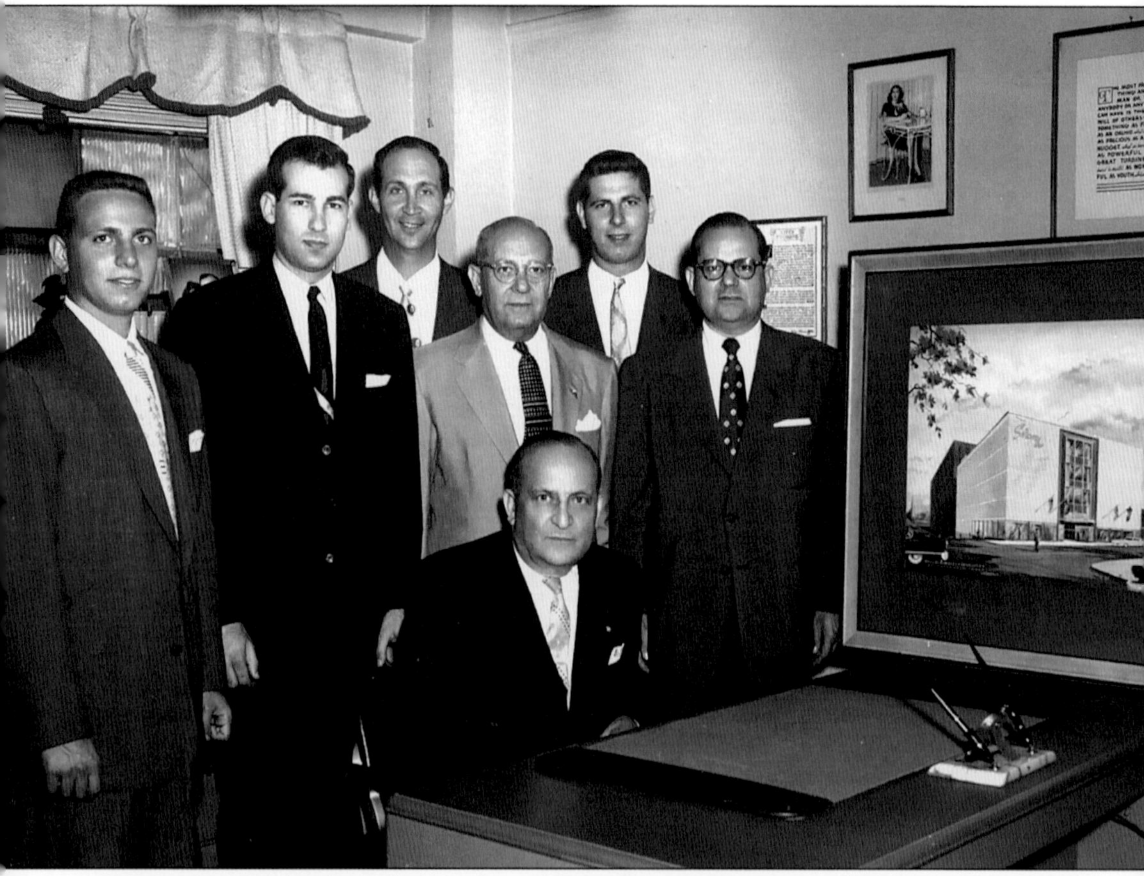

On August 1, 1954, the Selber Brothers Department Store announced and unveiled plans for a new downtown department store (see also pages 66, 82, 95). The store, then in its 47th year in Shreveport, had been located in the Ricou-Brewster Building for 29 years. The new building was built two blocks to the west on Milam and McNeill Streets. Shown are members of the Selber family and partners in the company on that date. From left to right are (standing) Leonard Selber, Mandel Selber Jr., Irving Selber, Aaron Selber, Aaron Selber Jr., and Mandel Selber; (seated) Louis Selber.

Upon the store's move to its new location in 1956, the Selber sign was taken down from the corner of the Ricou-Brewster Building. M. Levy's Sons department store would move into the former Selber's location that same year. In the background is Goldring's department store, located next door. The new Selber store (shown below), opened at 601 Milam in 1956. It would remain open for most of the next three decades, but today the building stands vacant and silent.

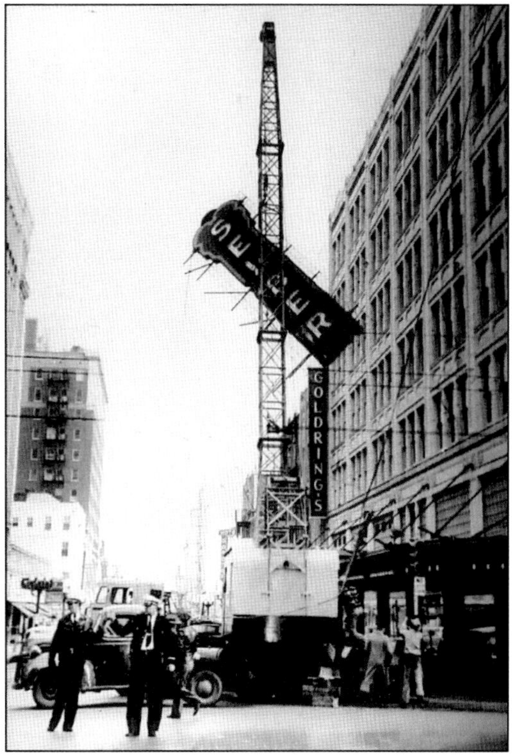

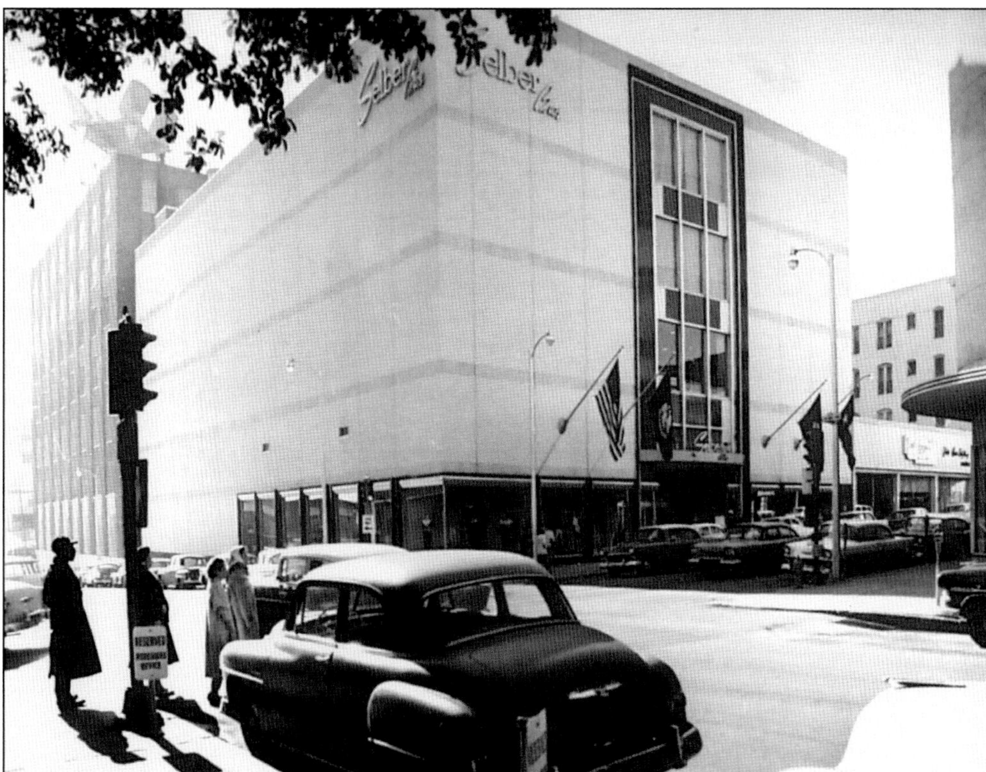

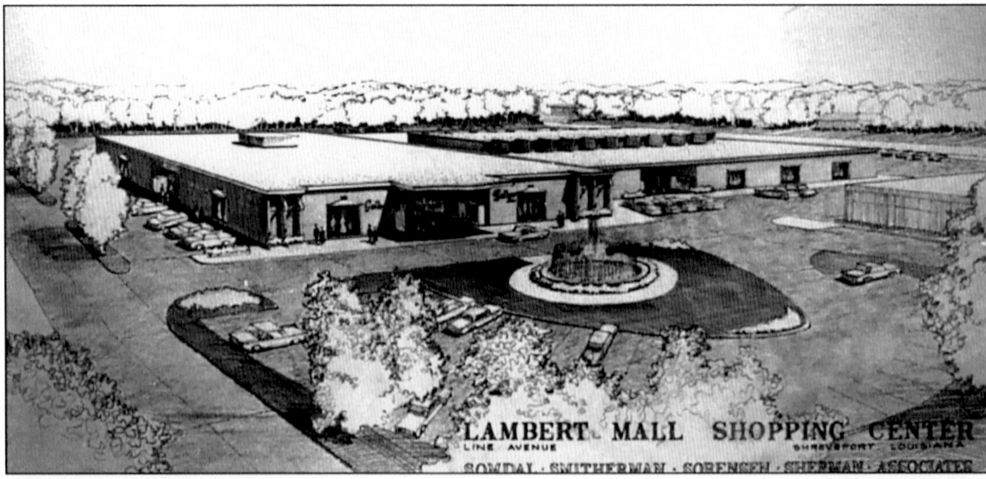

Pierremont Mall (first called the Lambert Mall and the Selber Mall) was the first enclosed shopping mall in the region. Opened in 1964, Pierremont Mall's first and principal anchor was the first of several suburban branches of Selber Brothers. Today the old Selber space is occupied by Stein Mart, a clothing store. Also in the mall are The Fashion, owned by the Hermer-Rosenfield family, and Toy Fair, owned by the Baskind and Laudenheimer families.

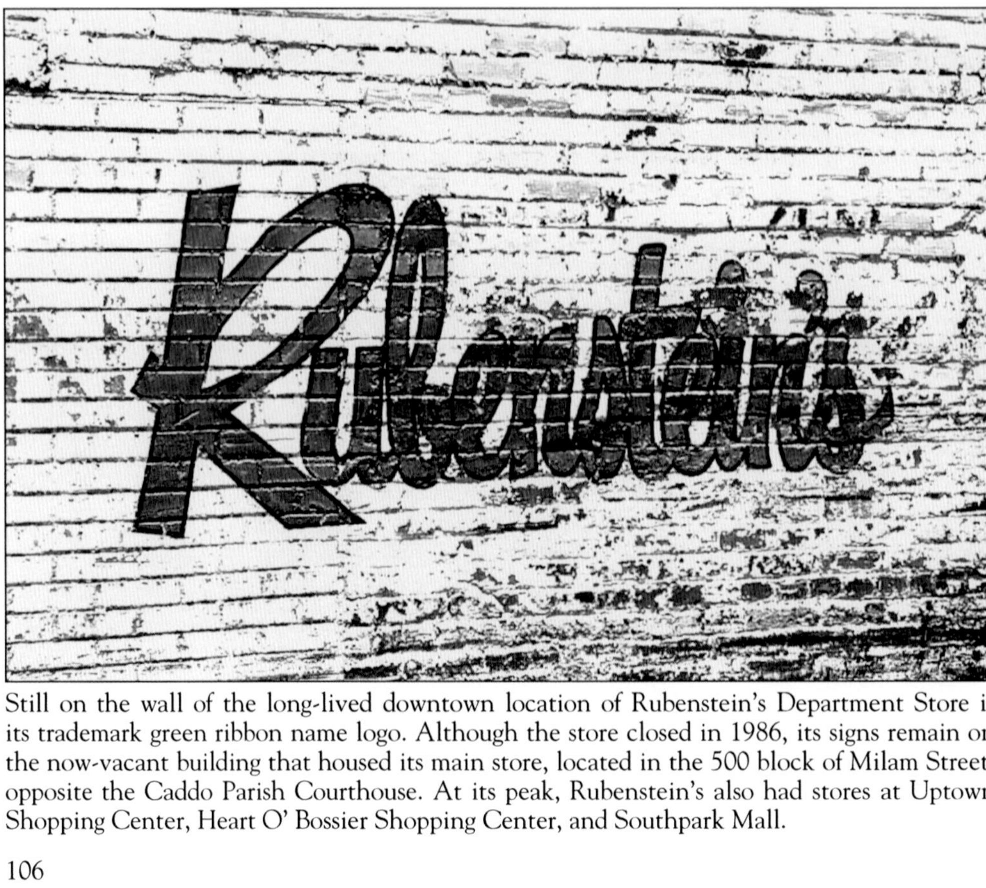

Still on the wall of the long-lived downtown location of Rubenstein's Department Store is its trademark green ribbon name logo. Although the store closed in 1986, its signs remain on the now-vacant building that housed its main store, located in the 500 block of Milam Street, opposite the Caddo Parish Courthouse. At its peak, Rubenstein's also had stores at Uptown Shopping Center, Heart O' Bossier Shopping Center, and Southpark Mall.

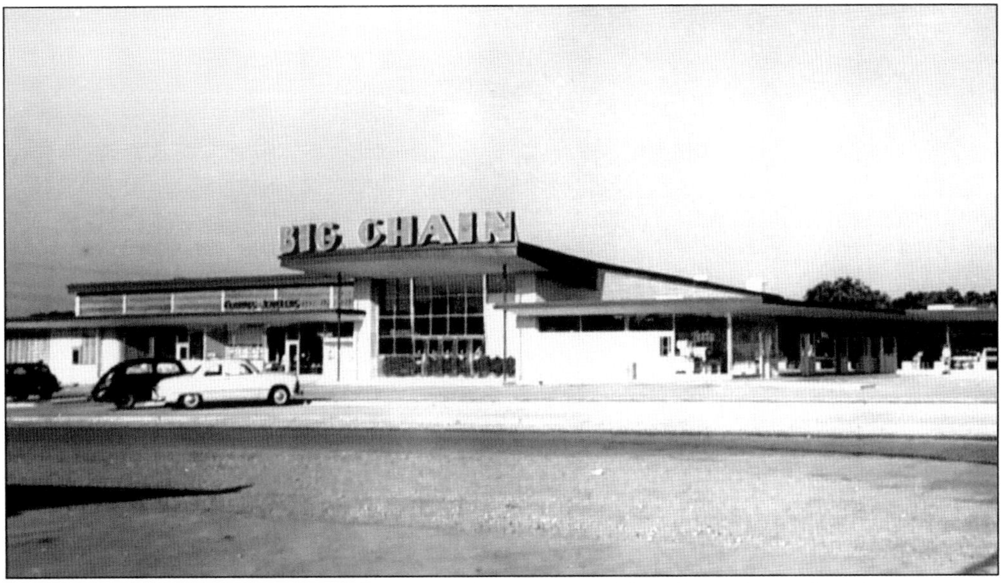

The Big Chain grocery store (above), at the corner of Jewella and South Lakeshore, was designed by S.G. and W.B. Wiener for I. Ed Wile. At its height, the firm included eight supermarkets in Shreveport and one in Bossier City. The stores were noted for their bakeries, kosher delicatessens, and wide variety of specialty items. The company also operated several cafeterias and was responsible for the construction of some of the city's major shopping centers. Another important supermarket operating in Shreveport at mid-century and after was Weingarten's (below), which had a number of local stores and later took over some of the Big Chain properties. Weingarten's was responsible for the erection of the Madison Park Shopping Center on Gilbert Drive, shown in the 1950s.

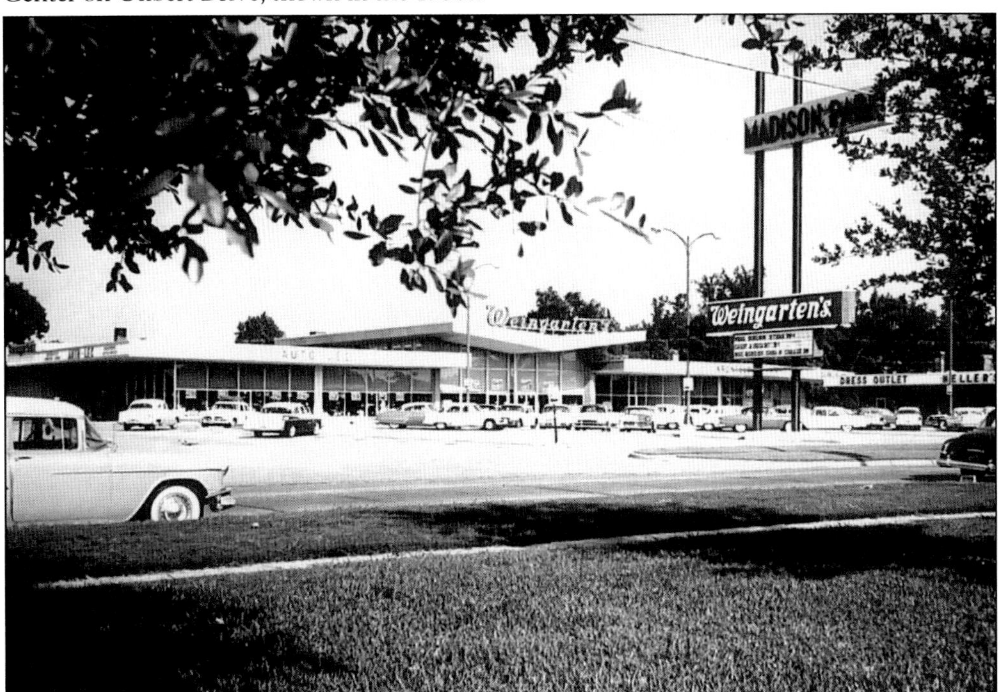

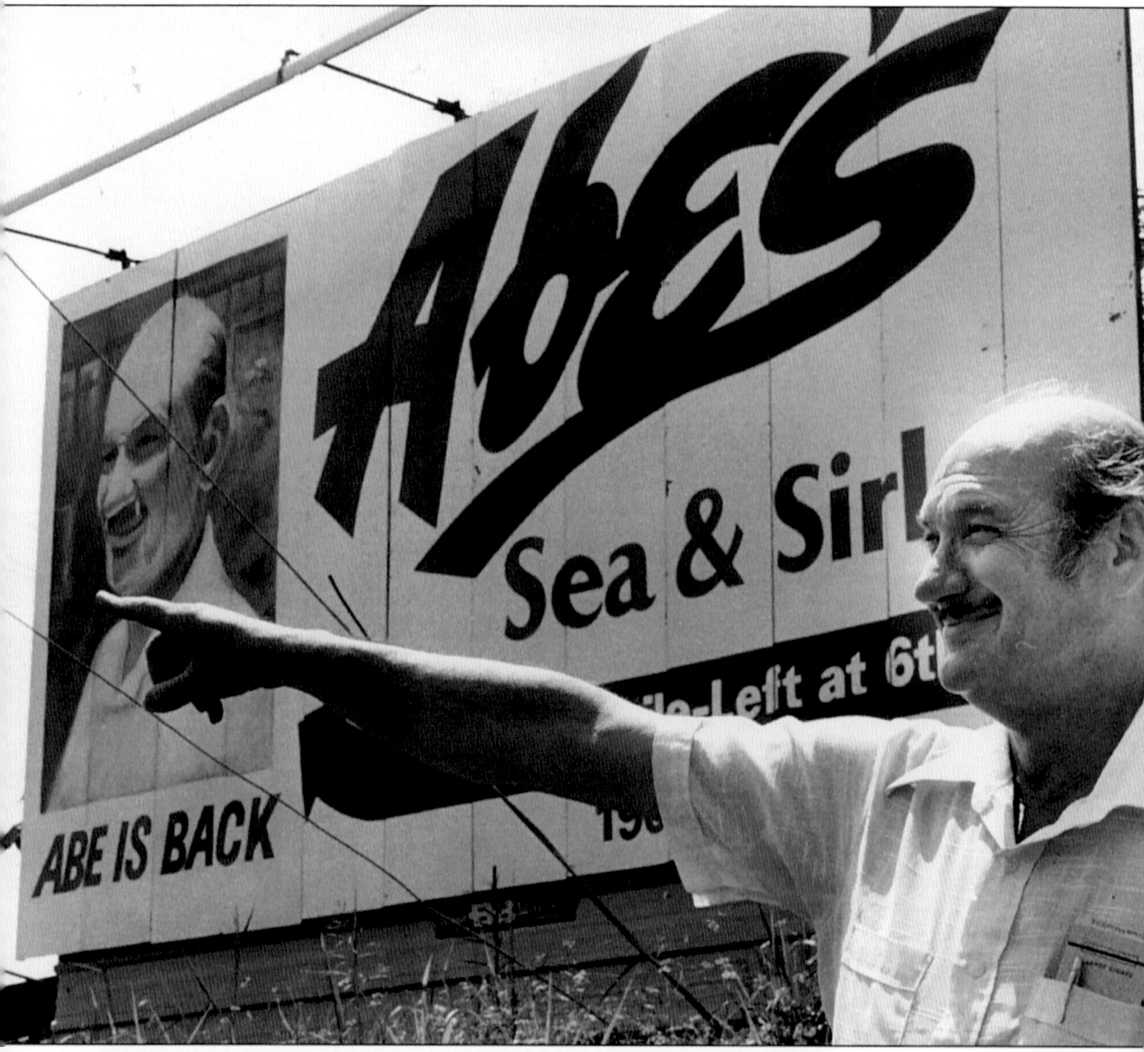

Abe Ritman (1928–1998) started Abe's Sea and Sirloin restaurant, a longtime Shreveport landmark, as the Derby Liquor Store in the late 1940s. From there it evolved into Abe's Derby Restaurant and then just plain Abe's, as people knew it for decades. Another landmark restaurant was Ablon's, located on Marshall Street downtown for many years. Started by George Ablon, it was later run by his widow Rosa. In the 1980s, the Pickle Barrell Deli was established by the Kupetz family. Other significant 20th-century businesses owned by members of the local Jewish community include Cuban Liquor Company, founded and long operated by the Greenberg and Meisel families (at its peak, Cuban had ten stores in Shreveport and Bossier City as well as stores in Baton Rouge and New Orleans); J.B. Bookshop; H.C. Silver and Company; Gilbert Pipe and Supply Company; Arnold Pipe and Supply Company; Louisiana Valve Company; and Marcus, Sun, and Schorr Furniture Companies, among others.

Dr. Harold B. Levy (1918–2001) was prominent in the field of pediatric medicine, which he practiced in Shreveport for 53 years beginning in 1947. A nationally recognized expert on children's learning disabilities, Dr. Levy was the recipient of numerous awards for his work. He was president of the American Academy for Cerebral Palsey and Developmental Medicine, a founder of the Caddo Foundation for Exceptional Children, and a fellow of the American Academy of Pediatrics. The Shreveport Jewish community has produced a number of notable physicians.

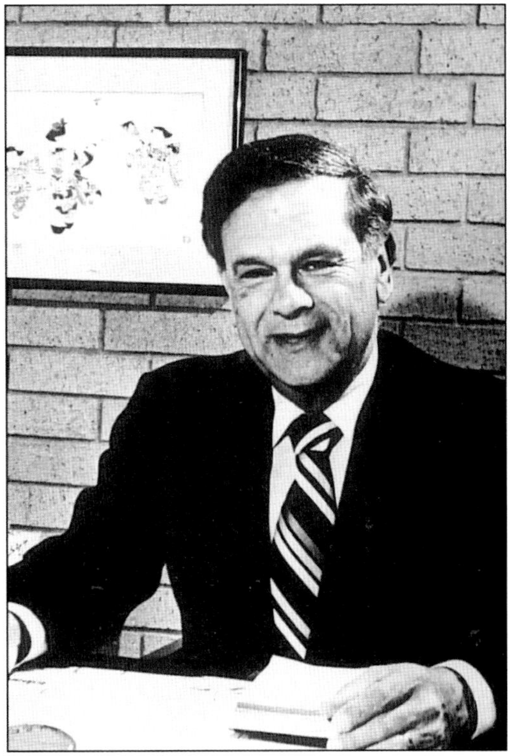

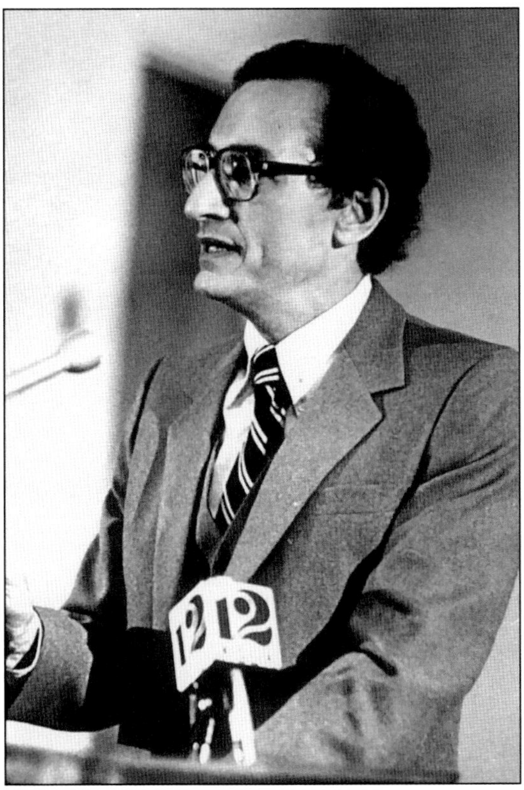

Paul Greenberg, a son of Benjamin and Sarah Greenberg, owners of Greenberg's Shoe Store in Shreveport, graduated from Centenary College in 1958. He later wrote for and edited the *Arkansas Democrat-Gazette* newspaper in Little Rock and then the Pine Bluff, Arkansas *Commercial*. In 1969, he was awarded the Pulitzer Prize for editorial writing. Today, Greenberg's column is nationally syndicated through the *Los Angeles Times*. His brother, Irving Greenberg (1928–1992), a partner in the law firm of Gamm, Greenberg, and Kaplan, served as president of B'nai Zion Temple from 1984 to 1986.

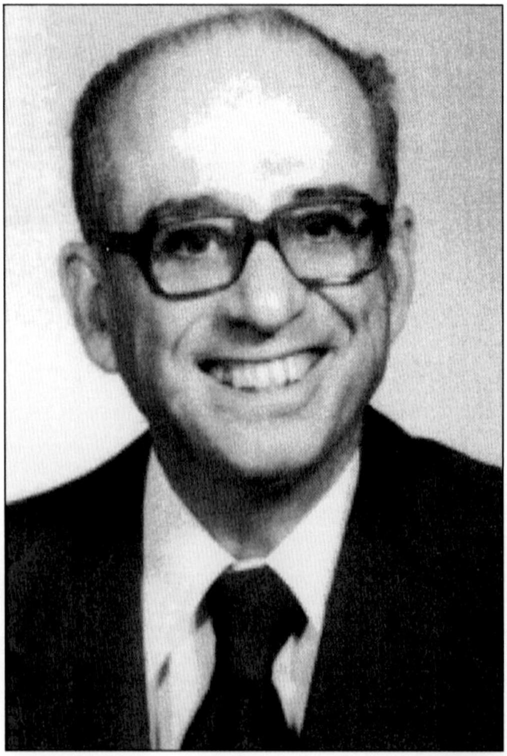

Rabbi Leo Brener, pictured to the left, served Congregation Agudath Achim continuously from 1934 to 1974 and as Rabbi Emeritus from then until his death in 1989. From 1980 to 1986, he and his wife Nanette Freeman (1916–1996), a native of Waco, Texas, relocated to Wichita Falls, Texas, returning to Shreveport afterward. Both now rest at Agudath Achim Cemetery. Rabbi Brener was succeeded by Rabbi Stanley Greenstein, pictured below. It was during his rabbinate that Agudath Achim made the shift from Orthodox to Conservative Judaism. He served the congregation from 1984 through much of 1978, one of the most notable periods in Agudath Achim's history.

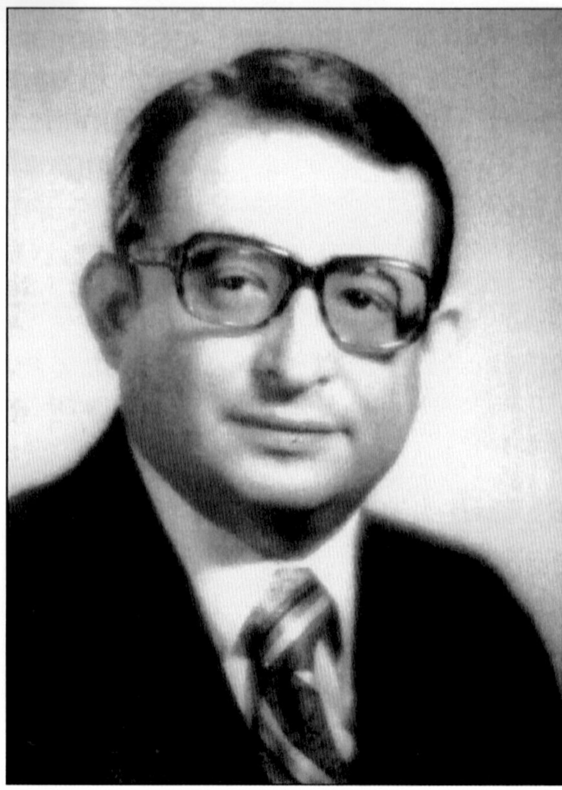

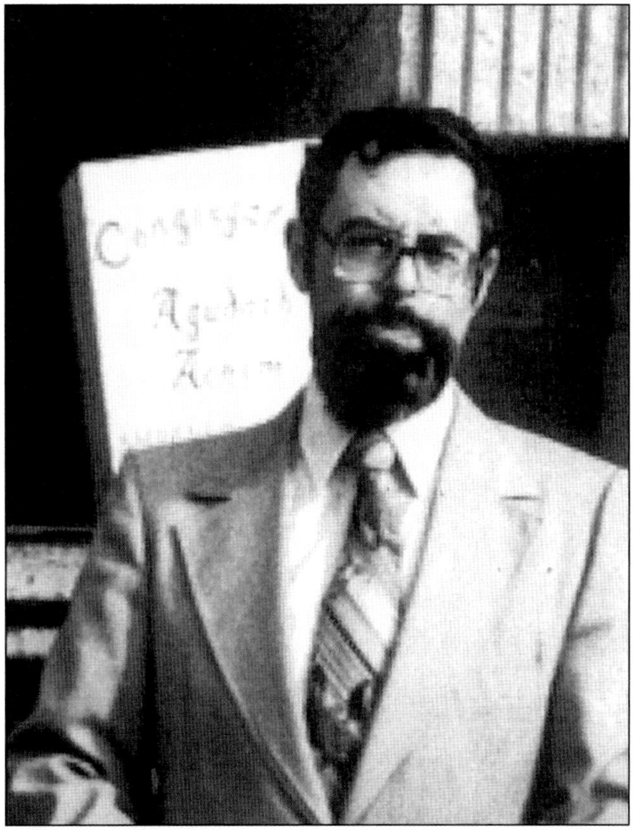

In 1979, Rabbi H.D. Uriel Smith, pictured to the right in 1980, was hired to serve Congregation Agudath Achim. A Londoner by birth, Smith was ordained a Reform rabbi in 1969, though in his tenure at Agdath Achim he would follow the form and ritual of the Conservative movement. During his five-year rabbinate, Agudath Achim would relocate to its third permanent synagogue in southeast Shreveport. On December 9, 1980, the cornerstone, pictured below, was laid.

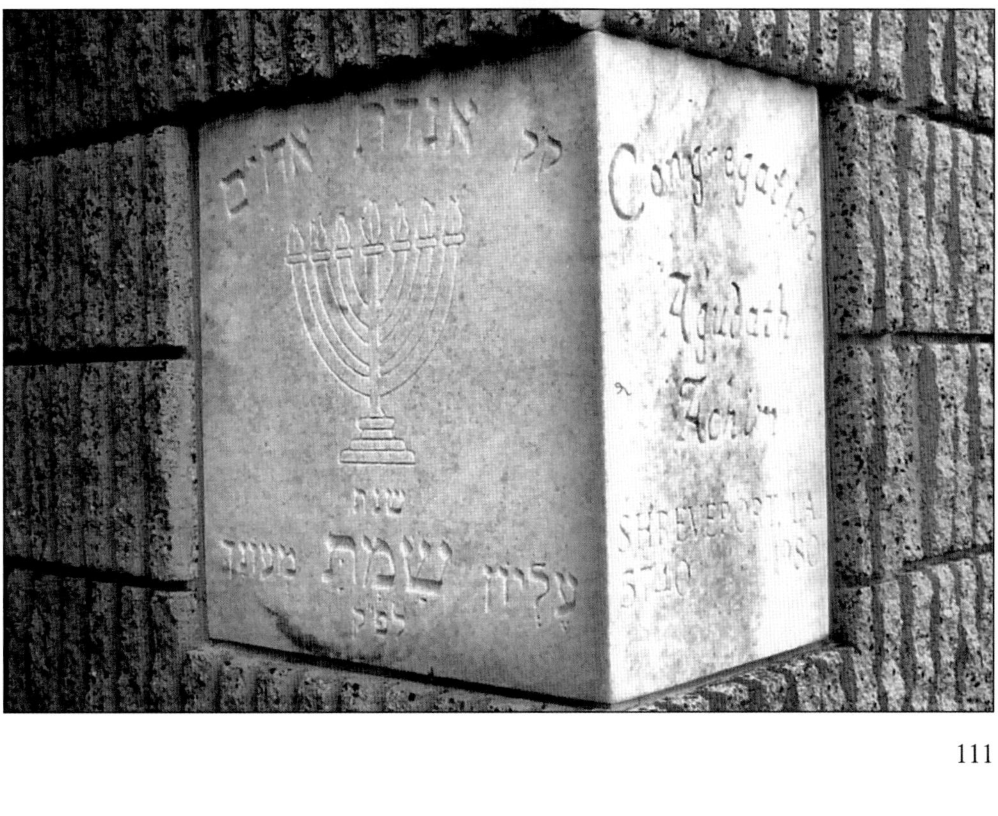

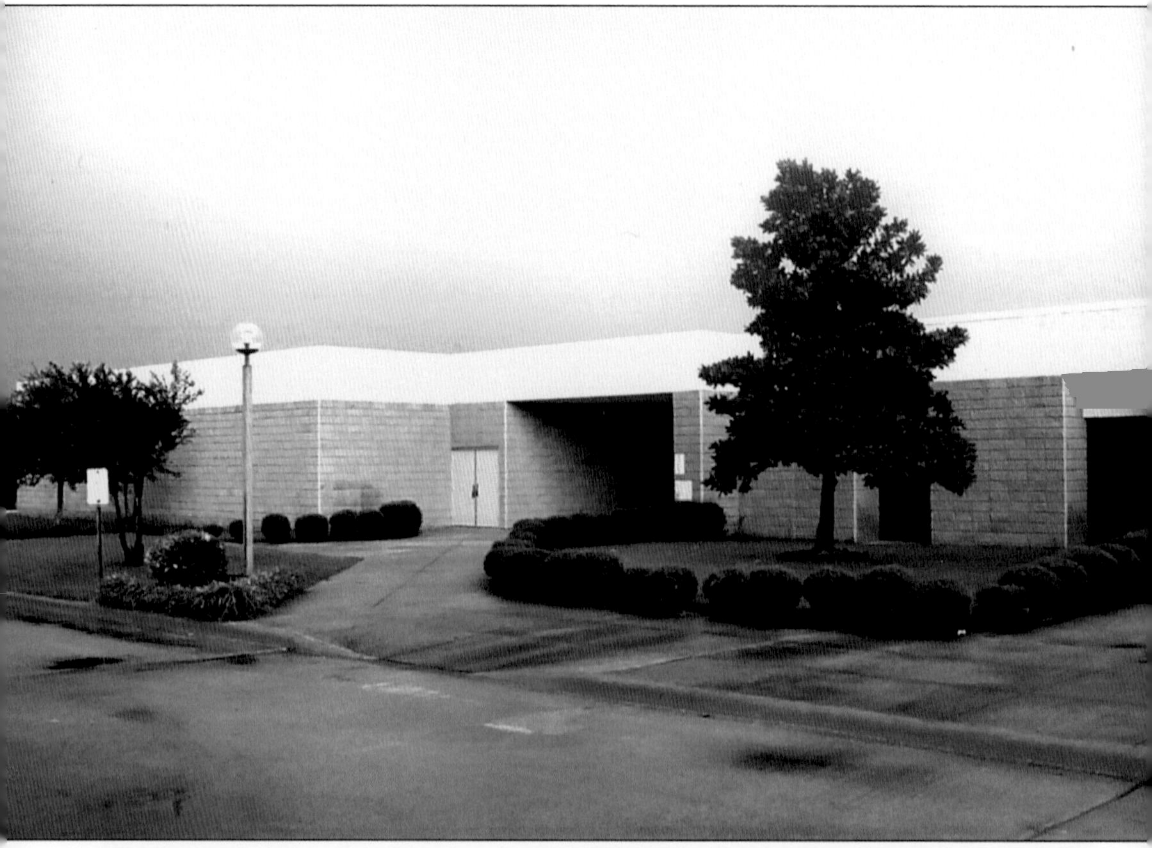

The third Agudath Achim Synagogue was designed by architect Warren Epstein of Atlanta, Georgia (brother-in-law of congregation member and later synagogue president Arnold Lincove), whose plans were unveiled in February 1980. On May 18, 1980, ground was broken for the new *shul*. Among the dignitaries present were Mayor Bill Hanna, city councilman and future mayor John Hussey (son-in-law of Ed Wile of the Big Chain Grocery firm), several other council members, two Louisiana congressmen, and both of Louisiana's United States senators. Built by the Florsheim Construction Company, the synagogue stands on five acres purchased by the congregation in 1966 at 9401 Village Green Drive. The view above is of the principal street front façade.

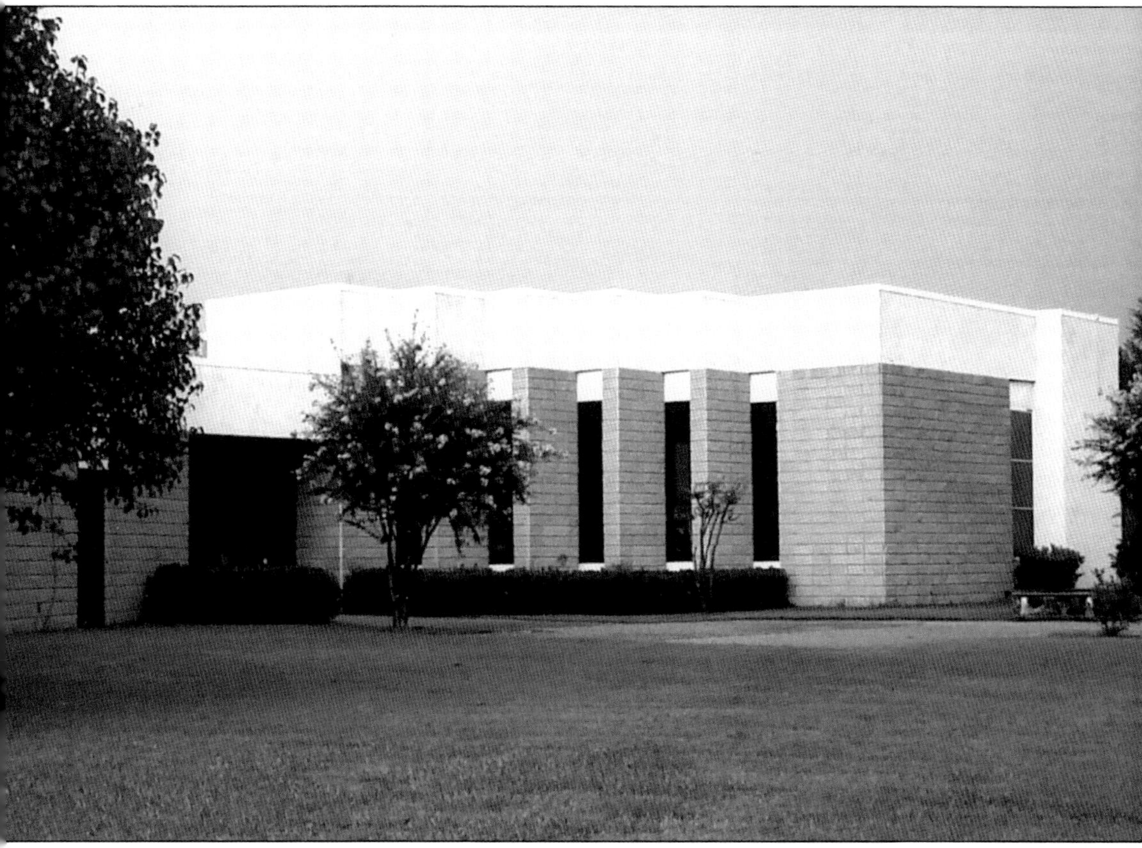

The new Agudath Achim Synagogue was formally dedicated on February 9, 1981, though dedication festivities ran through the entire month of February. Late in 1981, the Lisa Gaye Arnold Memorial Garden was dedicated behind the sanctuary, given in memory of Lisa Gaye Arnold (1969–1970), the daughter of Mr. and Mrs. Carl Arnold. Meanwhile, in 1980, the old *shul* on Line Avenue was sold to Rutherford House, a social service organization, which immediately began remodeling while allowing the congregation to continue holding services until the new building was complete. Above is a view of the sanctuary and main entrance to the Village Green Drive *shul*. The main entrance and "front" of the synagogue actually face away from the street and toward the gardens and parking lot.

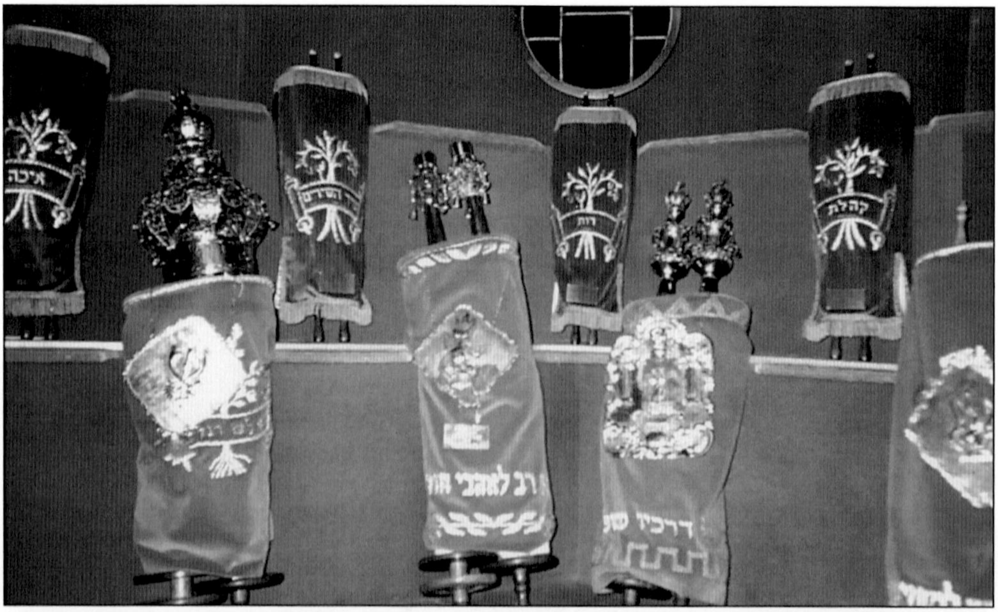

On January 11, 1981, the Torah scrolls of Agudath Achim were transferred from the Line Avenue synagogue to the new synagogue on Village Green Drive. Following a *minyan*, the Torahs were carried to decorated automobiles and a formal motorcade carried them to the new *shul*. Above is a view of the Torah scrolls in the ark today. The stained glass panel above them came from the Line Avenue ark as well.

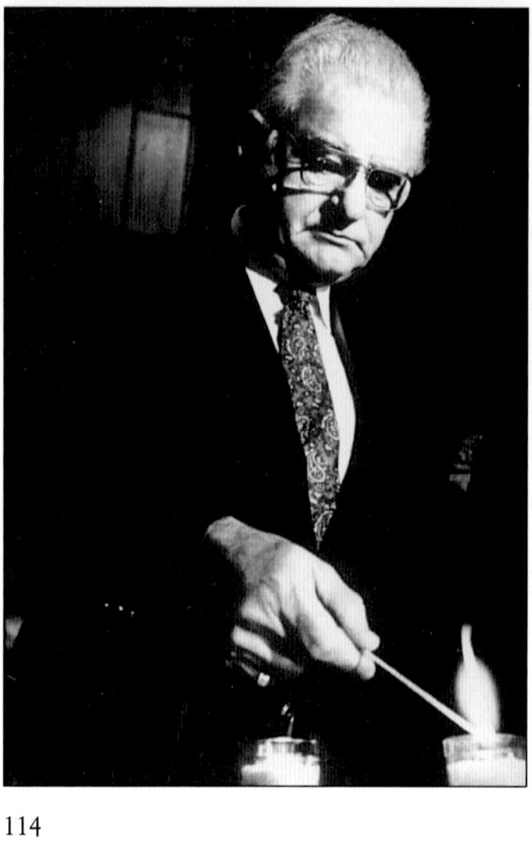

Bernard Rosenfeld, three-time president of Agudath Achim, served in that capacity at the time of the new synagogue's construction and dedication. Owner of Southern Gift and Fashion along with his wife Dorothy, for many years a landmark Shreveport specialty store, Rosenfeld lost much of his family in the Holocaust. An accomplished artist whose paintings grace the library and office of the synagogue, he has been one of Agudath Achim's most devoted and active members for many years.

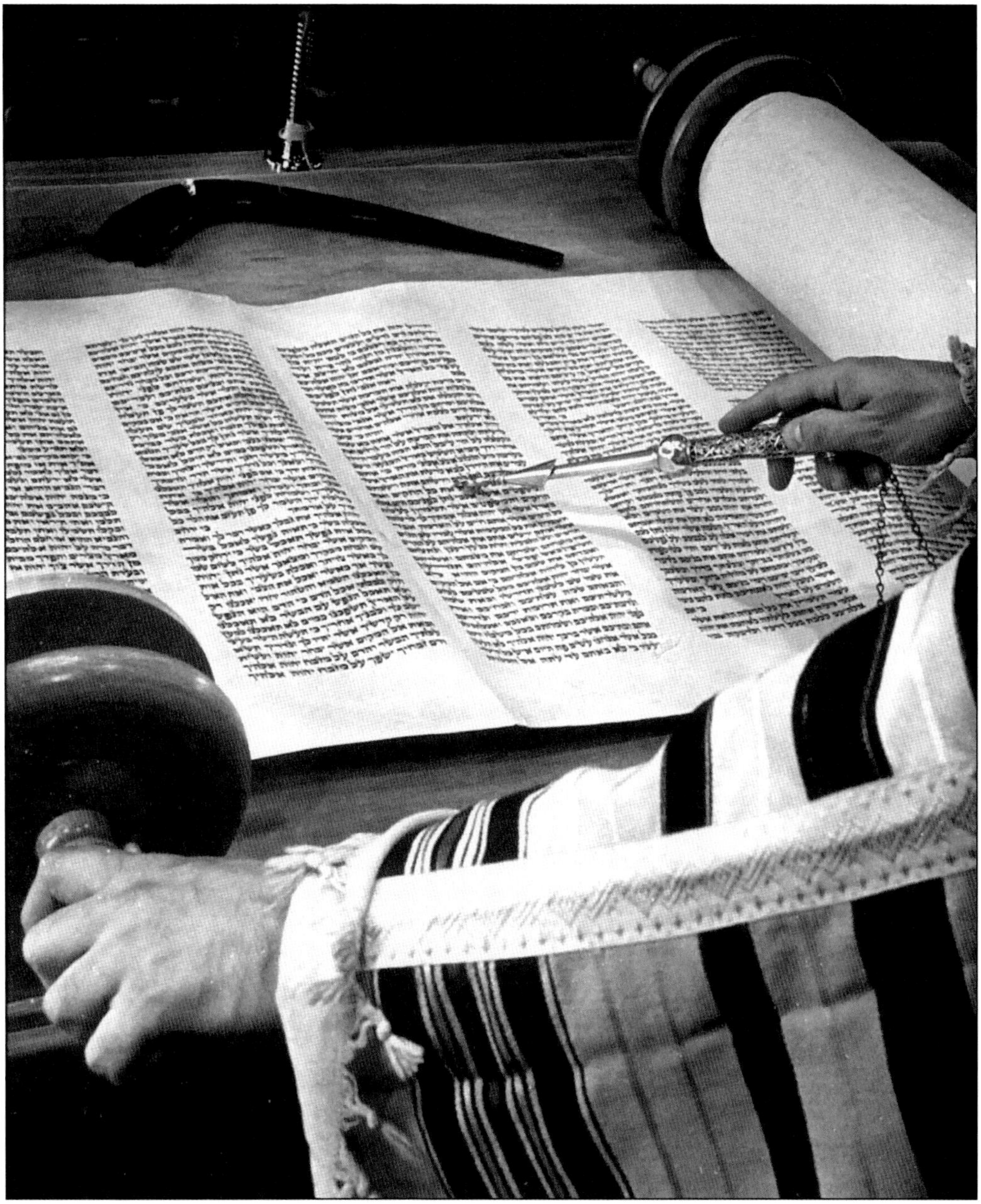

Here is a reader reading from the *Sefer Torah* at Agudath Achim. Of the synagogue's 10 Torahs, several date back to the first synagogue on Fannin Street. One was given to the congregation by the Falk family in 1952, and others were acquired by gifts or purchase during the years since. The Torah is read using a *yad*, or pointer (often of silver as this one, dating from the 1940s) so that human hands never touch the parchment or vellum on which the sacred text of the Bible's first five books is handwritten by Hebrew scribes. Creation of a *Sefer Torah* (Torah scroll) is time-consuming and costly. Many Torahs remain in continued use for generations, even hundreds of years, but when one is damaged or must be retired, it is disposed of by burial in the cemetery. The ram's horn, or *shofar*, seen on the reader's desk, is used to announce the opening and closing of the Days of Awe, which begin with Rosh Hashanah and end with Yom Kippur. The reader seen here wears a *tallit*, or prayer shawl.

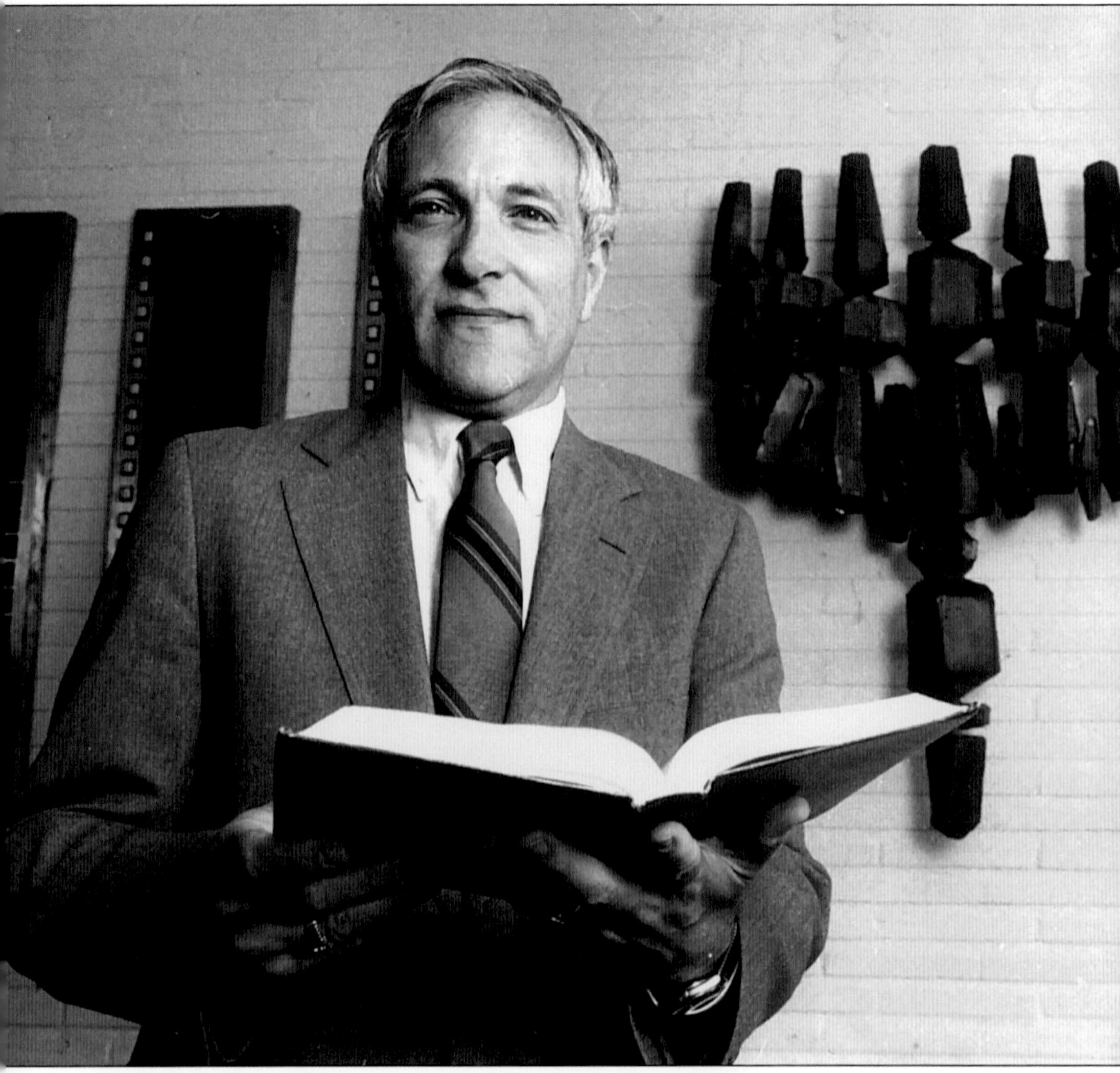

Rabbi Richard A. Zionts, a native of Pittsburgh, Pennsylvania, came to B'nai Zion Temple in 1972. Previously, he had been Rabbi of Congregation Mikveh Israel in Savannah, Georgia (the same congregation that B'nai Zion's third rabbi, Raphael de Costa Lewin, had served after leaving B'nai Zion in 1867). Prior to Savannah, Zionts had been associate rabbi of Temple Emanu-El in San Francisco, California. During much of his 16 years at B'nai Zion, Rabbi Zionts wrote a weekly religion column for the *Shreveport Journal* newspaper and served on the faculty of Centenary College of Louisiana, as did Rabbi David Lefkowitz Jr. It was during Rabbi Zionts's tenure that the *New Union Prayer Book* was introduced to B'nai Zion, replacing the long-used and much-beloved *Union Prayer Book*, a major change at the Shreveport temple, much as it was throughout American Reform Jewry. In 1988, Rabbi Zionts left Shreveport for Altoona, Pennsylvania where he served Temple Beth Israel until 1996 when he became rabbi of Temple Sinai in Palm Desert, California.

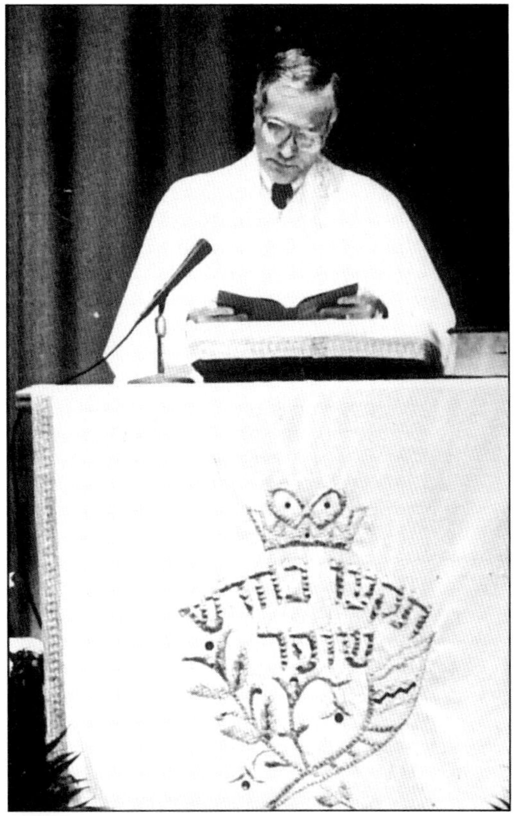

At right, Rabbi Zionts leads Yom Kippur services at B'nai Zion in about 1985. On the High Holidays—Rosh Hashanah, the Jewish New Year, and Yom Kippur, the Day of Atonement—services are held in the social hall (since 1997 called Lefkowitz Hall) to accommodate the overflow crowds that are typical then. Regular Friday evening Sabbath services are held in the main sanctuary. The congregational president and a lady of the congregation usually join the rabbi on the *bimah*, he to say the *kiddush* prayer over the wine, and she to light the *Shabbat* candles, welcoming the Sabbath. Below, in 1992, Rose Van Thyn joins B'nai Zion president Hamilton Benson during Friday evening services. Married couples from the congregation also often perform these rituals.

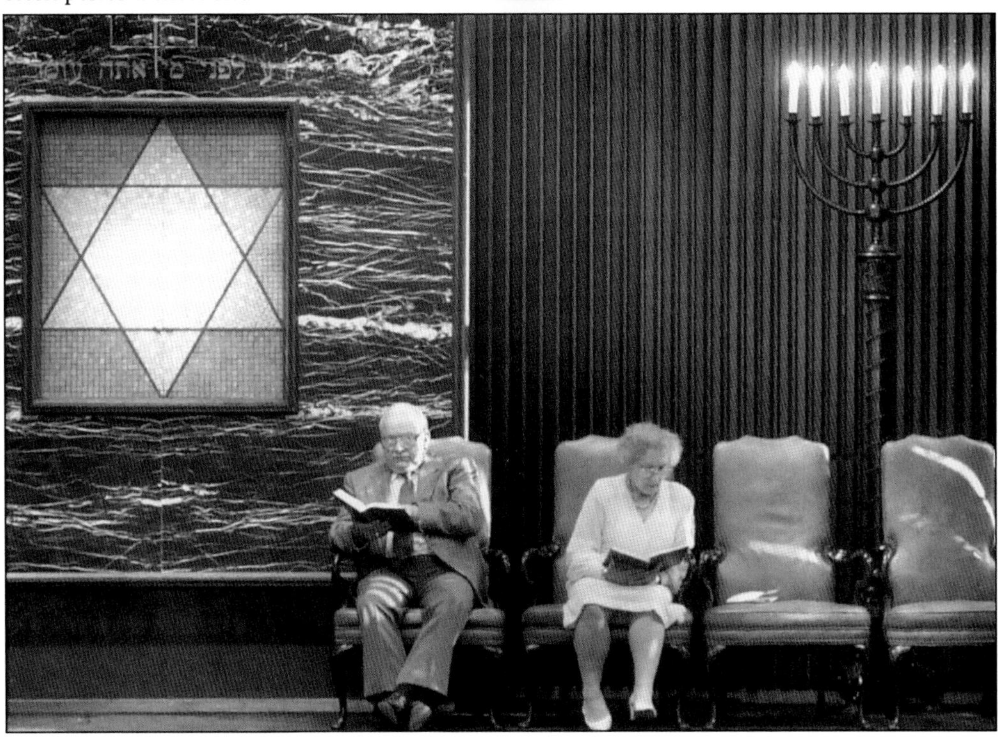

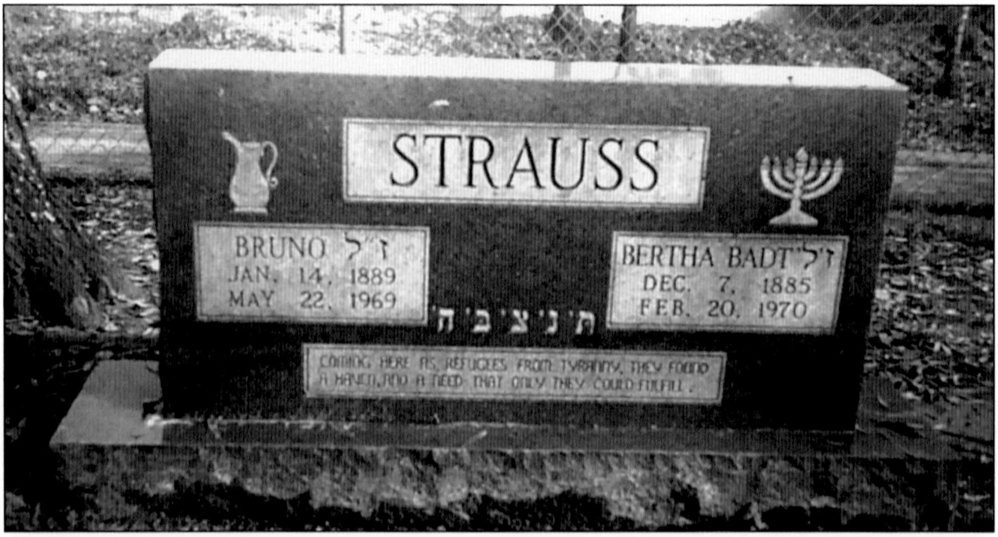

The Jewish section of Greenwood Cemetery, formally called Hebrew Rest Number Three, was consecrated in 1933 and has been the primary cemetery of Temple B'nai Zion since that time. Located in the southeast corner of Greenwood Cemetery, on East Stoner Avenue at Cornwell Street, this section is a large and shaded park-like spot. Of the many gravestones found here, most are typically modern, polished granite monuments bearing the *magen David* but otherwise largely indistinguishable from monuments in non-Jewish cemeteries. A few, such as the stone of Drs. Bruno (1889–1969) and Bertha Strauss (1885–1970), refugees from Nazi Germany and academics (he a longtime professor at Centenary College), bear some Hebrew and other Jewish symbols.

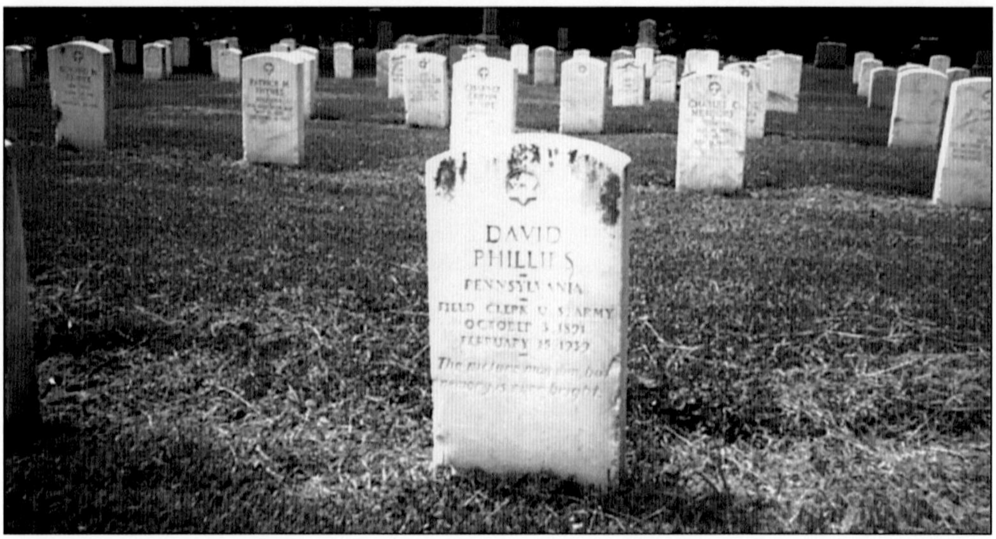

A few Jews are also buried in the non-sectarian part of Greenwood Cemetery, such as David Phillips (1891–1939), whose grave is seen here in the World War I veterans section of the cemetery where he rests with his comrades-in-arms. Others rest elsewhere at Greenwood also, as well as in the non-sectarian section of Oakland Cemetery and at the non-sectarian Forest Park Cemetery. Forest Park is the final resting place of a number of prominent local Jews, although there is no Jewish section there. Some members of the faith rest outside the Jewish cemeteries because of marriage to non-Jewish spouses, though this is not always the case.

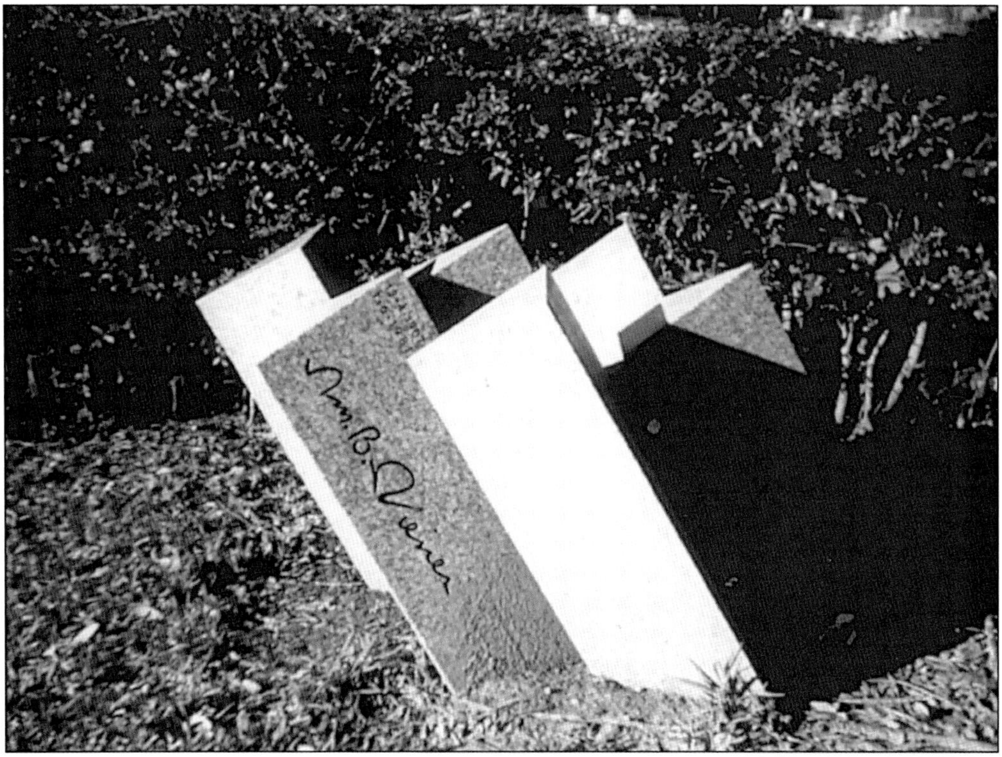

One of the most remarkable monuments in any of Shreveport's four Jewish cemeteries is that of architect William B. Wiener Sr. (1907–1981). Designed by his son, architect Bill Wiener Jr., the monument is made up of six triangular granite shafts embedded diagonally in the ground (top). From the side it appears simply to be a contemporary sculpture, which indeed it is, but from a certain angle it becomes a *magen David* (at right). Although of modern date, the monument is listed in the nationwide Save Outdoor Sculpture registry administered in Louisiana by the National Center for Preservation Technology and Training.

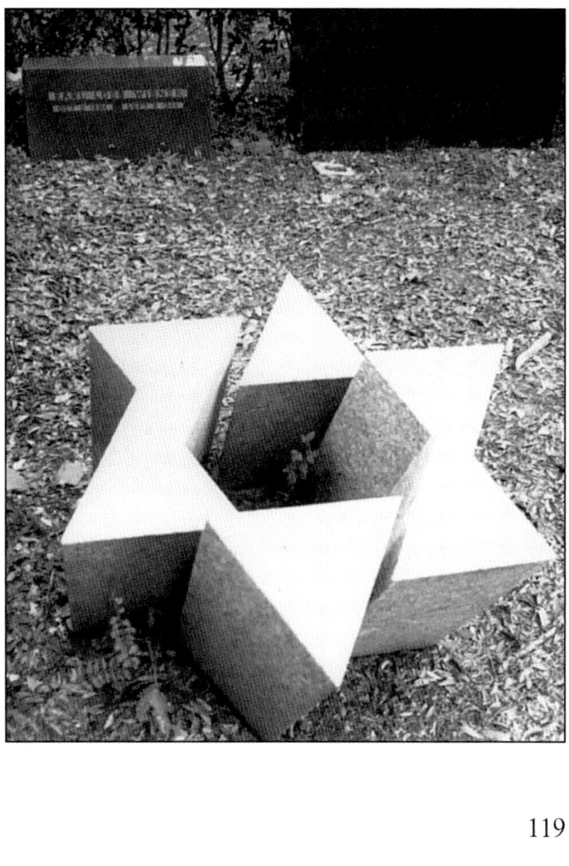

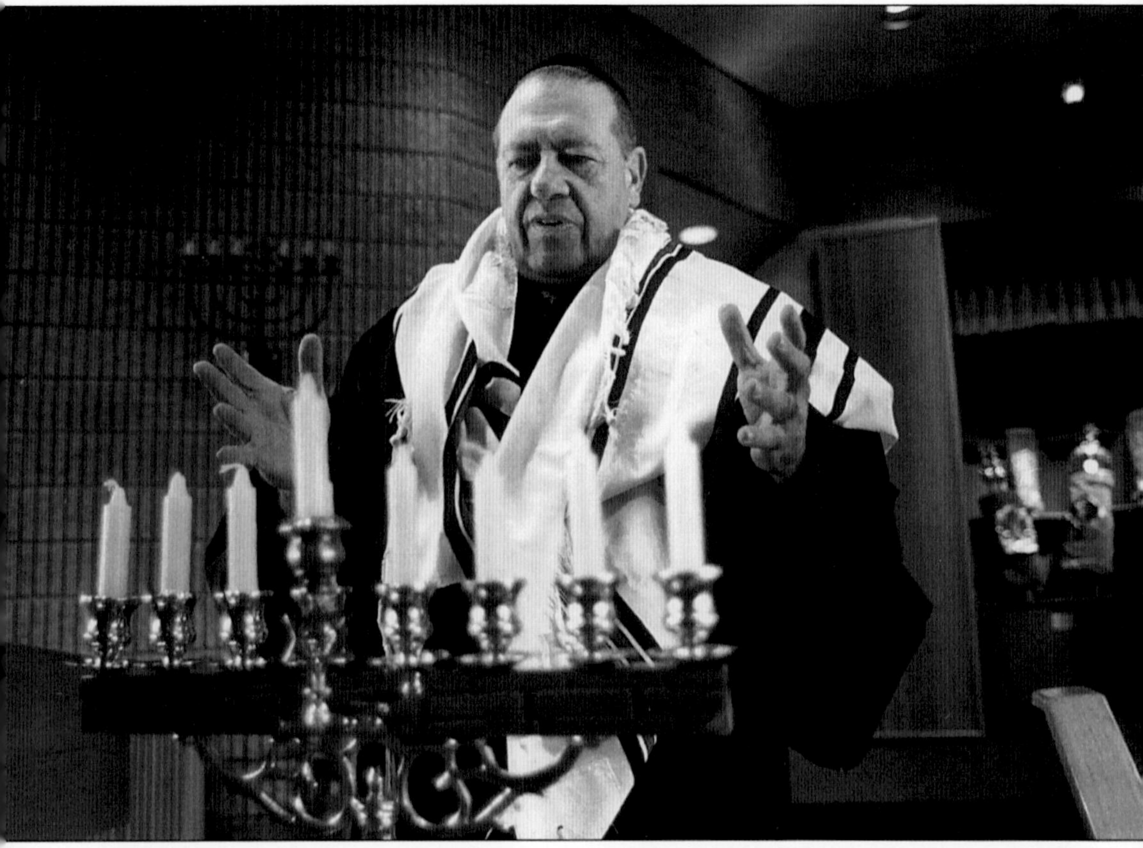

Rabbi Seymour Moscowitz, a native of New York and retired U.S. Army colonel, became rabbi of Agudath Achim Synagogue in 1986. During the years 1984 through1986, the *shul* was served by Rabbi Emanuel Kumin, director of the Shreveport Jewish Federation. Rabbi Moskowitz, his successor, was ordained in 1956 and had formerly been director of the Defense Language Institute at the Presidio of Monterey, California. He remained with Agudath Achim until 1993 when he and wife Selma relocated to Arizona. His successor was the present rabbi of Agudath Achim, Foster Kawaler, ordained in 1989 while serving as an officer in the United States Air Force. Above, Rabbi Moskowitz prepares for Hanukkah in 1990. Hanukkah, also known as "the festival of lights" or "the feast of the dedication," is a minor but popular holiday commemorating the rededication of the Jerusalem Temple in 165 b.c.e. as recounted in the apocryphal books of the Maccabes.

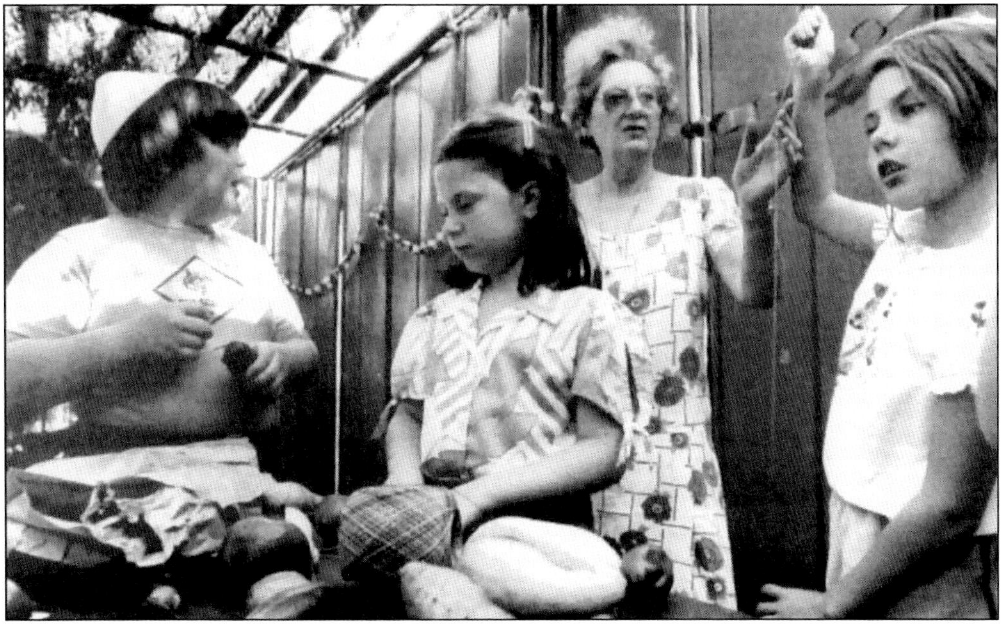

Here, children of Agudath Achim Synagogue celebrate the holiday of Sukkot in 1982. Sukkot is one of the three important "Pilgrim Festivals" (the others are Passover and Shavuot) by building a *sukkah* or booth of wood, metal, and vegetation. Sukkot is an ancient harvest holiday falling five days after Yom Kippur and is hallowed in all Jewish traditions. The children in this photograph are decorating the *sukkah* with artwork, fruits, and vegetables. Yetta Rubenstein assists.

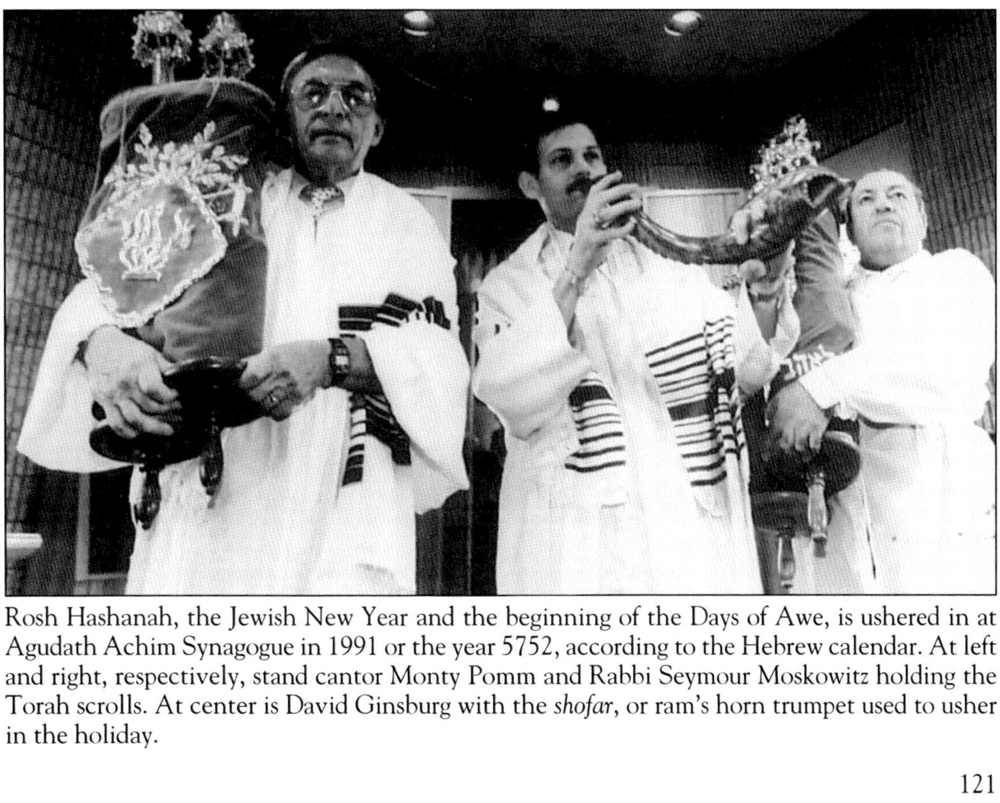

Rosh Hashanah, the Jewish New Year and the beginning of the Days of Awe, is ushered in at Agudath Achim Synagogue in 1991 or the year 5752, according to the Hebrew calendar. At left and right, respectively, stand cantor Monty Pomm and Rabbi Seymour Moskowitz holding the Torah scrolls. At center is David Ginsburg with the *shofar*, or ram's horn trumpet used to usher in the holiday.

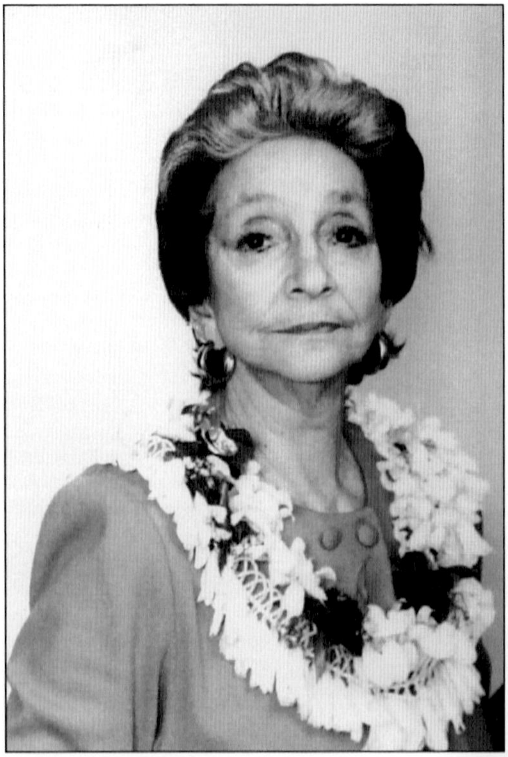

One of Shreveport's noted authors, Betty Eichenbaum Wiener (left), a native of Little Rock, Arkansas, was also an active humanitarian, philanthropist, and civic leader. She started Shreveport's Meals on Wheels program, was an ardent supporter of the Shreveport Symphony, taught Americanization classes for refugees from Nazi Germany, and was the recipient of numerous awards including the Alexis de Toqueville Award, presented to her in Washington, D.C. by Gregory Peck. She died in 1999 and was survived by her three children, including Judge Jacques Wiener, pictured below.

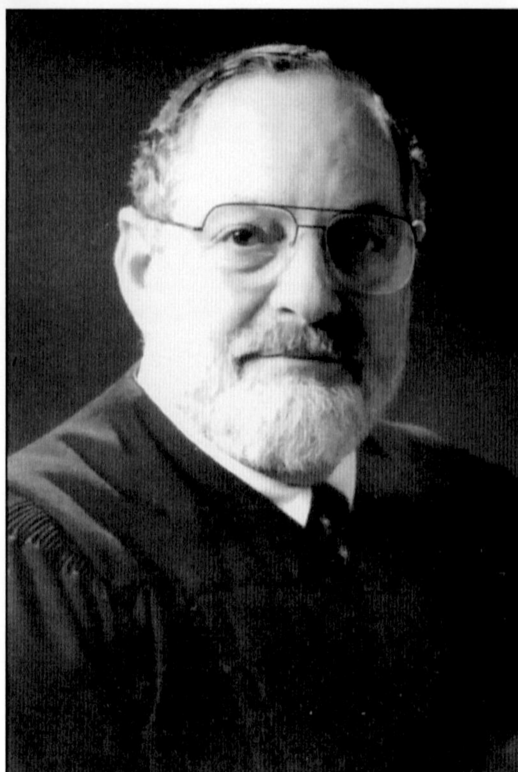

Judge Wiener of the United States Fifth Circuit Court of Appeals received his J.D. from Tulane in 1961 and was appointed to the federal bench by President George Bush in 1990.

Rabbi Michael Matuson (right), a native of Brooklyn, New York, came to B'nai Zion in 1989, serving until 1994. His charismatic and energetic style made him very popular, though his outspoken political and social stances sometimes found him at odds with the temple's lay leadership.

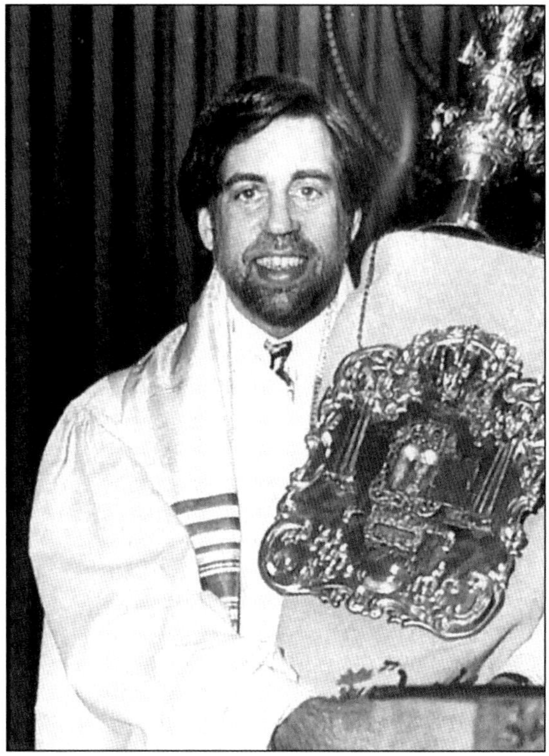

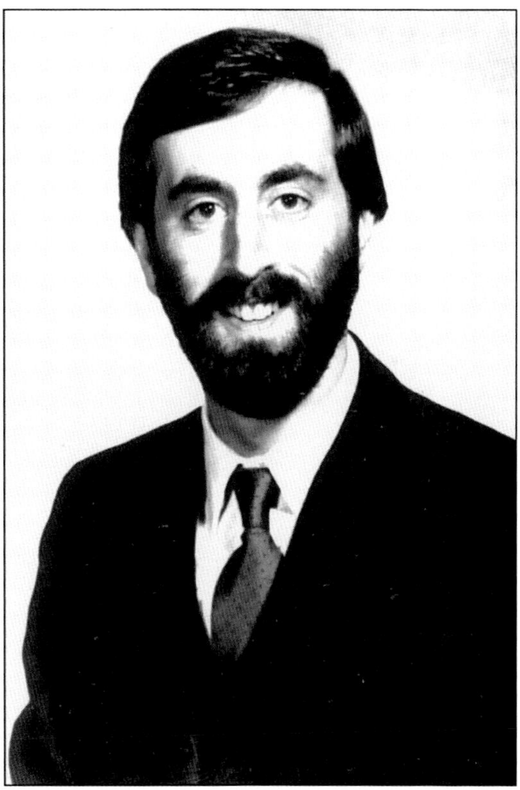

His successor was Rabbi Harold Floyd Caminker (left), a native of Detroit, Michigan, who came to Shreveport from West Hills, California, a suburb of Los Angeles. Rabbi Caminker served B'nai Zion from 1995 to 1997, during which time the congregation experienced substantial departures from its Classical Reform tradition. The trend toward greater traditionalism in Reform Judaism has continued and even accelerated under the leadership of Rabbi Harold Robinson, a former Bostonian and United States Navy chaplain, who serves the congregation at the time of this writing.

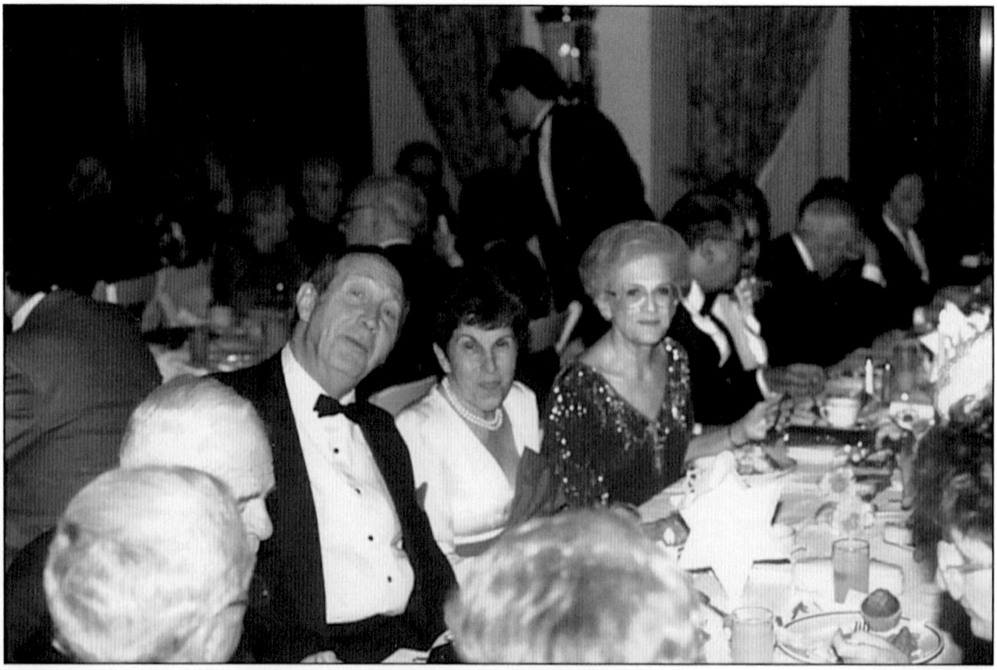

In January 1987, the B'nai Zion Temple Sisterhood celebrated its 80th anniversary. The Sisterhood is the organization of the women of the congregation and promotes programs to benefit the temple and the community as well as promote social activities, study, and the individual growth of its members. Within the structure of the congregation, the Sisterhood is the collective presence, voice, and strength of the female members. Hundreds turned out to celebrate the occasion, including the director of the National Federation of Temple Sisterhoods (now known as Women of Reform Judaism). On this page are two views of the gala dinner. In the tuxedo at top is Irving Selber, seen also on page 104. Beside him is his wife Flo. Below are Karl and Erna Levy, who came to Shreveport from Cologne, Germany in 1938, fleeing Nazi persecution. They became citizens in 1944.

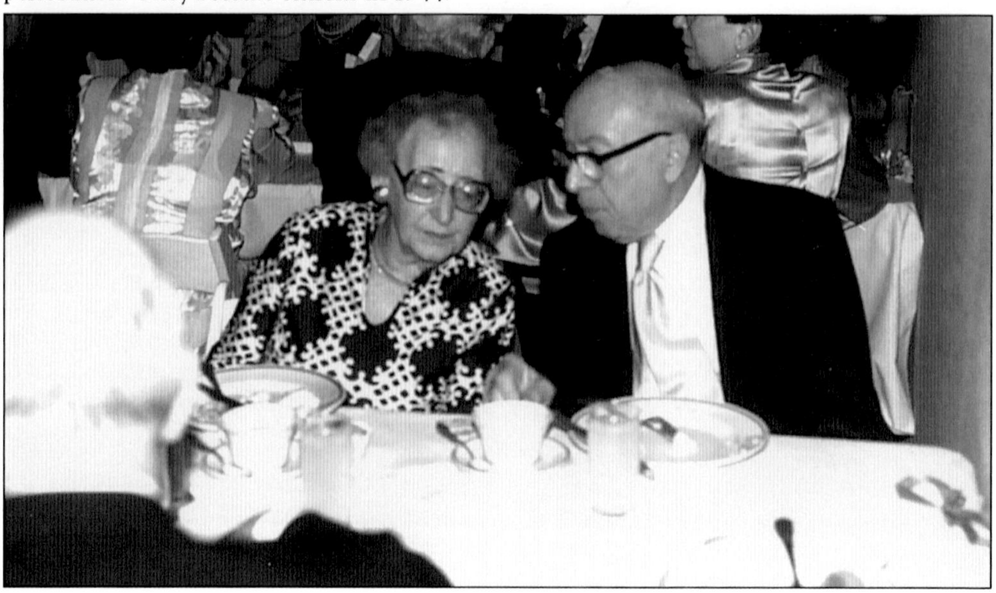

The Temple Sisterhood holds an annual Sisterhood Shabbat service in January, during which Sisterhood members lead the service, performing all rituals and emphasizing the role of women in the temple and the overall life of Judaism. To the right are, from left to right, Pamela Viviano Brock, Dr. Jana DeBenedetti, and Debbie Caminker, then wife of Rabbi Caminker, at the 1997 service. Pictured below is breaking *challah* on the temple's *bimah* following the 1999 service.

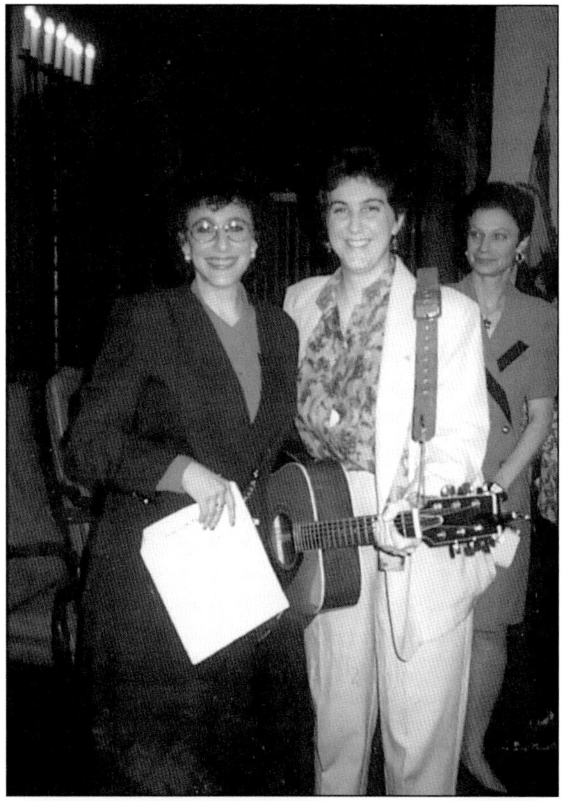

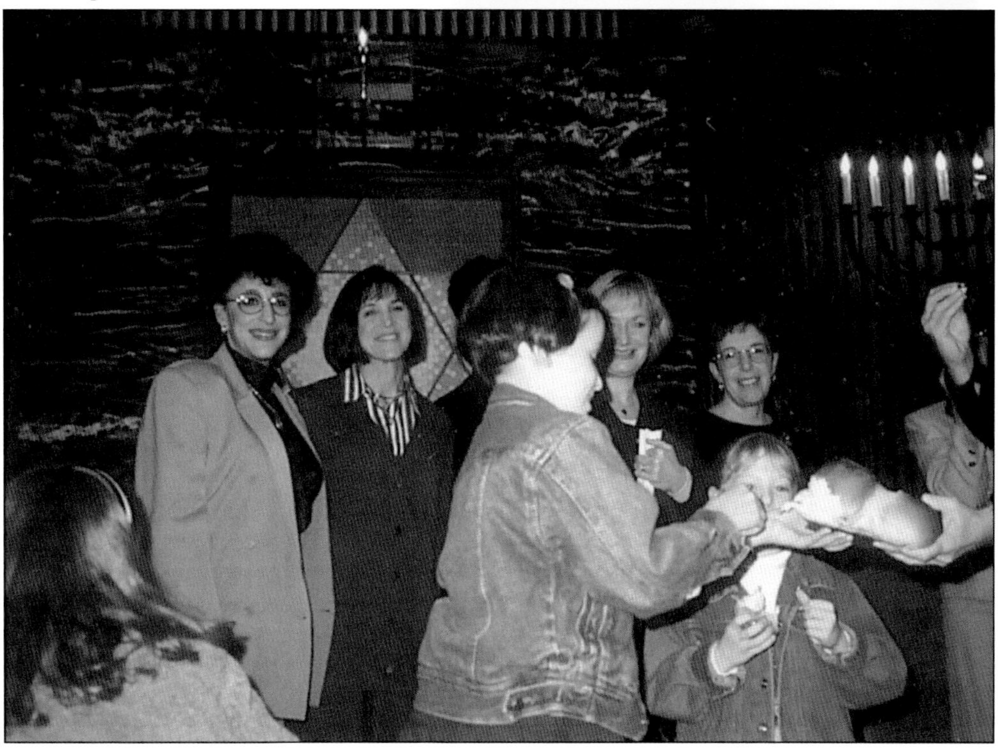

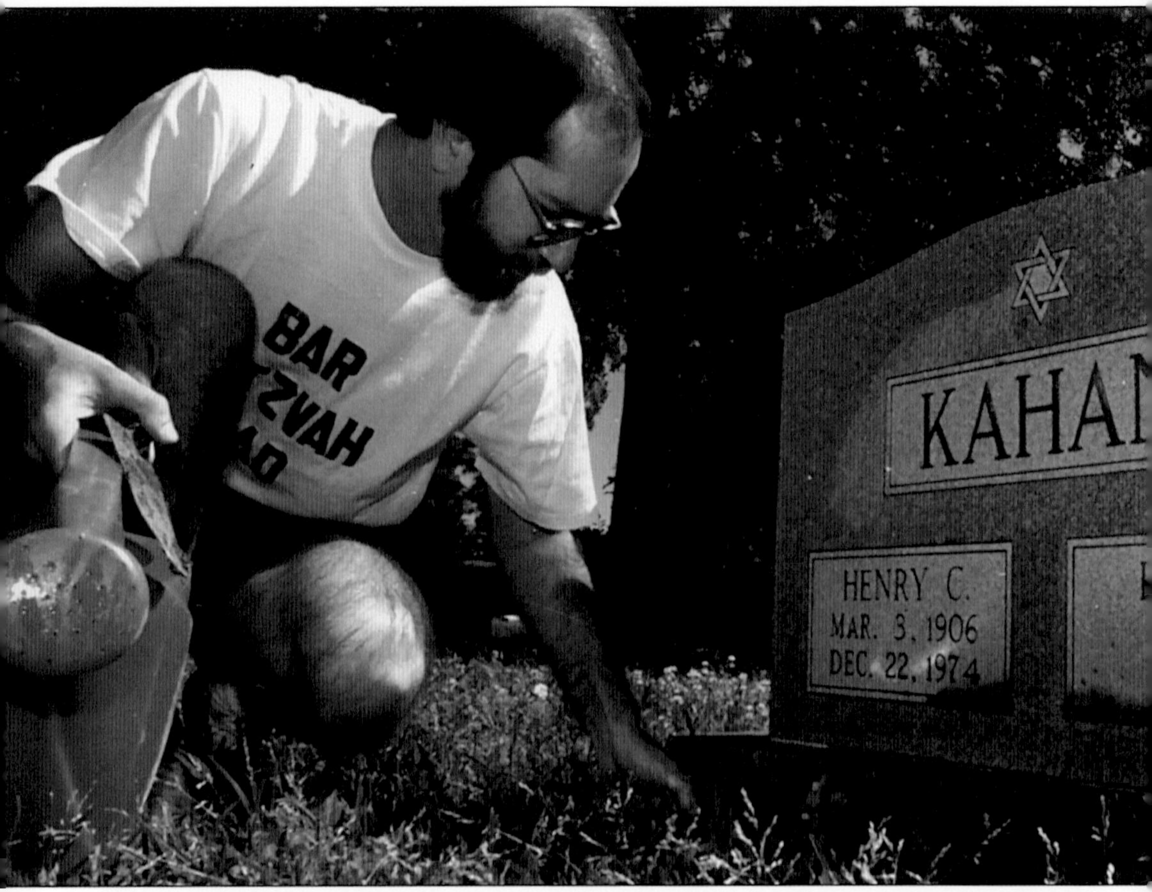

Here, Ron Nierman tends to the graves at Hebrew Rest Number Three, the Jewish section of Greenwood Cemetery. Cemetery cleanup and maintenance is a regular project of the Temple Youth of B'nai Zion. Death is but the final stage in the lifecycle around which all of Jewish life revolves. Judaism is a religion of life and the lives of those who went before are always celebrated in the hearts of their progeny. The departed are remembered annually on their *yahrzeit*, or anniversary of burial when the beautiful and poetic Aramaic prayer known as the *Kaddish* is recited. Remembering the past keeps it alive in the present and just as each member of the family of Judaism is remembered by those that come after, so too is the history of the ancient yet modern, permanent yet ever progressing, Jewish faith. In Shreveport, as throughout the world, we may say with pride *Am Yisrael Chai!*—"The People of Israel Lives!"

APPENDIX
SHREVEPORT RABBIS

RABBIS OF CONGREGATION HAR EL
Julius Lewin, 1860–1861 (occasional service as interim rabbi 1861–1865)
Ferdinand L. Sarner, 1861–1863
Moses Gabriel, (occasional service as visiting rabbi during Civil War)
A. Moses, (occasional service as visiting rabbi during Civil War)

RABBIS OF B'NAI ZION TEMPLE
Raphael de Costa Lewin, 1866–1867
Max Samfield, 1867–1871
M. Levine, 1871 (interim rabbi)
Meyer Greenblatt, 1871–1875
Emanuel L. Hess, 1876–1888
Israel Saenger, 1889–1901; emeritus 1901–1918
Moses P. Jacobson, 1901–1919
Abram Brill, 1920–1940; emeritus 1940–1942
David Lefkowitz Jr., 1940–1943; 1946–1972; emeritus 1972–1999
Max Merritt, 1943 (interim rabbi)
A. Stanley Dreyfuss, 1944 (interim rabbi)
Sanford Rosen, 1945 (interim rabbi)
Richard A. Zionts, 1972–1988
Michael Matuson, 1989–1994
Harold F. Caminker, 1995–1997
Harold Robinson, 1997–

RABBI OF CONGREGATION EMANU-EL
Nachman I. Benson, 1875–1877

RABBI OF CONGREGATION BETH EL
Joseph Getzler, *c.* 1890–1902

RABBI OF CONGREGATION BETH JOSEPH
J. Kallen (or Collins), 1895–1902

RABBIS OF CONGREGATION AGUDATH ACHIM
J. Kallen and Joseph Getzler, 1902–1904
Harriss Wolenske, 1904–1906
Mandell Horowitz, 1907–1914
Maurice Lesseraux, 1914–1915
Simon Smolensky, 1916–1917
Abram Abromowitz, 1917–1918
Phinehas Zissman, 1918–1922
Nathan Greenfield, 1922 (interim rabbi)
David Stern, 1922–1923
Charles Blumenthal, 1923–1926
Alexander Szandor Wiesel, 1926–1930
Israel Gerstein, 1930–1934
Leo Brener, 1934–1974; emeritus 1974–1989
Stanley Greenstein, 1974–1978
H.D. Uriel Smith, 1979–1984
Emanuel Kumin, 1984–1985 (interim rabbi)
Seymour Moskowitz, 1986–1993
Monty Pomm, 1993–1994 (acting rabbi)
Foster Kawaler, 1994–

ACKNOWLEDGMENTS

Except as noted below, the images in this book are from the collection of the author.

From the archives of B'nai Zion Temple: p.10 (top), p.31 (bottom), p.55 (bottom), p.56, p.57 (top), p.59 (bottom), p.63 (bottom), p.93 (both), p.97, p.123 (top), p. 124 (both), p.125 (both).

From the Archives of Congregation Agudath Achim: p.52 (top), p.66 (bottom), p.67 (bottom), p.68 (both), p.69 (bottom), p.87 (bottom), p.88, p.110 (both), p.121 (top).

From the Noel Memorial Library Department of Archives and Special Collections at Louisiana State University in Shreveport: p.13 (top), p.30, p.36, p.38 (top), p.40 (bottom), p.107 (top).

From the collection of Charlton E. Meyer Jr.: p.75 (bottom)

Photograph by J. Frank McAneny: p. 103 (bottom)

Photographs by Eric J. Brock: p.2, p.11 (top), p.12 (both), p.13 (bottom), p. 14 (both), p.15 (both), p.16 (both), p.17 (top), p.31 (top), p.35 (top), p.36 (bottom), p.37 (both), p.39 (top), p.43 (bottom), p.45 (top), p.52 (bottom), p.53 (top), p.59 (top), p.61 (top), p.67 (top), p.72 (bottom), p.84 (top), p.87 (top), p.94 (bottom), p.95 (bottom), p.99 (both), p.106 (bottom), p.111 (bottom), p.112, p.113, p.114 (top), p.118 (both), p.119 (both).